Management Accounting for spitality and Tourism

Tourism and Hospitality Management Series

Series Editors:

Stephen J. Page
Massey University – Albany, New Zealand

Professor Roy C. Wood
The Scottish Hotel School, University of Strathclyde, UK

Series Consultant:

Professor C. L. Jenkins
The Scottish Hotel School, University of Strathclyde, UK

Textbooks in this series:

Books in this series are available on free inspection for lecturers considering the texts for course adoption. Details of these and any other International Thomson Business Press titles are available by writing to the publishers (Berkshire House, 168–173 High Holborn, London WCIV 7AA) or by telephoning the Promotions Department on 0171 497 1422.

Management Accounting for Hospitality and Tourism

THIRD EDITION

Richard Kotas

Emeritus Professor, Schiller International University
formerly, Senior Lecturer, University of Surrey

INTERNATIONAL THOMSON BUSINESS PRESS
I(T)P® An International Thomson Publishing Company

London • Bonn • Johannesburg • Madrid • Melbourne • Mexico City • New York • Paris
Singapore • Tokyo • Toronto • Albany, NY • Belmont, CA • Cincinnati, OH • Detroit, MI

Management Accounting for Hospitality and Tourism: 3rd Edition

Copyright ©1999 Richard Kotas

First published by International Thomson Business Press

I(T)P A division of International Thomson Publishing
The ITP logo is a trademark under licence

British Library Cataloguing-in-Publication Data
A catalogue record for this book is available from the British Library

First edition published in 1977 as *Management Accounting for Hotels and Restaurants*.
Second edition published in 1986 as *Management Accounting for Hotels and Restaurants* by Blackie and Son Ltd.
This edition published 1999 by International Thomson Business Press.

Typeset by J&L Composition Ltd, Filey, North Yorkshire
Printed in the UK by TJ International, Cornwall

ISBN 1–86152–490–0

International Thomson Business Press
Berkshire House
168–173 High Holborn
London WCIV 7AA
UK

http://www.itbp.com

Contents

Series editors' foreword

The International Thomson Business Press Series in Tourism and Hospitality Management is dedicated to the publication of high quality textbooks and other volumes that will be of benefit to those engaged in tourism, hotel and hospitality education, especially at degree and postgraduate level. The Series is based on core textbooks in key areas of the curriculum. All the authors in the series are experts in their own fields, actively engaged in teaching, research and consultancy in tourism and hospitality. Each book comprises an authoritative blend of subject-relevant theoretical considerations and practical applications. Furthermore, a unique quality of the series is that it is student oriented, offering accessible texts that take account of the realities of administration, management and operations in tourism and hospitality contexts, being constructively critical without losing sight of the overall goal of providing clear accounts of essential concepts, issues and techniques.

The series is committed to quality, accessibility, relevance and originality in its approach. Quality is ensured as a result of a vigorous referencing process, unusual in the publication of textbooks. Accessibility is achieved through the use of innovative textual design techniques, and the use of discussion points, case studies and exercises within books, all geared to encouraging a comprehensive understanding of the material contained therein. Relevance and originality together result from the experience of authors as key authorities in their fields.

The tourism and hospitality industries are diverse and dynamic industries and it is the intention of the editors to reflect this diversity and dynamism by publishing quality texts that enhance topical subjects without losing sight of enduring themes. The Series Editors and Consultant are grateful to Steven Reed of International Thomson Business Press for his commitment, expertise and support of this philosophy.

Series Editors

Dr Stephen J. Page
Massey University – Albany
Auckland
New Zealand

Professor Roy C. Wood
The Scottish Hotel School
University of Strathclyde
United Kingdom

Series Consultant

Professor C. L. Jenkins
The Scottish Hotel School
University of Strathclyde
United Kingdom

Preface

It is now more than twelve years since the publication of the second edition in 1986. The present, third, edition has retained the basic structure of the book, but a number of significant alterations to the text have been made. Chapter 8 has been enlarged considerably by a new section on yield management and a full treatment of menu engineering. The two chapters 'Food cost control' and 'Beverage cost control' have been combined into a single chapter entitled 'Food and beverage control'. We have two new chapters. Chapter 11, 'Responsibility accounting', deals with the applications of responsibility accounting in hospitality. Chapter 20, 'Uniform system of accounts for the lodging industry', gives an outline of the ninth edition of the uniform system which is now well established throughout the international hospitality industry.

During the last decade or so many universities have introduced degree courses in tourism. The scope of the book has, therefore, been extended to cover tour operators, travel agents and other types of operation in tourism. It is hoped that *Management Accounting for Hospitality and Tourism* will appeal to an even wider academic audience as well as to practitioners in the hospitality and tourism industry. I am grateful to Kevin Collins of Thames Valley University and Michael Conlan of Bournemouth University who have, between them, read almost the entire manuscript and offered valuable comments.

London, 1998   Richard Kotas

Orientation | 1

INTRODUCTION

The last few decades have been characterized by unparalleled change. Information technology (IT) was still in its infancy some twenty years ago; and it is now having an immense impact on all of us as private individuals and on all business enterprises. Accounting and control systems throughout industry and commerce have, as a result, undergone a drastic change. Disposable incomes have generally shown a substantial upward trend—with obvious implications for eating out and international travel. The number of eating-out establishments has multiplied and travelling abroad for business and pleasure is now a fairly routine, commonplace occurrence.

There has also been, throughout Western Europe, a dramatic change in the structure of industry. Many of the traditional industries which used to be important employers of labour (agriculture, mining, shipbuilding, etc.) have declined very considerably. Other industries—and hospitality and tourism in particular—have established themselves as large, dynamic industries, and offer new and interesting careers to vast numbers of individuals. The hospitality and tourism industry—hotels, motels, restaurants, cafés, public houses, country clubs, leisure centres, tour operators, travel agents—now employs over 2.5 million people and is generally regarded as one of the UK's largest industries. Thus, from humble beginnings in the post-war years, the hospitality and tourism industry has become a substantial employer of labour, offering interesting and profitable opportunities to people with determination and imagination.

Even a brief examination of the nature of the hospitality and tourism industry will indicate that it is in many respects unique and different from other industries. Let us, therefore, now examine the major features of the industry, its main problems and the implications they have for accounting and control methods.

SALES INSTABILITY

Sales instability is a special characteristic and is inherent in almost all hospitality operations. Fluctuations which occur in the volume of business are of three kinds.

First, there is the annual pattern. Many hotels, restaurants and other establishments are seasonal, and whilst the degree of sales instability varies from one establishment to another, seasonality is generally regarded in the industry as a serious problem. Frequently, the volume of business achieved during the season is three times that in the off-season.

Secondly, we have the weekly pattern. Many city restaurants do little business during the first few days of the week, but operate at almost full capacity towards the end of the week. Numerous hotels both in London and the provinces find that the highest occupancies are achieved from Monday to Thursday, and the weekend is for them the least busy period of the working week.

Finally, to look at catering operations, there are fluctuations in the level of activity and the revenue inflow during the working day. Generally, peak periods are lunchtime and after 1800 hours. Thus, whatever the nature of the establishment, there are continuous changes in the volume of sales—daily, weekly and annually.

As far as tourism is concerned sales instability is also very much in evidence, and this is true both in relation to British holiday-makers travelling abroad and foreign tourists arriving in the UK. Most of the travel occurs during the summer months and has a most significant impact on hotel and restaurant occupancies and demand for public transport and various places of interest.

The effect of sales instability is to produce three problems. First, there is a degree of uncertainty about the future volume of sales. Secondly, where there is sales instability there is inevitably some spare capacity and the consequent failure to utilize fully the resources and facilities of the establishment. Spare capacity, coupled with a high level of fixed costs, tends, in turn, to result in a high degree of profit instability. During slack periods considerable losses may be incurred and these may take quite some time to recover during busy periods.

The implications of sales instability for accounting and control procedures are quite clear. As there is uncertainty about future revenue inflow, we must develop appropriate methods of prediction. In relation to food operations this means the maintenance of a well-developed system of volume forecasting. In relation to room sales it means the use of occupancy statistics to predict future occupancy levels with a fair degree of accuracy.

Secondly, it is necessary to adjust operating cost levels to the ever-changing volume of sales. Food costs will automatically be adjusted where there is a system of volume forecasting. Efforts must, therefore, be made to control labour costs and other non-fixed expenses to ensure that they stand in the correct relationship to the current volume of sales.

Thirdly, in order to cope with the problem of spare capacity it is essential to evolve an effective and often sophisticated approach to pricing. The pricing policy of the establishment must not only give it the fullest benefit of high occupancies in the peak-periods. Where demand in the peak-periods is more than can be accommodated by the establishment, the price structure must be such as to shift demand from peak to off-peak periods and thus ensure an increase in the overall volume of business.

During the last decade or so hotel operators have begun to appreciate more fully the implications of seasonality and sales instability for the profitability of the establishment. They have decided that as demand for hotel accommodation changes from one month/week/day to another—and the number of rooms remains constant—this must have a direct impact on room prices. The pricing system that has in consequence emerged is eminently demand-oriented, and is now known as 'yield management'. We consider the operation of yield management in Chapter 8. Prices charged by tour operators are equally sensitive to demand. A given holiday costing, say, £800 in the height of the season will frequently be offered for less than £500 during the low season. Finally, readers who travel by rail will, no doubt, have noticed that the price paid for a given journey will vary depending on the day of the week and indeed the time of the day. Thus throughout the field of hospitality and tourism we see a pricing system which is complex, sophisticated and invariably demand-oriented; we see a pricing system that is, essentially, conditioned by seasonality and spare capacity.

COST STRUCTURE

Most hospitality establishments have a high proportion of fixed costs, and this applies particularly to hotels and other residential establishments. Considered from the point of view of the various revenue-producing departments, the position is this. Overall approximately three-quarters of the total cost of a hotel is fixed and uncontrollable. The relative proportions of fixed and variable costs will, however, vary from one department to another. In the rooms department we see a very high level of fixed costs, though in most cases such fixed costs are not apportioned to the rooms department but treated as (common) costs of the hotel as a whole. Variable costs such as laundry, linen and guest supplies constitute a very small percentage of departmental revenue—frequently less than 5 per cent. Departmental payroll is usually a semi-fixed cost.

Hotel food and beverage operations incur a considerably higher level of fixed costs, and this consists mainly of wages and salaries in the kitchens, dining rooms, bars, etc. Also the level of variable costs—essentially food and beverage costs—is considerably higher than in the rooms department.

Restaurants have considerably lower fixed costs—in many cases 40–50 per cent of total sales. Their variable costs tend to average 40–45 per cent of total sales volume.

Tour operators are, in this respect, similar to hotels, and also operate at a high percentage of fixed costs. Costs such as salaries and wages of head-office staff, rents, rates, etc. tend to be fixed and quite unaffected by current sales volumes. Salaries paid to couriers/guides and company representatives in the relevant destinations are also essentially fixed, though some of the employees would only be engaged during the high season. Finally the cost of air transport, hotel accommodation and excursions also tends to be fixed in that the tour operator has to purchase a fixed amount of such services and pay for them regardless of actual take-up.

Retail travel agents act on behalf of tour operators and other principals (railway companies, coach operators, etc.). Their remuneration tends to be based on a fixed percentage of sales—frequently in the region of 10 per cent. Some additional revenue is secured from the sale of foreign currency and insurance policies. The most important operating costs of a travel agent are staff costs and the rent paid for the premises. Most travel agents are situated in prime high-street locations where rents are high.

Mention has already been made of the effects of sales instability. The combined effect of a high percentage of fixed costs, fluctuations in the sales volume, and spare capacity is to produce a condition of profit instability which is quite uncommon in many other industries. The higher the percentage of fixed costs the more difficult it is to maintain adequate profitability through cost manipulation. In such circumstances, whilst paying adequate attention to cost control, one should be more concerned with the control of the revenue of the business. The main implication of the high fixed-cost structure of the business unit is that the traditional cost-oriented approach to accounting and control problems is only partly relevant. Cost analysis, cost control, cost statements, etc., are not the right weapons with which to attack obstacles to hospitality and tourism profitability. We must, instead, look at the other side of the profit and loss account and look for solutions in the total sales volume, sales mix, departmental profit margins, occupancy rates, pricing devices, etc.

NATURE OF 'PRODUCT'

The nature of the product sold by an industry is of considerable importance for a number of reasons. A product which is durable may be stored for long periods and held in large quantities to meet peaks of consumer demand. During inflationary periods there is often the added advantage of selling at an increased price a product which was manufactured some months previously at a relatively low cost.

The product of the hospitality industry is entirely different. A hotel bedroom which has not been sold is an irretrievable loss. Similarly, food is perishable both in raw material form and as a prepared meal.

With regard to accommodation the solution to the problem of product perishability requires a dual approach. First, we must have adequate predictions of hotel occupancy levels which, by definition, will indicate what spare capacity will obtain over a future period. Secondly, we must ensure imaginative pricing and effective marketing: price concessions, off-season rates, mini-weekends, conferences and business meetings all have a great contribution to make. The management accountant, though not a marketing expert, certainly has an important part to play in this context.

Finally, hospitality establishments do not sell a single product, but a multiplicity of mainly low-priced items. Whatever the wisdom of it, many restaurants have menus containing well over one hundred items, each of which has to be separately costed, prepared, served and accounted for on the customer's bill. In the case of hotels there is an even greater multiplicity of products and services offered to the customer. To quote from a well-known American text

(E. B. Horwath, L. Troth and J. D. Lesure, *Hotel Accounting*, New York: Ronald Press, 1963, p. 9):

> There is hardly any other business in which the amount involved in each individual transaction is so small and where these transactions, cash or credit, follow each other with such rapidity. A guest may arrive and take a room, have his baggage delivered, use the telephone and valet service, have his meal in his room or in the dining room, send a telegram, purchase cigars and dictate a few letters to the public stenographer, all within little more than an hour. During the same time he must be registered; his name must be listed so that mail and telephone calls can reach him; an account must be opened for him; the baggage porter, telephone operator, valet, restaurant cashier, telegraph office, cigar stand and the public stenographer must all record the charges for their services, and must report the charges to the bill clerk, who, in turn, must post them to the guest's account.

Of course, all the postings to the guest's account must be made as soon as possible so that his bill may, if necessary, be ready for presentation virtually within minutes. There must be few other industries where the speed of sales recording and an efficient cash collection system are so important.

The tourist product is an amalgam of elements such as transport, hotel accommodation, food and drink as well as the facilities available and the characteristics of a given destination. It is somewhat similar to the hotel meal in that it consists of a number of different components. It is, importantly, also similar to the hotel room in that it is highly perishable. As far as the tourist product is concerned, therefore, tour operators are in the same situation as hotels. A holiday package that remains unsold cannot be stored and sold subsequently: it is an irretrievable loss.

CYCLE OF OPERATIONS

In some industries the time taken from the purchase of raw materials to the sale of the finished product is long, sometimes a matter of months. In hospitality establishments the cycle of operations is, on the other hand, very short. Food delivered early in the morning is often processed later that morning and sold the same day.

Unless there are adequate checks and control devices at each stage of the catering cycle it will be very difficult for the establishment to reach an acceptable level of profit. The checks and control devices must be such as to cover the whole of the catering cycle, i.e. (a) buying, (b) receiving, (c) storing and issuing, (d) food preparation, and (e) selling.

In addition to adequate and comprehensive controls of both revenue and operating costs, each establishment needs a reporting system related to this particular cycle of operations. There must, therefore, be relatively more short-term reporting than is the case in other industries. It will be found that most well-managed establishments have a variety of daily and weekly reports in addition to monthly and quarterly operating statements.

As far as tour operators are concerned, the cycle of operations is quite different. Holidays planned for any given period must be arranged at least a year in advance, resulting in a fairly long cycle of operations. It should be noted, however, that, unlike in manufacturing industries, this long cycle of operations does not necessitate the holding of large stocks of materials over long periods.

The retail travel agent sells services made available by tour operators and other principals. The sale of a holiday or train ticket requires no previous arrangements to make these services available. The cycle of operations is, in such circumstances, practically non-existent.

Business orientation

In the first half of this chapter we have stressed several times that the two most powerful factors which militate against hospitality profitability are sales instability and high fixed costs. It is, in fact, the stability or otherwise of demand and cost structure that jointly determine what may be described as business orientation.

When one considers the various sectors of the hospitality industry, one can distinguish two types of operation. Some establishments operate at low fixed costs and enjoy a relatively stable volume of business. Others have a high percentage of fixed costs and are subject to a high degree of sales instability. In the first category we have various kinds of welfare catering: industrial canteens, hospital catering, school meals, university and college catering, etc. In the second category we have hotels, motels, guest houses and similar operations. The two groups of establishments, though integral parts of the industry, are so different in many respects that it is useful to be able to summarize such differences by attaching to each group a different label. For our purposes here we will refer to the first group as 'cost-oriented' and to the second as 'market-oriented'.

Of course, where there is a broad classification such as the one suggested above, it is inevitable that there should be borderline cases, i.e. types of operation which are partly cost- and partly market-oriented. It is thought nevertheless that the two labels are valuable and may serve many useful purposes.

In order to determine the degree of cost or market orientation of a business we may use a *business orientation chart*. This measures, vertically, the respective proportions of fixed and variable costs and, horizontally, the stability or otherwise of consumer demand. Having drawn the two axes, we may show the positioning of any one type of hospitality operation and thus decide to what extent it is cost- or market-oriented. From Figure 1.1 it will be seen that the most market-oriented establishments are positioned in the top right-hand area, and those most cost-oriented in the bottom left-hand area of the chart.

From the figure it would appear that the most market-oriented types of business unit are hotels (H) and tour operators (TO). On the other hand, canteens (C) and university catering (UC) tend to be essentially cost-oriented. It is possible to argue about the exact positioning of any one type of business. What, however, matters here is the general principle. It is difficult to plot

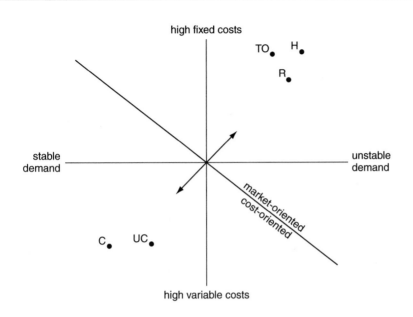

Figure 1.1 Business orientation chart

'typical' or 'average' types of operation. It is much easier to show the exact positioning of a particular business.

Implications of business orientation

Let us now look at the main differences between cost-oriented and market-oriented establishments. Hotels, motels, restaurants and tour operators have a high percentage of fixed, and in the short-run, uncontrollable costs. They are, therefore, less able to adjust or manipulate costs. In order to secure adequate profitability, attention must in such circumstances be shifted to the revenue side of the business. In the cost-oriented sectors of the industry, most of the operating costs are of a variable nature, and there is a great deal of scope for cost control and, generally, for adjusting operating cost levels to changes in the volume of sales.

Thus the approach to accounting and control problems in the market-oriented sector should be revenue-based, whilst in the cost-oriented sector it is cost-based. This basic approach should be reflected in all accounting and control procedures. Hence the nature and selection of all the accounting records should reflect the orientation of the establishment. For example, there is no point in a market-oriented establishment analysing in detail all the fixed expenses, as this is of little use for management control purposes. There is, on the other hand, a very strong case for keeping detailed records relating to sales mix, occupancy, prices charged and other factors which affect the revenue of the establishment.

Similar considerations apply to management reports. In both sectors of the industry we should find a different emphasis. The greater the degree of market orientation the more essential it is to keep fixed expenses in the background and highlight elements which determine the profitability of the business; and this, again, points to revenue-based accounting information.

Accounting methods and terminology

It is essential to realize that most accounting methods and control procedures had their origin in largely cost-oriented manufacturing industries. This is quite evident from accounting terminology: standard costing, cost accounting, cost control, cost analysis, cost accountant, etc. It is clear that this pronounced cost orientation cannot be right from the point of view of the market-oriented establishment. Also, it seems that the indiscriminate application of cost-oriented accounting and control methods in the market-oriented sectors of the industry will result in poor standards of management accounting. What is required for the market-oriented sectors of the industry is a new and rather different approach to accounting and control methods—a concept of *revenue accounting*. It is hoped to present the subject matter in this volume accordingly.

PROBLEMS

1. Enumerate the principal characteristics of each of the following:
   (a) resort hotel
   (b) hamburger bar
   (c) museum
   (d) retail travel agent.
2. Describe the business orientation of each of the four units mentioned in Question 1.
3. Draw a business orientation chart and show the positioning of
   (a) four-star London hotel
   (b) popular resort restaurant
   (c) industrial canteen.
4. If business orientation has important implications for accounting and control techniques, it must also have some implications for the choice of senior accounting personnel. Do you agree?
5. List five cost-based and five revenue-based accounting and control techniques. Explain how the cost-based techniques should be adapted for use in a market-oriented business.
6. Suggest what meaning might be attached to the concept of 'revenue accounting', and explain how this differs from the traditional concept of 'cost accounting'.

The accounting framework

2

BASIC ACCOUNTING CONCEPTS

The purpose of the first part of this chapter is to present, in outline, several concepts, principles and conventions which are basic to all accounting processes.

These concepts, principles and conventions have been evolved over a long period. Indeed, one of the most basic accounting principles—double entry—was first postulated some five hundred years ago. Accounting as we know it today, however, is very largely a set of man-made principles and methods, evolved in more recent times as a response to practical business problems. Whenever a new problem arises, accountants suggest solutions, and invariably one of these becomes generally regarded as the most practical, relevant and acceptable. In due course it tends to acquire the status of an accounting principle or otherwise becomes the generally accepted method.

Thus the visitors' ledger and the monthly summary sheet are examples of a man-made solution to the problem of a large volume of guest transactions. In the sphere of food control, the standard recipe is now regarded as the most effective method of controlling portion costs. However, in the pages which follow we are going to explore the most basic 'rules of the game' which regulate and condition all accounting processes. More detailed methods and procedures will be examined elsewhere in this volume. It should be added that some of these basic concepts are so obvious that accountants do not bother to state them explicitly. Nevertheless they do constitute part and parcel of the accounting framework and regulate all accounting and control procedures. Readers who have not had much formal training in accounting will, it is hoped, find this first part of the present chapter particularly useful.

The fundamental equation

The balance sheet of a business shows essentially two things: assets (i.e. business property) on the one hand, and proprietors' interest (i.e. the amount due from the business to its proprietors) and any amounts owing to third parties (i.e. liabilities) on the other.

Since finance for the acquisition of the assets must have come either from the proprietors or third parties, it is clear that proprietors' interest plus the liabilities of the business (if any) must be equal to the sum total of the assets.

The balance sheets we show here have the traditional double-sided form.

This makes the effect of transactions clearer and easier to understand. Elsewhere in this volume we use what is known as the 'vertical method' of presentation which is now in general use.

Let us assume that on 1 January 19. ., X starts in business as a restaurant operator. He pays £100,000 into the bank account of the restaurant and, immediately, buys the following assets; premises £60,000; equipment £20,000; furniture £10,000.

His balance sheet will then appear as follows:

Balance sheet

	£		£
Capital (proprietor's interest)	100,000	Premises	60,000
		Equipment	20,000
		Furniture	10,000
		Cash	10,000
	£100,000		£100,000

Let us assume that some days later he buys food and beverage supplies on credit for £10,000. His balance sheet after this transaction will appear as follows:

Balance sheet

	£		£
Capital	100,000	Premises	60,000
Creditors	10,000	Equipment	20,000
		Furniture	10,000
		F & B stocks	10,000
		Cash	10,000
	£110,000		£110,000

As may be seen from the second balance sheet, every business transaction is recorded twice. In this particular case the increase in the assets of the restaurant (food and beverage stocks) is matched by a corresponding increase in the liabilities (creditors).

The same applies to all transactions of the business which are recorded by means of double entry. Each transaction is entered in the records twice. This stems from the basic premise that where money or value is given by one party money or value must necessarily be received by another party. Traditionally we record the giving aspects by means of credit entries and the receiving aspects by means of debit entries. Hence, whatever the transactions of a business ultimately the two sides of its balance sheet will be equal.

Let us assume that some time later the restaurant sells a banquet for £5,000. Food and beverage stocks used amounted to £2,000 and labour and other costs were paid for in cash and amounted to £1,000. The profit on this banquet was, therefore, £2,000. The balance sheet of the restaurant would then appear as follows:

Balance sheet

	£		£
Capital	100,000	Premises	60,000
Profit	2,000	Equipment	20,000
Creditors	10,000	Furniture	10,000
		F & B stocks	8,000
		Debtors	5,000
		Cash	9,000
	£112,000		£112,000

Again, the sum total of assets is equal to the proprietor's interest plus the liabilities. It should be noted that the proprietor's interest is now £102,000, as the profit made by the restaurant on the banquet belongs to the proprietor.

The business entity concept

One of the firmly established accounting conventions is that accounts are kept for business entities and not for the individuals who are the proprietors, shareholders or persons otherwise associated with the business.

The distinction between the business as such and its owners is not always immediately obvious. With regard to the limited company the legal position is quite clear. The company has a separate legal existence from its members and in the eyes of the law is a separate legal person. The partnership has no legal existence separate from its members. Thus 'Jones and Brown' is a mere expression and not a separate legal entity. The same applies to the sole trader. Whether he trades as 'A. B. Brown' or 'Brown's Hotel' or 'The A. B. Brown Organization: Travel Experts,' the business has no legal existence separate from Mr Brown himself.

Whatever the legal position, from the point of view of accounting the affairs of the business must be kept quite separate from those of its owners. This results in numerous complications, particularly in smaller residential establishments. Where the proprietors live in, it is necessary to separate many items of expenditure. The rent of the premises must be apportioned so that the correct portion of it is charged against the profits of the business. Part of the food and beverage cost should presumably also be deducted and regarded as the owners' private consumption. Where cash is withdrawn to pay the owner's private bills, this should also be recorded as a non-business cash outlay. The same frequently applies to several expenses such as gas, electricity, telephone and similar expenses. The fact that the business belongs to the owners is, in this context, of no consequence.

The money measurement concept

Accounting records show only what is capable of being expressed in terms of money. In other words there are many things and events which accounting records do not show. Thus, while the degree of satisfaction of customers who attended a recent banquet or the current state of relations between the head chef and the head waiter are obviously quite important matters, accounting records are, unfortunately, not capable of recording them or, for that matter, anything else that cannot be expressed in terms of money.

Accounting and control are adjacent and very much allied fields. And whilst in accounting proper almost all records are expressed in terms of money, the requirements of control procedures are different. Here many facts and events are expressed in terms of units, percentages or otherwise. Sales histories and volume forecasts will be concerned with numbers of covers and numbers of menu items. Occupancy statistics are invariably expressed in terms of percentages. Although some of the matters controlled cannot or need not be expressed in terms of money, they may nevertheless be quantified and presented in a meaningful fashion.

The going-concern concept

In most situations we assume that the business will continue in operation for an infinite period. As we intend to continue indefinitely, it is presumably our intention to keep the fixed assets. If so then, naturally, we are not interested in the disposal or current market value of such assets. Consequently we record all the fixed assets at cost, less any depreciation.

One of the effects of this accounting approach to the valuation of fixed assets is that our records do not necessarily (indeed, do not usually) show the true value of the resources of the business generally and fixed assets in particular. However, the argument for the above course of action is strong and clear. Fixed assets are acquired for the purpose of increasing the profit-earning capacity of the business and not for resale. As long as it is our intention to continue in business, the possible disposal value of such assets is generally irrelevant.

However, during periods of prolonged inflation it is not always possible to ignore the true value of fixed assets. Indeed, there are numerous occasions when the approach outlined above has to be modified. One such occasion, when the going-concern concept has to be modified, is the measurement of return on capital. During inflationary periods it does not make sense to relate the current net profit to historic asset values. Consequently, some hotel companies undertake periodic asset revaluations, as a result of which it is possible to relate current profits to the current (present) value of capital employed.

Accrual accounting

A hotel may purchase a larger quantity of beverages towards the end of one accounting period, and sell the beverages in the next accounting period. If the cost of the beverages were charged against the revenue of the first period, and the revenue from the sale of the beverages added to the revenue of the second period, there would be an over-statement of the profits of the second period and a corresponding under-statement of the profits of the first period. This, quite clearly, would not be the right thing to do.

In order to ensure that we show the correct profit for each accounting period it is essential to *match revenue and expenses over time*. This in accounting terminology is referred to as *accrual accounting*. On the revenue side, it is immaterial when cash is collected by the business. What matters is when the income is earned. Let us assume that a hotel's accounting year runs from January to December. The hotel holds a banquet on 15 December, but the clients do not pay until the end of January. Although the cash was collected in the second year the income was earned in the first year and should be credited to the first year's profit and loss account. Similarly, if a hotel guest arrives a week before the end of the accounting year and stays for a fortnight, charges debited to him must be allocated to the two accounting years irrespective of when he settles his account.

The same applies on the expense side of the business. What matters here is not when cash is paid out but the *actual expense incurred*. Let us, again, assume that the accounting year runs from January to December. A restaurant takes out an insurance policy from 31 March and pays the full annual premium of £600. Although £600 has, in fact, been paid out the restaurant has had the benefit of the insurance cover for nine months only. The correct debit for insurance in the profit and loss account is, therefore, £450. The remainder of £150 represents a benefit still to come and is, at least technically, an asset at the end of the accounting year.

An obvious example of accrual accounting is depreciation. A billing machine may be purchased for £4,200. If the estimated life of the machine is seven years then (assuming what is known as straight-line depreciation) £600 will be regarded as the annual cost of the machine. Thus the initial cost of the asset will be spread over its effective life. In this way the periodical cost of the billing machine will be matched with the periodical revenues which this particular asset helps to generate.

Consistency

One of the important conventions of the accounting practitioner is consistency. In the preparation of accounting statements the accountant will, therefore, endeavour to apply the same accounting treatment and procedures from one year to another. Any change in the treatment of an item will not be decided upon lightly. Thus once it has been decided to treat the cost of printing the menus as 'advertising' rather than 'printing and stationery', the cost will be regarded and recorded as such from one year to another.

Similarly once it has been decided to apply a particular method of depreciation, the method will be applied consistently from one year to another. It will be realized that consistency in the preparation of accounting statements is of paramount importance. Without it, comparisons from one accounting period to another could be very difficult indeed.

Materiality

Accountancy, as a profession, is dedicated to accuracy and precision. Absolute accuracy is, however, prohibitive on economic grounds. It is for this reason that the accountant must ensure a sensible compromise between his desire to record and report as accurately as possible and the cost of such accuracy.

Let us take an example. An office stapler, costing say £10, will normally have a useful life of several years, and should ideally be regarded as a fixed asset. Whatever the theoretical aspects of the case, the accountant would not be able to spare the time to deal with such 'trivial' fixed assets, and would probably require the cost of the stapler to be written off to the office expenses account. Which items are or are not trivial depends on the size of the business. Where, for instance, the beverage stocks of a hotel are valued at £40,000 an error in stocktaking of £40 would not be considered material. A similar error in a small licensed restaurant could make a material difference to the restaurant's bar profit.

Conservatism

Conservatism is another well-established convention. The convention refers to the accountant's attitude in the valuation of assets and computation of profits. Briefly, the attitude is this: *provide for all possible losses, but do not anticipate profits.*

Thus, where there is some doubt as to the value of a fixed asset, the accountant will prefer to show a lower valuation rather than one which is more optimistic. The lower the valuation of fixed assets the larger the depreciation written off, and the lower the net profit of the business.

What applies to fixed assets applies equally in other directions. When, at the end of an accounting period, there is an amount of outstanding debtors, it is quite likely that some of these will prove bad. Though often there is no proof that some of the debtors will fail to pay, the accountant will tend to create a provision for bad and doubtful debts. This will be debited in the profit and loss account and thus result in a decreased figure of net profit. Conservatism, therefore, means in this context nothing more than a degree of cautiousness.

BRANCHES OF ACCOUNTING

Before the 1960s accounting was characterized by a backward-looking approach, a preoccupation with the recording of past transactions. The accountant was regarded as a financial chronicler rather than a member of the management team. Accounting meant accounting for past events; effective techniques for dealing with the present and the future were still to be developed.

Quite certainly more progress in the development of accounting methods has been made since the second World War than any comparable period preceding it. It is in the last four decades that we have witnessed the most important developments in accounting. New techniques such as marginal costing, break-even analysis, discounted cash flow and the application of electronic data processing to accounting have all taken place since 1955. Similarly it has been during this period that we have identified, though not always with a great degree of precision, the main branches, functions or orientations of accounting.

The precise line of division between one branch of accounting and another is not always easy to draw. The accumulation and classification of basic accounting data is the function of book-keeping. The information so obtained is, however, used in all branches of accounting. The same applies to various techniques. Discounted cash flow is used most frequently in decision accounting, but it is often used in different aspects of financial accounting. Marginal costing had its origin in cost accounting but is now extensively applied in decision accounting. Indeed the practising accountant would find it difficult to isolate the different branches or orientations of accounting in his day-to-day routine of accounting.

Historical accounting

Historical accounting is the term used to describe the now out-of-date backward-looking approach to accounting. This is, in fact, the approach which was quite prevalent until three or four decades ago.

The main characteristics of historical accounting are as follows. First, there is a great deal of emphasis on what has already taken place, i.e. past transactions. Where such an approach prevails the books of the business are 'opened' at the commencement of the accounting period; transactions are then recorded for twelve months. Some weeks later the external accountants (auditors) take over, and some fifteen months after the commencement of the accounting year would present the final accounts to management.

The difference between historical accounting and the more modern approach lies not only in the accountant's preoccupation with a particular segment of the accounting time-scale. Quite apart from the undue concentration on past transactions, this particular approach detracts from the most vital functions of accounting: it fails to assist management in its task of planning, controlling and decision-making.

Additionally there is in this approach an inordinate stress on the relationship between the business and the outside world. Thus the bought ledger is maintained to enable the business to decide exactly how much is due to its suppliers. The sales or visitors' ledger is kept to ensure that all amounts owing from customers are in due course collected from them. Wages books are similarly kept to make sure that the correct wages are paid to the employees. The fact is that all accounting records, including the sales and bought ledgers and payroll, contain a great deal of valuable information which is vital to management. Yet it is the requirements of management that historical accounting ignores.

Historical accounting is a matter of both orientation and emphasis; and elements of this approach will even now be found in many hotels and restaurants. Whilst some of the larger hospitality organizations have been employing management accountants, revenue accountants, credit controllers and budget accountants for a generation, many of the smaller units still rely on part-time or full-time book-keepers or accountants, whose time is limited and tends to be devoted to the maintenance of basic historical records.

Cost accounting

Whilst financial accounting tends to concentrate on external financial relationships, cost accounting is concerned with the essential internal operational processes of the business. Similarly, it is concerned much more with flows of income and expenditure and is only to a lesser extent related to the management of the financial resources of the business.

Traditionally the principal function of cost accounting is to record expenditure and supply cost information to management. Hence, the cost accountant has two major responsibilities: (a) to design a system of cost recording and supervise its operation; and (b) to supply information for management purposes.

Cost accounting is closely allied to the modern concept of management accounting. In many respects the nature of these two branches of accounting and, as some would claim, their objectives are very similar. This is, in fact, evidenced by recent additions to accounting literature and the numerous courses offered on 'cost and management accounting'.

As explained in Chapter 1, cost accounting had its origin in mainly cost-oriented manufacturing industries. The orientation of cost accounting is, therefore, alien to the nature of hotel and restaurant operation. Hence in the chapters which follow the traditional cost accounting approach will be modified so as to accord with the requirements of the market-oriented business unit.

Financial accounting

In some respects financial accounting is the opposite of cost accounting. Whilst in the latter we concentrate largely on the internal transactions, in the former there is a great deal of emphasis on the relationship of the business with the outside world.

In addition to the preparation of final accounts, the financial accountant will be responsible for the provision of information to shareholders, bankers and government departments.

Much of the financial work done is undertaken by professional accountants in practice. These are concerned with the accuracy of the accounts prepared internally, compliance of final accounts with current company legislation, the computation of tax liabilities and similar matters.

Other aspects of accounting work which fall into the area of financial accounting are: company formation, sources of capital, issue of shares and debentures, the management of short- medium- and long-term capital, consolidated accounts, liquidations, bankruptcies and investigations. Financial accounting, therefore, is not much oriented towards the actual business operations.

Decision accounting

The concept of decision accounting is relatively new. It is essentially the sum total of accounting techniques which aid the decision-making process. Some of the principal techniques used in decision accounting are: marginal costing, break-even analysis, ratio analysis and discounted cash flow.

Where there are a number of alternatives, it is the function of decision accounting to secure sufficient relevant information regarding each alternative, evaluate the possible consequences of each alternative and suggest appropriate solutions. Decision accounting is essentially of a non-routine nature as important decisions are, clearly, not made every day or even every week. Each major problem is somewhat different and requires a different approach.

A hotel company may have spare cash resources of £2,000,000 and a number of alternatives may be open to it: to take over an additional hotel; to modernize its existing units: to diversify by acquiring a chain of restaurants in another part of the country; to invest the cash in a subsidiary company, etc. Quite obviously, the greater the number of alternatives the more difficult the decision.

Decision accounting is a collection of techniques drawn from several branches of accounting, particularly cost accounting and financial accounting, and is generally regarded as an integral part of management accounting. It is not a method of accounting (e.g. as budgetary control or departmental accounting) but a sum of techniques applied on an *ad hoc* basis whenever a decision has to be made.

Control accounting

Control is the process by which the management ensures that actual results are in conformity with the policy of the business. Thus the starting point for control accounting is the formulation of policy and the translation of such policy into practical terms: budgets, standard procedures and operating instructions.

Most of the work associated with control accounting is of a routine nature. Current actual results have to be ascertained, compared with budgeted results (or measured against other appropriate yardsticks) and reported on regularly and expeditiously. The work of the control accountant, or controller, will, therefore, encompass budgetary control, costing and pricing methods, food and beverage control and operating statistics. Ability to present information and write reports are indispensable attributes of the controller.

The main task of the controller is to identify revenue-producing and other departments, ensure that there is a budget for each department, arrange a suitable means of recording current performance and, finally, present appropriate reports to management.

Though most of the work involved in control accounting is of a routine nature, it is no less important than other branches of accounting. This is particularly so in market-oriented businesses which, as explained earlier, have a short cycle of operations and are subject to a high degree of profit instability.

Management accounting

The term 'management accounting' was first used in Britain (following the visit of the Anglo-American Council on Productivity Management Accounting Team to the United States) in 1950. The term is, therefore, of comparatively recent origin. Even if not all agree on the precise definition of management accounting, its nature and functions are now well understood.

In many ways management accounting is the opposite of historical accounting. In the latter the accountant's main concern is the recording of past transactions. In management accounting there is, on the other hand, a forward-looking approach: we are more interested in the present and the future.

The second distinguishing feature of management accounting is a question of attitude and outlook: the management accountant does not stand aloof, but takes an active interest in all management problems and provides information designed to help management in the day-to-day running of the business. In the process of providing such information, the management accountant makes use of many techniques which are also used in other branches of accounting: marginal costing, discounted cash flow, break-even analysis, budgetary control, ratio analysis, etc.

Finally, management accounting deals with individual departments rather than the business as a whole. The management accountant will, therefore, spend a great deal of time on activities such as analyses of departmental performance, pricing procedures, budget reports and the provision of cost, revenue and profit information to top management. Also, an active interest in, and familiarity with, departmental operations is indispensable.

Revenue accounting

In Chapter 1 we looked at the characteristics and problems of the market-oriented sector of the hospitality and tourism industry. Our conclusion was that the traditional, cost-oriented accounting approach was not appropriate to this sector of the industry; and that consequently, accounting methods and procedures should have a market-oriented, or revenue-oriented, approach. This approach to accounting may, for our purposes here, be described as a 'revenue accounting' approach.

Market orientation implies a high degree of dependence on market demand, a situation where almost all major problems arise on the revenue (as opposed to cost or production) side of the business. It is also on the revenue side of the business that the most successful solutions will be found to such problems.

The implications of this situation for management accounting are clear. The management accountant in a market-oriented business must adopt a revenue accounting approach to all his work. He must realize that many accounting methods and techniques have a cost-oriented origin and are not, therefore, wholly relevant to the problems that arise in the market-oriented business. Secondly, he must accept that, at least in the short run, most of the costs of his organization are fixed and uncontrollable. His attention must, consequently, be shifted from the debit to the credit side of the profit and loss account. This applies equally, whether he is engaged on control accounting or preparing an *ad hoc* project for a special decision.

What may be achieved in the cost-oriented business through cost manipulation and cost control, should in the market-oriented business be attempted through revenue control. Revenue accounting, therefore, is a matter of outlook and a particular accounting orientation which stems from the nature and problems of the market-oriented business.

PROBLEMS

1. Explain, using assumed figures, why the balance sheet always balances.
2. Why is it necessary to distinguish between the business and its proprietors?
3. 'Accounting records can only show what is capable of being expressed in terms of money.' Explain.
4. Explain what is meant by the 'going-concern concept'.
5. What do you understand by the term 'accrual accounting'?
6. Why is it that the accountant insists on consistency in accounting procedures from one period to another?
7. What do you understand by the term 'materiality'?
8. Is the accountant right in refusing to anticipate profits but making provision for all possible losses?
9. Write short, explanatory notes on:
   (a) historical accounting
   (b) cost accounting
   (c) financial accounting
   (d) decision accounting
   (e) control accounting.
10. It has been said that 'the essential aim of management accountancy should be to assist management in decision-making and control'. Does it follow that the principal ingredients of management accounting are decision accounting and control accounting?
11. Quote any three definitions of management accounting and identify their common elements.
12. 'The management accountant in a market-oriented business must adopt a revenue accounting approach to all his work.' Discuss.
13. A 300-bedroomed city hotel has decided to appoint a management accountant. Write a job specification for this appointment, making any assumptions that may be neccessary.
14. State what qualifications and attributes you would expect to find in a potential management accountant of a tour operator, quite apart from formal accounting qualifications.

3 | Basic cost concepts

INTRODUCTION

The word 'cost' is not easy to define. When a cost is incurred there is clearly some diminution or reduction in the value of an asset; something is sacrificed or forgone now in order to secure some benefit at a later stage.

Costs may arise in two main ways. When a hotel buys a dishwasher there is no immediate cost. Initially, at least, one asset (cash) is decreased and another (kitchen plant) increased. The total of the assets is unchanged. The dishwasher will—unlike 'cash at bank', especially that on deposit—last only a given number of years, and the initial value of the asset will inexorably be decreasing from one year to another. The initial 'cost' (i.e. cash outlay) of the dishwasher will therefore give rise to an annual 'expense' over a period of time, and so cost is incurred at a point in time. Expense is related to the accounting time scale in accordance with the concept of accrual accounting. Expense is thus the expired cost.

When cash is spent on labour, rent, insurance, etc., costs are incurred in a different manner. There is a decrease in cash, but no corresponding immediate increase in another asset. The calculation of the annual expense in this second case is considerably easier than in the first, where estimates and assumptions have to be made with regard to the technological properties of the asset and its consequent effective life.

Accounting is often referred to as the 'language of business'. If, as such, it is to be an effective means of communication, it must not only operate within the framework of a set of well-developed rules, but also have the characteristic of precision. Thus to say that something cost £x is vague and potentially misleading. In order to add precision to a statement it is essential that the noun 'cost' is preceded by the appropriate adjective.

Let us take an example. The statement that 'the cost of running the banqueting department last year was £200,000 could be interpreted in several ways. It may refer to (a) the food and beverage cost of that department; (b) the cost of food, beverages and banqueting labour, (c) the cost of food, beverages, banqueting labour and direct departmental expenses; and finally (d) all expenses listed in (c) plus a proportion of fixed expenses such as: management salaries, administration and office expenses, advertising and depreciation.

In order, therefore, to give a precise meaning to the noun 'cost' it is necessary to precede it by some adjective such as 'fixed', 'controllable', 'budgeted', 'direct', etc. In this way we develop purpose-oriented and unambiguous cost concepts, all of which will be used in different settings and different situations. It is essential for the manager to be familiar with these cost concepts: otherwise he will find it difficult not only to think about business problems with the requisite degree of precision but also to communicate with his accounting advisers. The aim of the pages which follow is, therefore, to introduce the reader to the principal cost concepts and explain what cost concepts are appropriate in particular situations.

FIXED AND VARIABLE COSTS

Definitions and examples

From the point of view of the behaviour of costs in response to changes in the volume of sales (or rate of activity) it is possible to distinguish three categories of cost.

Fixed costs are those which do not respond to changes in the volume of sales. Whatever the sales, fixed costs remain constant. Examples of fixed costs are rent, rates, management salaries, administrative and office expenses and depreciation. All these accrue with the passage of time, and are, therefore, sometimes referred to as *period costs*.

Variable costs are those which vary in proportion to the sales volume. Whatever the change in sales there is, for practical purposes, a proportional change in variable costs. The best examples of variable costs are food and beverage costs. When the volume of business increases by ten per cent there is normally a ten per cent increase in food and beverage costs. Conversely, a particular percentage decrease in the sales volume will be matched by that percentage decrease in food and beverage costs.

In addition to costs which are fully fixed or fully variable there is a group described as *semi-fixed costs* (also referred to as semi-variable costs). These are costs which move in sympathy with but not in proportion to the volume of sales. Examples of semi-fixed costs are gas, electricity, telephone, breakages and renewals.

Let us take an example. Suppose the cost of kitchen fuel required to produce 1,000 meals is £10. Quite clearly, if the output of the kitchen is increased by 100 per cent to 2,000 meals, there will be some increase in the cost of kitchen fuel. As all experienced caterers know, the increased cost of kitchen fuel will not be as much as £20. What happens then in the case of semi-fixed costs is that we have a change in the same direction, but not quite at the same rate as the change in the volume of sales. To revert to our example, the increased cost of kitchen fuel may be £13, £14, £15 or some such figure, depending on the nature of the meals prepared, the equipment used and the cost-consciousness of the kitchen staff.

The response of semi-fixed costs to changes in the level of activity will, therefore, vary from one semi-fixed cost to another and from one establishment to another. Where there is a change in the volume of sales of 20 per cent and this results in a change in a semi-fixed cost of ten per cent, we say that the semi-fixed cost is 50 per cent variable. Thus when sales rise from £1,000

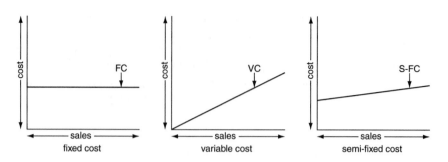

Figure 3.1 Fixed, variable and semi-fixed costs

to £1,400 (i.e. 40 per cent) and a semi-fixed cost rises from £100 to £110 (i.e. 10 per cent) the semi-fixed cost is only 25 per cent variable.

It is useful for many purposes to represent costs graphically. The three categories of cost may be represented as shown in Figure 3.1.

FIXED COSTS: SOME QUALIFICATIONS

We have said that fixed costs are fixed in amount irrespective of the volume of sales. In the real world, however, fixed costs are not as fixed as many might imagine. Let us, therefore, look at one or two qualifications.

Over a long period of time the general price level may change very considerably. Indeed, from time to time we have inflation running at well over 10 per cent—when all costs, including those described as fixed, display a distinct upward trend. One should remember, however, that such fixed costs are rising because of general inflationary conditions and not in response to changes in the sales volume. It is, in such circumstances, still correct to describe them as fixed costs. In other words, a cost is fixed or variable depending on its response to changes in the sales volume; its behaviour in conditions of inflation is, in this respect, quite irrelevant.

A fixed cost is fixed only within a particular range of activity called the *relevant range*. Thus if a restaurant serves between 200 and 400 covers per day, its fixed cost will be determined by the operational requirements of that level of food production and food service. This implies a particular mix of full-time, part-time and casual labour, a particular quantity of plant and equipment, a particular outlay on repairs, maintenance, etc. Should the restaurant occupancy show, for one reason or another, a permanent change then after some inevitable time lag the level of fixed costs will also change. We should, therefore, refer to fixed costs only in relation to the relevant range of activity. The concept of the relevant range for fixed costs is illustrated in Figure 3.2.

SEMI-FIXED COSTS

We have defined a semi-fixed cost as one which moves in the same direction as, but not quite in proportion to, the volume of sales. The main reason for

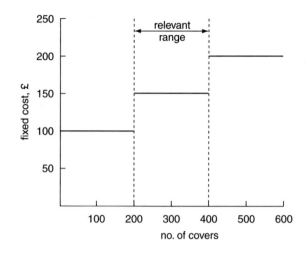

Figure 3.2 Fixed costs and the relevant range

this kind of cost behaviour is that semi-fixed costs are really a mixture of fully fixed and fully variable costs. Where a cost is shown as semi-fixed it is only because it is too costly, or too time-consuming or not immediately essential to isolate the fixed and variable elements of the cost.

The degree of responsiveness of semi-fixed costs to changes in the volume of sales depends on the respective proportions of the fixed and variable elements of each semi-fixed cost. Where the variable element is high a 100 per cent change in sales will result in, often, as much as a 75 per cent change in the semi-fixed cost. Conversely, where the fixed element is high a 100 per cent change in sales may only result in a very modest change in the semi-variable cost.

Let us look at some real examples. One of the typical semi-fixed costs is the cost of the telephone. This is made up of two elements: the periodical rental which is fully fixed and the fully variable element which depends on the number of calls made. Space heating in the hotel is in the same category. Even when the occupancy is nil, it is still necessary to heat—continuously or intermittently—certain areas of the premises. As the rate of occupancy rises, more and more rooms have to be heated and this is reflected in a steady rise in the semi-variable cost. Another typical semi-fixed cost is the cost of labour in a seasonal establishment. Here, again, it is possible to isolate the fixed component—which presumably is the key personnel—and the variable component which changes with the volume of business. The head-office staff of a tour operator are normally permanent employees. A large proportion of guides and hotel representatives are, however, employed during peak periods only.

In many aspects of management accounting work it is inconvenient to deal with all the three cost categories: fixed, semi-fixed and variable costs. It is certainly much easier if all the operating costs can be divided into fully fixed and fully variable costs. There are four methods of dividing semi-variable costs into fully fixed and fully variable components. These are: the high–low method, the regressions chart method, the least squares method and, finally, the practical segregation method.

High–low method

Under this method one picks a high and a low point in the rate of activity (e.g. hotel occupancy, number of covers, etc.) and ascertains the semi-fixed cost relevant to each point. The difference between the two semi-fixed costs is then divided by the difference in the rate of activity. The resulting figure is the increase in the variable element of the semi-fixed cost for each point increase in the rate of activity. An example will make this quite clear.

Example

The table which follows shows the cost of gas consumed in a hotel over a period of eight months.

Month	% Occupancy	Cost of gas, £
January	20	250
February	25	275
March	40	370
April	50	385
May	60	450
June	70	515
July	80	550
August	75	510

To apply the high–low method:

	% Occupancy	Cost of gas, £
High point—July	80	550
Low point—January	20	250
Change	60%	£300

As may be seen, the change in the hotel occupancy is 60% and this has caused a change in the variable element of this semi-fixed cost of £300. If we divide the latter by the former we get a change of £5.00 in the variable element for every one per cent rise in hotel occupancy. We may now ascertain the fixed element.

In January the variable element was (occupancy times the variable element per point of activity), i.e. $20 \times £5.00 = £100$; the fixed element must therefore have been £150. In July the variable element was $80 \times £5.00 = £400$ and, again, the fixed element must have been £150.

The high–low method is simple but not always very accurate. Semi-fixed costs do not always display a linear behaviour; and it is essential to ensure that the periodical figures chosen are reasonably typical. Thus, if we applied the method to the figures available for the first six months the result would have been rather different:

	% Occupancy	Cost of gas, £
High point—June	70	515
Low point—January	20	250
Change	50%	£265

If we divide the change in the variable element by the change in the occupancy of the hotel, we get £5.30 for each point increase in the rate of activity. It is clear, therefore, that the high–low method has its limitations.

Regression chart method

This method is equally easy to apply but is rather more accurate than the high–low method. The procedure is as follows. The semi-fixed cost is measured vertically and the rate of activity horizontally. The periodical semi-fixed costs are then plotted and a *line of best fit* drawn. The line should cut through as many points as possible, leaving (if possible) an equal number of points above and below the line. The regression chart in Figure 3.3 is based on our initial example used to explain the high–low method.

By reference to the regression chart it is immediately apparent that the variable element for each point change in the rate of activity is £5.00. For example, the increase in occupancy from 50 to 70 per cent is one of 20 per cent. This results in an increase in the semi-fixed cost of £100. The increase in the variable element for each one per cent increase in hotel occupancy is therefore £5.00.

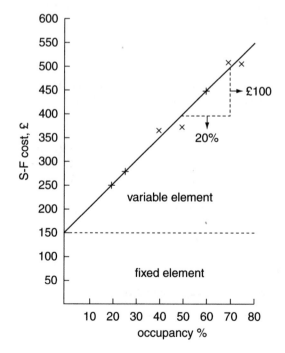

Figure 3.3 Regression chart

The method of least squares

In addition to the high–low and the regression chart method we may use the method of least squares to calculate the fixed and variable element of a semi-fixed cost. It will be remembered that in the high–low method our results depend on which particular high and low points are chosen. With the regression chart method there is frequently more than one way of drawing the line of best fit. In the case of the method of least squares, such anomalies are avoided, and the results obtained are mathematically precise and wholly reliable.

The application of the method requires us to solve two equations. These are known as the 'normal equations' and are given below.

$$\Sigma XY = a\Sigma X + b\Sigma X^2 \qquad (1)$$
$$\Sigma Y = na + b\Sigma X \qquad (2)$$

Where X = measure of volume
Y = semi-fixed cost
a = fixed cost
b = variable cost per unit
n = number of observations
and Σ signifies summation

We use the letter Y to designate the 'dependent variable', i.e. the one we are trying to predict. The letter X is used to designate the 'independent variable', i.e. the one we think affects the dependent variable. In the example which follows, Y is the total semi-fixed cost and X is a measure of volume (i.e. the number of rooms serviced).

Example

Listed below we have, in respect of a six-week period, the weekly number of rooms and the departmental payroll (the semi-fixed cost) in the Rooms Department of a hotel.

Week	Rooms serviced	Departmental payroll (£)
1	160	357
2	180	397
3	170	366
4	190	404
5	200	398
6	220	434

Set out below are the necessary calculations:

Week	X	Y	X^2	XY
		£		
1	160	357	25,600	57,120
2	180	397	32,400	71,460
3	170	366	28,900	62,220
4	190	404	36,100	76,760
5	200	398	40,000	79,600
6	220	434	48,400	95,480
	1,120	2,356	211,400	442,640

If we substitute the relevant values in the normal equations we obtain the following:

$$£442,640 = 1,120a + 211,400b \qquad (1)$$
$$2.356 = 6a + 1,120b \qquad (2)$$

We have two equations and two unknowns. In order to ascertain the values of the unknowns we must use the techniques for solving simultaneous equations. It would appear that the easiest method here is to solve for b by eliminating a. We may eliminate a by multiplying equation (1) by n, which is 6, the coefficient of a in equation (2), and equation (2) by 1,120, which is the coefficient of a in equation (1). We proceed as follows:

$$£2,655,840 = 6,720a + 1,268,400b \qquad (3)$$
$$£2,638,720 = 6,720a + 1,254,400b \qquad (4)$$

Subtracting equation (4) from equation (3) we get:

$$£17,120 = 14,000b$$

therefore $$b = £1.22286$$

and so, for practical purposes, we would say that the variable cost per serviced room is £1.22.

We are now able to substitute the value of b in either equation and solve for a. We substitute £1.22286 for b in equation (2) and get:

$$£2,356 = 6a + (1,120 \times £1.22286)$$
$$£2,356 = 6a + £1,369.6$$
$$£986.4 = 6a$$
$$a = £164.40$$

and so, of the total semi-fixed cost of our departmental payroll in the Rooms Department, the fixed element is £164.40 per week.

Now that we have split the total semi-fixed cost into the fixed and variable elements, we may predict the cost of departmental payroll in relation to any one level of activity in the Rooms Department.

If in week 7, 140 rooms will require to be serviced, the cost of departmental payroll will be:

	£
Fixed element	164.40
Variable element 140 × £1.22286	171.20
Departmental payroll	335.60

In practice, of course, we would not strive for such a high level of precision and would work to the nearest penny, multiplying the projected rooms to be serviced by £1.22.

Practical segregation method

There are a number of hospitality operations in which the composition of certain semi-fixed costs is such as to lend itself to easy segregation into fixed and variable elements. This is particularly so with regard to the cost of labour. Let us look at two examples.

Most outdoor catering companies engage a relatively small number of full-time permanent employees, and a high proportion of staff are reasonably permanent, but part-time and hourly paid. In respect of any one function it is fairly easy to ensure that, for instance, the number of waiting staff is in line with the projected number of covers. Thus, depending on the price per cover, we may have a ratio of anything from eight to fifteen covers per waiter or waitress. In a situation like this the segregation or division of the total (semi-fixed) cost of labour presents no problem at all, as it is abundantly clear which elements of the labour cost are fixed and which are fully variable.

A similar situation obtains in the rooms departments of certain hotels. Here again, whilst the total cost of departmental labour is a semi-fixed cost, there are some elements which are, clearly, fixed (e.g. salaries of executive housekeeper, floor housekeepers, florist, etc.) and others—particularly chambermaids' wages—which are a fully variable cost. The division of the total payroll of the rooms department will be facilitated through the establishment of relevant performance standards. For instance, in some hotels a chambermaid is expected to service a room in 30 minutes. If we can predict occupancy levels then we can also predict the number of rooms that will need to be serviced from one day to another.

Day	Rooms to be serviced	Labour hours required	Chambermaids required
Sunday	100	50	10
Monday	60	30	6
Tuesday	70	35	7
Wednesday	80	40	8
Thursday	110	55	11
Friday	120	60	12
Saturday	100	50	10

Where chambermaids are employed on the basis of 5 hours per day and the standard time is 30 minutes per room, a simple forecast of the daily number of chambermaids required is possible.

If we can secure a degree of adjustment in labour costs such as shown in the above table, the division of the total departmental cost of labour into fully fixed and fully variable elements may be achieved without resorting to methods such as the three already described in this chapter.

Fixed and variable costs: importance and applications

The distinction between fixed and variable costs is of fundamental importance in almost all areas of management accounting.

In break-even analysis we project for various levels of activity the fixed cost and the appropriate variable costs, to find the break-even point and obtain other useful information. Pricing is a most complex problem and here the distinction between fixed and variable costs helps in several respects to find a rational solution to the pricing problem. In budgeting we are concerned with several cost concepts, including to a very large extent fixed and variable costs. The same applies to the technique of discounted cash flow. Finally, the whole field of decision accounting rests on the distinction between fixed and variable costs.

Most certainly of all the cost concepts discussed in this chapter, fixed and variable costs are the most immediately relevant and most commonly applied in a variety of situations.

DIRECT AND INDIRECT COSTS

The distinction between direct and indirect costs flows from the traceability of costs to a unit of output or a department. A cost may be direct in relation to a department but indirect in relation to a unit of output.

Let us look at some examples. Food cost is a direct cost from both points of view. It may be traced to a unit of output (e.g. a menu item, a complete meal). Also it is clear in which department the cost has arisen. Food cost is, therefore, also a direct cost from the point of view of its traceability to a particular department. Kitchen labour is a direct cost as it is clear in which department it originates. It is an indirect cost in relation to a unit of output as it is impossible in normal circumstances to calculate the labour absorption of any one item produced in the kitchen. The typical member of the kitchen crew will, during the course of his working day, perform a variety of tasks. By the end of the day it will be quite impossible to apportion his time between the various items of food he has helped to produce.

> For example, fowl and turkey, which constitute one of the units in food control, go into many dishes and are handled by many persons in the kitchen. To calculate the cost of labour of the butcher in preparing a fowl for the kitchen, of the assistant cook in looking after the boiling, and of the cooks in making chicken salad, chicken a la king, chicken patties,

croquettes, hash, etc. would perhaps be possible, but the cost of the calculation would be disproportionate to the advantage gained.

(E. B. Horwath, L. Troth and J. D. Lesure, *Hotel Accounting*, New York: Ronald Press, 1963, pp. 313–14)

Indirect costs are also referred to as 'common costs' or 'joint costs': they are incurred on behalf of the business as a whole or on behalf of a particular department. The distinction between direct and indirect costs is important in the production of management information.

When compiling unit costs we must only take into account costs which may be traced to a unit of output. When building up departmental costs we should only take into account costs traceable to departments. To do more than this is both difficult and frequently misleading.

Most hotels operate some kind of departmental accounting. The usual approach is to charge against departmental revenue costs which are direct or otherwise controllable at the departmental level. By deducting such costs from departmental revenue we obtain a figure of departmental profit. In order to arrive at the net profit of a department one would have to deduct from the departmental profit a proportion of indirect costs such as management salaries, rent, rates, depreciation of premises, etc.

There is no scientific or accurate method by which such costs could be apportioned to departments. Thus the general manager's salary could be apportioned on the basis of departmental revenues, the number of persons employed in each department, the departmental profits of the various departments, etc. Rent and rates could be apportioned on the basis of space occupied. But, then, is a square metre in the basement equivalent to a square metre on the first floor or the seventh floor? The whole process of apportionment of indirect costs is at best a matter of estimation and opinion and does not guarantee any degree of accuracy. The final figures of departmental net profits depend on what bases of apportionment are chosen and thus do not have much significance or serve any useful purpose. It is for these reasons that most systems of departmental accounting do not attempt to show net profit figures of revenue-producing departments.

Similar considerations apply to unit costs of menu items. The usual procedure is to arrive at the food cost of each item: no attempt is made to add to such food costs a proportion of kitchen or dining-room labour or, indeed, a proportion of general administration expenses. A total unit cost so built up is quite artificial and wholly meaningless.

CONTROLLABLE AND UNCONTROLLABLE COSTS

The distinction between controllable and uncontrollable costs depends on management's ability to influence cost levels or, tautologically, on the controllability of costs.

Examples of controllable costs are food costs, beverage costs, part-time and casual labour. Uncontrollable costs are insurances, rent, rates, depreciation and similar items. Whether a cost is controllable or otherwise depends in some cases on the level of management. Thus if the establishment for the kitchen personnel is twenty, it is not within the power of the executive chef to vary this by employing an additional sous-chef or dismissing a plongeur. The cost of labour, assuming that the establishment is non-seasonal, is therefore uncontrollable at the departmental level. The general manager of the establishment has the authority to vary the staffing of all the departments, and at this level of management the labour cost of the kitchen is controllable.

The concepts of controllable and uncontrollable costs are particularly useful in the area of accounting sometimes referred to as 'responsibility accounting'. A full treatment of responsibility accounting will be found in Chapter 11.

An important feature of responsibility accounting is the division of the business into clearly defined divisions, areas or departments and the assignment of responsibility for each division to a particular manager. Quite clearly when calculating the net profit of a division of a business it would be inequitable to take into account items over which the manager has no control. Thus the banqueting manager should be fully responsible for food and beverage costs and the relevant profit margins; also for labour costs, the cost of music, entertainment, stationery and similar items. He should not be held responsible for the cost of the space his department occupies nor be charged with a proportion of general administration expenses of the hotel. His responsibility for the trading results of his department must correspond with the authority he has for incurring expenditure. Responsibility and authority must be co-extensive.

ESTIMATED BUDGETED AND STANDARD COSTS

There is a great deal of confusion regarding the respective and precise meanings of estimated, budgeted and standard costs.

When we estimate we are making a prediction of some future happening. For example we may say that the cost of so-and-so was £10 two years ago, £12 last year and that it is likely to be £14 this year. We are simply looking at the trend of events indifferently and dispassionately.

When we budget, however, our intention comes into play. We might then say 'although the cost was £10 two years ago and £12 last year, we just cannot afford to pay £14 this year and will make every effort to maintain the cost at £13'. A budgeted cost then is a 'normative' cost in that it reflects the management's intention with regard to what a particular cost ought to be.

The main difference between budgeted and standard costs is one of detail. Standard costs are also normative costs but are built up from a multitude of detail. A good example of the way in which such costs are built up is the standard recipe. It pre-determines the quality and quantities of ingredients, the yield obtainable and shows a detailed step-by-step procedure for the production of the item of food concerned.

Budgeted and standard costs are used mainly in various areas of control accounting particularly—of course—in budgetary control. The current trend is to show in most management reports actual and budgeted (or standard) figures rather than actual and 'previous period' figures. The former is more meaningful than the latter, as any budgeted figures would normally have been arrived at in the light of what happened during the corresponding period of the previous year. Estimated costs and revenues tend to be used in areas of decision accounting, where budgeted and standard costs tend to figure quite prominently too.

AVERAGE COST AND MARGINAL COST

Average cost is normally understood as total cost divided by the number of units produced or sold. Thus if a hotel accommodated 500 clients during a particular week and incurred a total cost of £20,000 the average cost per client would be £40.

Marginal cost may be defined as the increase in total cost resulting from one more unit (or batch of units) being produced. Hence, if in the following week the hotel accommodated 501 clients and had a total cost of £20,010 the marginal cost would be £10. Whilst average cost shows the proportion of total cost, i.e. both fixed and variable cost, per unit of output, marginal cost reflects the changes occurring in the variable portion of total cost.

The distinction between these two cost concepts is of paramount importance. Whilst in some situations it is, so to speak, right and proper to look at average costs, in other situations it is essential to think in terms of marginal costs. As a general rule we use the average cost concept in strategic, long-run situations and the marginal cost concept in tactical, short-run situations.

It will be appreciated that the essential difference between these two situations is this. In the short run fixed costs remain fixed; whatever decision is made the amount of fixed costs will not be affected. In such circumstances it is as well to keep the fixed costs in the background and concentrate on the consequences of decisions on variable costs. If, on the other hand, a decision is to be made which will have consequences over a long period—at least months but normally years—it is obvious that both fixed and variable costs have to be taken into account.

To take a simple example, a hotel charges £50 per room. Its total cost is £45 and the latter consists of fixed costs of £40 and a variable element of £5. The net profit per room is therefore £5. Let us assume that one day during a relatively slack period a customer arrives, but is unwilling to pay as much as £50 and says 'if you'll have me for £20, I'll stay'. The reception manager has obviously two alternatives: to accept or not to accept the customer. If he accepts the customer he will increase the sales of the hotel by £20 and increase the variable costs by £5. He will thus add to the net profit of the business £15 or decrease the net loss by that amount. If he rejects the customer's offer he will deprive the hotel of that little additional profit. It should be noted that, whatever the reception manager's decision, the fixed costs of the hotel are not affected. The appropriate cost concept to use in such circumstances is that of marginal, not average, cost.

It is clear, however, that it would not be right for the hotel to sell its accommodation at prices below total cost or just above marginal cost over a long period. By the end of the accounting year it is essential for the business to cover all its costs and show a fair rate of net profit.

OUTLAY COST AND OPPORTUNITY COST

An outlay cost is the financial expenditure which is recorded in accounting records. An opportunity cost is the profit from some alternative venture which is foregone by using resources for a particular purpose.

Outlay costs are easy to comprehend: they are there, recorded in the books; they have in fact taken place; they may be measured, related to units of output, sales, etc.

The concept of the opportunity cost is, however, more difficult to appreciate. Suppose a restaurant company has a spare cash balance of £600,000. The immediate possibilities for investing the cash may be: (a) to take over an existing restaurant for £600,000; (b) to modernize the existing units operated by the company.

If the company decides in favour of alternative (a) then, clearly, the outlay cost will be £600,000. However, by deciding in favour of this alternative the company fails to modernize its existing units, and this certainly will affect their decor, atmosphere and efficiency which, in turn, will make it more difficult for them to attract business. The opportunity cost of the new unit is, therefore, what the company forgoes by not deciding in favour of alternative (b). To quote from a well-known textbook of managerial economics (J. Dean, *Managerial Economics*, Englewood Cliffs, NJ: Prentice-Hall, 1951, p. 260):

> in business decisions the message of opportunity costs is that it is dangerous to confine cost knowledge to what the firm is doing. What the firm is not doing but could do is frequently the critical cost consideration which it is perilous but easy to ignore.

Where several alternatives exist, opportunity cost is the profit of the most profitable venture forgone by using resources for some other purpose.

The concept of opportunity cost is especially useful in the field of decision accounting and particularly in cases involving the allocation of scarce resources. Numerous examples could be given in relation to hospitality operations. Let us look at just one example. In the case of a new hotel a decision has to be made on the allocation of space to various revenue-producing and other departments. The greater the allocation to, say, the banqueting department the smaller the allocation to the other departments. What matters is not only the outlay cost of the additional x square metres of space but also the effect of a more modest space allocation elsewhere.

PROBLEMS

1. Explain what you understand by the noun 'cost'.
2. Define the following:
   (a) fixed cost

(b) semi-fixed cost

(c) variable cost.

3. What is the practical usefulness of the concept of the 'relevant range'?

4. Explain the high–low method and the regression chart method.

5. Given below are the daily numbers of covers served by a catering organization and the total cost of labour. Using the method of least squares calculate the daily fixed element and the variable element (i.e. the variable cost per cover).

Day	Covers	Labour cost £
Monday	2,000	1,600
Tuesday	3,000	2,450
Wednesday	5,000	3,850
Thursday	4,000	3,050
Friday	1,000	1,100
Saturday	2,500	2,000

6. Compare and contrast the following cost concepts:

(a) fixed and variable costs

(b) direct and indirect costs

(c) controllable and uncontrollable costs

(d) estimated and budgeted costs

(e) average and marginal costs

(f) outlay and opportunity costs.

7. 'The word "cost" has many meanings in different settings. The kind of cost concept to be used in a particular situation depends upon the business decision to be made' (J. Dean, *Managerial Economics*, Englewood Cliffs, NJ: Prentice-Hall, 1951). Discuss.

8. 'In particular, it is important to remember that there is no such thing as "the" cost of something in any situation in which joint or common costs are involved, and they usually are' (R. N. Anthony, *Management Accounting*, 3rd edn, Homewood, Illinois: R. D. Irwin, 1964).

(a) State, giving reasons, whether you agree with the above view.

(b) What implications has the above statement for the compilation of unit costs?

9. Set out below are particulars of rooms serviced and the monthly cost of payroll in the Rooms Department of a 100-bedroomed hotel.

Month	No. of rooms serviced	Departmental payroll £
January	1,000	8,000
February	1,100	8,400
March	1,300	8,800
April	1,600	9,800
May	2,000	11,000
June	2,400	12,200
July	2,900	13,800
August	2,800	13,400

September	2,500	12,400
October	2,100	11,200
November	1,700	10,200
December	1,400	9,200

You are required to calculate the fixed and variable elements of the total payroll in the Rooms Department using: (a) the high–low method; (b) the regression chart method and (c) the method of least squares. Comment on the results obtained from each of the three calculations.

10. Give three examples of each of the following cost concepts:
    (a) fixed and variable costs
    (b) direct and indirect costs
    (c) average and marginal costs
    (d) outlay and opportunity costs

    by reference to: (i) a tour operator and (ii) a retail travel agent.

4 Sales–cost–profit relationships

COST STRUCTURE AND PROFITABILITY

As mentioned in previous chapters one of the most important features of the market-oriented business is a high proportion of fixed costs. Most hospitality and tourism businesses operate at a high proportion of fixed costs, though this applies more to the former than the latter.

High fixed costs tend to produce a condition of *profit instability*, particularly when the sales volume fluctuates from one trading period to another. Let us look at a simple example.

Let us assume that there are two restaurants, Hifix and Lofix. Both have an identical volume of sales and operate at the same percentage of net profit on sales. Their cost structures are, however, dissimilar. Let us also assume that, for some reason, the volume of sales is in both cases reduced by 10 per cent.

As may be seen from the table below, the 10 per cent decrease in the volume of sales has affected the net profit of the two restaurants quite differently. In the case of Hifix restaurant the net profit has decreased from £1,000 to £300—a reduction of 70 per cent. In the case of Lofix Restaurant the net profit has decreased from £1,000 to £600—a reduction of 40 per cent.

The conclusions which may be drawn from the above example are as follows. First, the higher the percentage of fixed costs the more important it is to secure an adequate volume of sales. Where the percentage of fixed costs is very high, it is primarily the volume of sales that determines the net profit of the business. Needless to say, the higher the percentage of fixed costs the greater the effect of any one change in the sales volume on the net profit of the business.

	Hifix		*Lofix*	
	Period 1	*Period 2*	*Period 1*	*Period 2*
	£	£	£	£
Sales	10,000	9,000	10,000	9,000
Fixed costs	6,000	6,000	3,000	3,000
Variable costs	3,000	2,700	6,000	5,400
Total cost	9,000	8,700	9,000	8,400
Net profit	£1,000	£300	£1,000	£600

Secondly, where fixed costs are high it is dangerous to operate at a low percentage of net profit. The lower the net profit on sales, the greater the impact of sales fluctuations on profitability. Had the two restaurants in our example started with a net profit on sales of 20 per cent, the impact of the 10 per cent decrease in their sales would have been appreciably less. This is shown in the table below.

	Hifix		*Lofix*	
	Period 1	*Period 2*	*Period 1*	*Period 2*
	£	£	£	£
Sales	10,000	9,000	10,000	9,000
Fixed costs	5,500	5,500	2,500	2,500
Variable costs	2,500	2,250	5,500	4,950
Total cost	8,000	7,750	8,000	7,450
Net profit	£2,000	£1,250	£2,000	£1,550

The position now is materially different. The net profit of Hifix Restaurant has been reduced by 37.5 per cent. That of Lofix Restaurant has been reduced by 22.5 per cent. It is quite obvious, therefore, that if the market-oriented business is to enjoy a reasonable degree of profit stability it must operate at an adequate net profit on sales.

FIXED COSTS AND FLUCTUATING SALES

Let us now take a closer look at the effect of sales instability. The fluctuations in the volume of sales experienced by hotels and restaurants occur during the working day, over the working week and throughout the calendar year. Where there is a high proportion of fixed costs such changes in the sales volume will have a profound effect on profitability.

Figure 4.1 shows the effects of cost fixity and sales instability on a larger restaurant.

As may be seen from Figure 4.1, the beginning of the week is slack and both Monday and Tuesday show a loss. The number of covers rises on Wednesday and this enables the restaurant to make a modest profit of £120, after which there is a progressive improvement in profitability. This is shown diagrammatically in Figure 4.2.

However, it will be appreciated that it takes the restaurant almost until the end of Thursday to offset the net loss incurred on Monday and Tuesday. The result is that the net profit for the working week is just in excess of the profits made on Friday and Saturday. This is illustrated in Figure 4.3 which shows the cumulative results over the working week.

The consequences of this weekly pattern of sales instability are similar to those which flow from the annual problem of seasonality. Hospitality establishments of a seasonal nature operate at a net loss at the beginning of the

Day	Mon	Tue	Wed	Thu	Fri	Sat	Total
No. of covers	100	120	150	170	220	240	1,000
	£	£	£	£	£	£	£
Av. spending power[1]	12	12	12	12	12	12	12
Sales	1,200	1,440	1,800	2,040	2,640	2,880	12,000
Fixed costs	960	960	960	960	960	960	5,760
Variable costs[2]	480	576	720	816	1,056	1,152	4,800
Total cost	1,440	1,536	1,680	1,776	2,016	2,112	10,560
N. profit (N. loss)	(240)	(96)	120	264	624	768	1,440
Cumulative results:							
Sales	1,200	2,640	4,440	6,480	9,120	12,000	
Total cost	1,440	2,976	4,656	6,432	8,448	10,560	
N. profit (N. loss)	(240)	(336)	(216)	48	672	1,440	

1 Average spending power means the average amount spent per customer, i.e. sales divided by the number of customers.
2 Here assumed to be 40 per cent of sales.

Figure 4.1 Effect of cost fixity and sales instability on profit

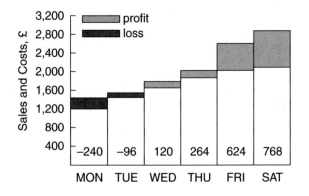

Figure 4.2 Effect of cost fixity and sales instability on profits

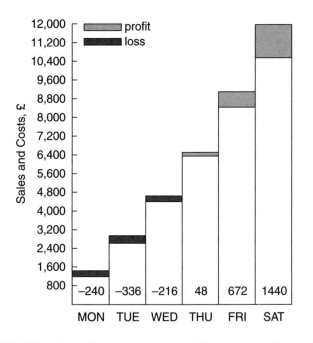

Figure 4.3 Effect of cost fixity and sales instability on cumulative weekly results

calendar year, and in many cases it takes them until May or June to offset losses incurred and start making a profit. The total net profit accumulated by the end of the season may then be quite appreciably eroded by low occupancies towards the end of the calendar year.

THE BREAK-EVEN POINT (BEP)

A business is said to break even when its total sales are equal to its total cost. In other words, it is a condition where there is no net profit and no net loss.

Let us look at an example. A café has fixed costs of £3,000 per week and serves up to 1,000 covers. Its average spending power (ASP) is £8.00, of which 40 per cent is needed to pay for the café's variable costs.

As of the £8.00, £3.20 is required to cover variable cost, £4.80 is the balance (frequently referred to as 'contribution'—see next section of this chapter) available, first to cover the fixed costs and secondly as net profit. It follows, therefore, that if we divide the weekly fixed cost by the balance of £4.80 (i.e. contribution per cover) we shall obtain the number of customers required by the café to break even. Hence:

$$\frac{£3,000}{£4.80} = 625 \text{ customer (or covers)}$$

Proving that the above calculation is correct:

625 covers @ £8.00 = sales		£5,000
Less: Variable cost (VC) = 40% of sales	£2,000	
Fixed costs	3,000	5,000

Total sales of the café are equal to its total cost, there is no net profit and no net loss. The formula, therefore, for calculating the break-even point in terms of the number of covers is:

$$\frac{\text{Fixed costs}}{\text{ASP less VC per cover}} = \text{BEP}$$

In order to calculate the break-even point in terms of the volume of sales, the formula is:

$$\frac{\text{Fixed costs} \times \text{sales}}{\text{Sales} - \text{variable costs}} = \text{BEP}$$

Therefore:

$$\frac{£3,000 \times £5,000}{£5,000 - £2,000} = £5,000$$

From what has been said so far, it will be realized that the break-even point is reached when the excess of sales over variable cost is equal to the fixed costs.

An example will make this clear. A snack bar has weekly fixed costs of £9,000. Its number of covers varies from 200 to 2000 per week. The average spending power is £10, and variable costs are equal to 25 per cent of sales. Figure 4.4 shows that 1,200 covers are required to reach this break-even point.

To apply the first formula which expresses the break-even point in terms of the number of covers:

$$\frac{\text{Fixed costs}}{\text{ASP less VC per cover}} = \frac{£9,000}{£7.50} = 1,200 \text{ covers}$$

To apply the second formula which expresses the break-even point in terms of the volume of sales:

$$\frac{\text{Fixed costs} \times \text{sales}}{\text{Sales} - \text{variable costs}} = \frac{(£9,000 \times £12,000)}{(£12,000 - £3,000)} = £12,000$$

No.of covers	Sales	Variable costs	Sales less variable costs	
	£	£	£	
200	2,000	500	1,500	
400	4,000	1,000	3,000	
600	6,000	1,500	4,500	
800	8,000	2,000	6,000	
1,000	10,000	2,500	7,500	
1,200	12,000	3,000	9,000	→ Equal to fixed costs
1,400	14,000	3,500	10,500	
1,600	16,000	4,000	12,000	
1,800	18,000	4,500	13,500	
2,000	20,000	5,000	15,000	

Figure 4.4 Explanation of the concept of break-even point

Sales instability in tourism

The examples we have given so far relate to hospitality operations. Students will, on reflection, realize that the whole field of tourism is affected by seasonality. Tour operators have always been subject to substantial fluctuations in their volume of business, the peak months being July, August and September. During the last decade or so we have seen an increase in the popularity of cheap off-peak holidays; and now a significant proportion of the tour operator's business consists of cheap and frequently long holidays of 4–6 weeks. This relatively new business has had a positive effect on both the employment of staff and the utilization of resources in the tourist destinations concerned.

The retail travel agent is very much in the same category. Most travel agents—as already noted in Chapter 1—operate at a high percentage of fixed costs. Their revenue—commission from the sale of package holidays and railway tickets—tends to fluctuate considerably over the calendar year. In consequence, both tour operators and travel agents suffer from a high degree of sales and profit instability.

CONTRIBUTION AND THE C/S RATIO

'Contribution' may be defined as the excess of sales over variable cost.

Contribution is, therefore, a surplus which in the first instance is available to cover fixed costs and, when fixed costs have been covered, as net profit. This is illustrated in Figure 4.5. Of the total sales of £1000, £400 is required to pay for the variable costs: contribution thus amounts to £600. This may be divided into two slices: £400 to pay for the fixed costs, and the residue of £200 which is net profit.

Contribution as a percentage of sales will vary quite considerably from one business to another; also from one revenue-producing department to another in the same establishment.

We have defined contribution as the excess of sales over variable cost. It follows, therefore, that contribution as a percentage of sales will depend on

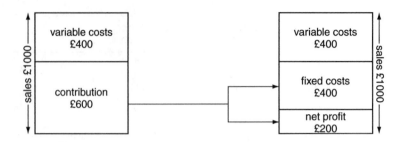

Figure 4.5 The concept of contribution

the cost structure of the business. The higher the variable cost, and the lower the fixed cost, the lower the contribution—and vice versa. The majority of hospitality businesses operate at a high percentage of fixed costs. Most of them will, therefore, have a high percentage of contribution in relation to their volume of sales. Tour operators are in a similar situation to hotels and operate at a high percentage of contribution. Travel agents, on the other hand, have a very modest percentage of contribution—frequently of the order of 10 per cent.

From the point of view of business dynamics, a high percentage of contribution is very significant. In the short run fixed costs are, by definition, fixed. Where contribution is high, changes in the volume of sales will have a powerful impact on net profit. Once fixed costs have been covered, every increase in contribution is an addition to net profit. This may be verified by reference to the example on the Hifix and Lofix Restaurants at the beginning of this chapter.

The three basic 'products' sold by hotels are accommodation, food and beverages. In the case of room sales variable costs are commonly very low, frequently in the region of 5–10 per cent. Contribution will, in such circumstances, be very high. In the case of food and beverage sales variable costs tend to account for 40–50 per cent of the sales volume. Contribution will, therefore, vary between 50 and 60 per cent. To take an additional example, the variable cost in the case of cigarettes and tobaccos is very high, usually 80 to 90 per cent. Contribution as a percentage of sales in this case will be very low indeed.

From the point of view of the profitability of hospitality businesses what matters is not only the total volume of sales but also what is described as 'sales mix', i.e. the composition of sales. An increase in the sales of cigarettes and tobaccos of £300 will invariably bring less net profit than an increase in room sales of £100. Quite clearly the greater the percentage differences in departmental contributions the more important it is to monitor closely the sales mix of the business as a whole.

Contribution/sales ratio

The concept of the C/S ratio (contribution to sales ratio) is closely related to that of contribution. The former is a percentile expression of the latter. To revert to the example in Figure 4.5 the position is as follows:

	£	%
Sales	1,000	100
Less variable costs	400	40
Contribution	£600	60 = C/S ratio

The C/S ratio is a convenient method of measuring the impact of changes in the volume of sales on net profit. Where the C/S ratio is 60 per cent, of each £100 of additional revenue £40 will be absorbed by variable costs and £60 will be the addition to net profit, assuming of course that the break-even point has already been reached. Similarly every loss of revenue of £100 will decrease the net profit by £60. We are, of course, now referring to short-term fluctuation in the volume of sales during which fixed costs remain fixed.

FIXED COSTS: IMPACT ON UNIT COSTS

Whilst in some situations it is the total cost of an operation which is looked at, in others it is more appropriate to look at unit costs. The impact, or incidence, of fixed costs on cost per unit is generally well understood. It is, however, worth stressing that in market-oriented (high-fixed-cost) industries that impact is particularly powerful. And, of course, it goes without saying that the higher the proportion of fixed costs the more dramatic the effect of fixed costs on the total cost per unit.

Example

A sports club holds an annual dinner dance. The organizers have decided on the venue of the next function and engaged a band. From available information it appears that fixed costs will be incurred as follows:

	£
Hire of hall	350
Band	500
Floral decorations	150
Total	1,000

Agreement has been reached with a firm of outdoor caterers, who have undertaken to supply all food and beverages at £10 per head. The capacity of the hall is 300 persons and the organizers are confident that at least 50 persons will attend. A projection of revenue, costs and profits or losses on the assumption that the price charged will be £20 per head could take the following form:

	Number of persons					
	50	100	150	200	250	300
	£	£	£	£	£	£
Sales	1,000	2,000	3,000	4,000	5,000	6,000
Fixed costs	1,000	1,000	1,000	1,000	1,000	1,000
Variable costs	500	1,000	1,500	2,000	2,500	3,000
Profit (Loss)	(500)	—	500	1,000	1,500	2,000

As may be seen from the above table the break-even point is 100 persons, after which there is a sharp increase in the net profit on the function with each increase in the number of persons attending. This is due to the incidence of fixed costs on the total cost per unit, and is illustrated by the table below:

	Number of persons					
	50	100	150	200	250	300
	£	£	£	£	£	£
Fixed cost (per person)	20.00	10.00	6.67	5.00	4.00	3.33
Variable cost (per person)	10.00	10.00	10.00	10.00	10.00	10.00
Total cost (per person)	30.00	20.00	16.67	15.00	14.00	13.33

As the total of fixed costs is high there is a sharp decrease in the total cost per unit with every increase in the number of persons attending the function. This is further illustrated in Figure 4.6.

BREAK-EVEN CHART

Consideration of basic sales–cost–profit relationships would not be complete without a brief introduction to break-even charts.

A break-even chart is a device in graphic form designed to portray the principal sales–cost–profit relationships of an operation. To be more specific, it shows for each level of activity the sales revenue, operating costs and the resulting net profit or net loss. The construction of a break-even chart is simple. Sales and costs are plotted vertically. The rate of activity is measured horizontally. This may be expressed in terms of the rate of (hotel or restaurant) occupancy, number of covers or percentage rate of activity.

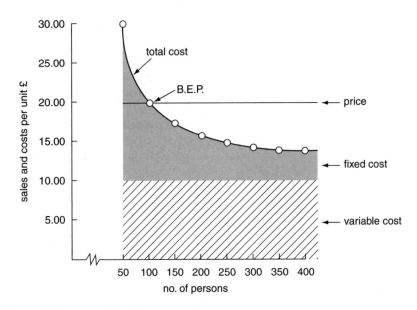

Figure 4.6 Impact of fixed costs on unit costs

Example

During the quarter ended 31 March 19 . ., a restaurant served 10,000 covers and its average spending power was £15.00. The fixed costs of the restaurant amounted to £60,000 and variable costs were incurred at the rate of 40 per cent in relation to the sales volume.

Notes on construction of break-even chart:

(a) Fixed cost, because it is fixed irrespective of the number of covers, will be represented by a straight line parallel to the horizontal axis.
(b) The total cost line is obtained by superimposing variable cost on fixed cost. When the number of covers served is nil, no variable costs are incurred and total cost is equal to the fixed cost. Hence the total cost line starts at £60,000 and then goes up to £120,000.
(c) Sales line starts at the point of origin and is drawn so as to indicate that the sales volume reaches £150,000 when the number of covers is 10,000.

From the break-even chart in Figure 4.7 it may be seen that the restaurant breaks even when it serves just over 6,500 covers. In order to find the precise break-even point, as explained earlier in this chapter, fixed cost is divided by the contribution per cover.

$$\frac{\text{Fixed cost}}{\text{Contribution per cover}} = \frac{£60,000}{£9} = 6,66\dot{6} \text{ covers}$$

A more comprehensive treatment of break-even charts will be found in Chapter 5.

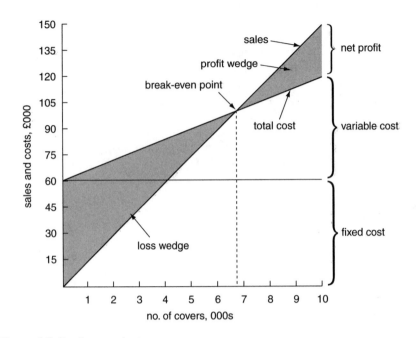

Figure 4.7 Break-even chart

PROBLEMS

1. Explain the relationship between cost structure and profit stability.
2. 'Where fixed costs are high, it is dangerous to operate at a low percentage of net profit.' Explain.
3. Explain what you understand by:
   (a) contribution
   (b) C/S ratio
   (c) break-even point.
4. A and B are two snack bars. Given below is a summary of their trading results for 19 . . .

	A	B
	£	£
Sales	40,000	40,000
Fixed cost	24,000	10,000
Variable cost	10,000	24,000
Total cost	34,000	34,000
Net profit	6,000	6,000

You are required to construct a break-even chart for each snack bar and comment on the profit stability of each business.

5.

No. of covers	Average spending power	Sales	Variable costs	Contribution	Fixed costs
	£	£	£	£	£
100	4	400	160	240	1200
200	4	800	320	480	1200
300	4				1200
400	4				1200
500	4				1200
600	4				1200
700	4				1200
800	4				1200
900	4				1200
1000	4				1200

You are required to:
(a) complete the above table
(b) ascertain the break-even point
(c) calculate the C/S ratio
(d) state what net profit/loss will result when the number of covers is:
    (i) 400
    (ii) 800.

6. The particulars given below relate to the monthly trading results of three restaurants.

	X	Y	Z
Sales	£5,000	£15,000	£20,000
Av. spending power	£10	£15	£10
C/S ratio	50%	60%	60%
Fixed costs	£2,000	£6,500	£7,500

Calculate—both in terms of the number of covers and the sales volume—the break-even point of each restaurant.

7. The City Hotel has three revenue-producing departments: rooms, food, and beverages. The following is a brief summary of the operating results of the Rooms Department in respect of month 6 of 19 . .

Rooms Department—Operating Statement
Month 6, 19. .

	£	£
Sales		210,000
Less allowances to customers	3,000	
agency commission	7,000	10,000
Net sales		200,000
Less Departmental expenses:		
wages and salaries	49,000	
staff meals	6,000	
staff accommodation	5,000	
laundry and dry cleaning	4,000	
cleaning contracts	2,000	
linen	2,000	
domestic supplies	3,000	
other expenses	4,000	75,000
Departmental profit		£125,000

It is expected that net sales will increase by 20 per cent in month 7. Departmental expenses should rise in accordance with the cost-behaviour criteria given below.

(a) Wages and salaries: £32,000 is fixed and the balance a fully variable cost.
(b) Staff meals: £4,000 is fixed and the balance variable.
(c) Staff accommodation: £4,000 is fixed and the balance variable.
(d) Laundry and dry cleaning: £3,000 is fixed and the balance variable.
(e) Cleaning contractors: a fixed cost.
(f) Linen: one-half is fixed, the balance being variable.
(g) Domestic supplies: £2,000 is fixed and the balance variable.
(h) Other expenses: £2,000 is fixed and the balance variable.

You are required to:

(i) calculate the departmental profit for month 7
(ii) ascertain the C/S ratio of the Rooms Department
(iii) prepare a break-even chart of the Rooms Department for month 6 and comment on its break-even point
(iv) state, giving reasons, what justification there is for not showing in the Rooms Department's break-even chart a proportion of fixed expenses such as rates, depreciation, management salaries, etc.

8. Set out below in summary form is the profit and loss account of a hotel.

PROFIT & LOSS ACCOUNT

Department	Sales	Cost of sales	Dept. payroll	Dept. expenses	Dept. profit
	£000	£000	£000	£000	£000
Rooms	900	—	180	90	630
Food and beverages	800	300	400	50	50
Sundries	300	120	60	50	70
Total	2,000	420	640	190	750

Less undistributed operating expenses   550

Net profit before income tax   £200

You are required to assume that of the total of departmental payroll and departmental expenses (£830,000) 90 per cent is fixed and 10 per cent is the variable cost. Calculate the overall and departmental C/S ratios and comment on the profitability of the hotel.

9. Abdel is the owner of the Crêperie Touristique and specializes in selling pancakes to foreign tourists. He is renting his premises from his cousin at 5,000 dinars a month. He is selling one type of pancake only at 4.00 dinars each and the variable cost is 0.50 dinar per pancake. Abdel reckons he needs a net profit of 3,000 dinars per month.

Calculate his monthly net profit for the following monthly levels of turnover:

    2,000 pancakes
    2,500 pancakes
    3,000 pancakes

Also calculate his break-even point and state how many pancakes he has to sell each month to earn a net profit of 3,000 dinars.

10. Henri Dupont sells souvenirs to British tourists in Normandy. His fixed costs are FF 200,000 per month. The average transaction per tourist amounts to FF 200, and his variable costs amount to 60 per cent of turnover. A summary of his profit and loss account for July 1999 is given below.

PROFIT & LOSS A/c

	FF
Sales	600,000
Less variable costs	360,000
Contribution	240,000
Less fixed costs	200,000
Net profit	40,000

You are required to:

(a) calculate Dupont's break-even point
(b) draw his break-even chart
(c) calculate the number of customers he needs each month to earn a net profit of FF 50,000.

Break-even analysis

5

INTRODUCTION

A simple break-even chart has already been illustrated. The purpose of the present chapter is to describe different kinds of break-even charts and show their applications to a variety of different situations.

The term 'break-even chart' is rather unfortunate in that it focuses attention on one particular aspect of what is, in fact, a complex set of sales–cost–profit relationships. The principal aim of the break-even chart is not merely to ascertain the actual or potential break-even point, but also to show what net profit or loss will obtain over the whole range of activity, at what rate net profit will accrue when sales increase above the break-even point, the degree of profit stability of the business, etc.

One of the main objectives of the break-even charts is to show, preferably in simple terms and without excessive detail, the total sales–cost–profit picture of the business. If it is to achieve this objective, it must be presented as an elegant, well thought-out document and create the right kind of visual impression. It is, consequently, better for the break-even chart to show only the essential data; other information may be given in appropriate schedules, profitability statements and similar documents.

BASIC BREAK-EVEN CHART

The basic break-even chart is the starting point for a more detailed consideration of break-even analysis. Let us therefore take a simple example, construct a basic break-even chart and then look at some of its main features.

It is assumed that a business has up to 10,000 customers per month and that its ASP is £10.00. Monthly fixed costs are £40,000 and variable costs are incurred at the rate of 40 per cent in relation to the volume of sales. The break-even chart for this operation would appear as shown in Figure 5.1. The information disclosed by the break-even chart is as follows.

Break-even point

This is reached when the number of covers is over 6,500. As explained in the previous chapter, the expected break-even point (in terms of the number of

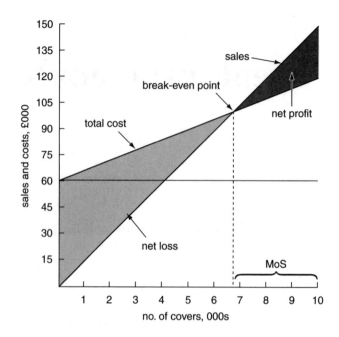

Figure 5.1 Basic break-even chart

covers) may be calculated by dividing fixed costs by the contribution per cover, which in the present example is £6.00. Hence:

$$\frac{\text{Fixed costs}}{\text{Contribution per cover}} = \frac{£40,000}{£6} = 6,667 \text{ covers}$$

Contribution and C/S ratio

As variable costs are maintained at 40 per cent of the sales volume, the C/S ratio of the business is 60 per cent. Out of every increase in sales of £100, £40 is spent on variable costs and £60 is the contribution. When the business has more than 6,667 customers (or sales of £66,667) every addition of £100 to its sales volume will add £60 to its net profit.

Margin of safety (MoS)

The margin of safety is that range of activity over which some profit will always be made. This range is, therefore, regarded as 'safe'.

The margin of safety may be expressed in terms of the number of covers (here 6,667 to 10,000); the sales volume (£66,667 to £100,000); in terms of the percentage level of activity (66.7 per cent to 100.0 per cent) or the rate of hotel or restaurant occupancy.

The width of the margin of safety depends primarily on the cost structure of the business: the higher the percentage of fixed costs the narrower the margin of safety, and vice versa. This is illustrated in Figure 5.2, where Business A has high fixed costs, low variable costs and a relatively narrow margin of

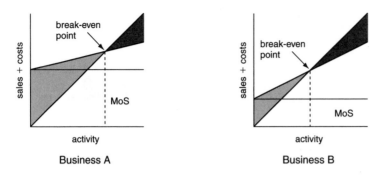

Figure 5.2 Cost structure and the margin of safety

safety; Business B has low fixed costs, high variable costs and, therefore, a wide margin of safety. Incidentally, it should be noticed that there is a clear relationship between the width of the margin of safety and the C/S ratio: the wider the margin of safety the lower the C/S ratio, and vice versa.

The margin of safety is a measure of the profit stability of a business: the wider the margin of safety the greater the degree of profit stability. From what has already been said in the previous chapters it follows that, generally, market-oriented businesses will tend to be subject to a greater degree of profit instability than cost-oriented businesses. The greater the degree of market orientation the more attention should, therefore, be paid to all aspects of revenue control: total sales, sales mix, price structure, profit margins, etc.

PRICING BREAK-EVEN CHART

Break-even charts are frequently applied in various pricing problems. There are basically two possible approaches.

One is to assume that variable cost will be a fixed ratio of sales and project different price levels to see what net profit will be achieved at various levels of activity. This particular approach is more relevant in market-oriented situations, where there is relatively little scope for cost manipulation. The other approach is to take the price per unit as given and project different levels of variable cost. In this second approach it is implied that there is adequate scope for cost manipulation; and that it is, therefore, possible to offer the product or service at various levels of variable cost to the establishment. For example, a catering establishment might offer a meal at a food cost of 40p, 50p or 60p. Where there is this scope for cost manipulation there is quite certainly a fairly high percentage of variable costs and thus a fair degree of cost orientation.

It is, of course, possible to project both—several price levels and a number of variable cost levels. The resulting break-even chart would, however, tend to be unduly complex and make it difficult to 'see the wood for the trees'.

As may be seen from Figure 5.3, each projected price level will produce a different profit wedge and result in a different margin of safety.

In Figure 5.4 Total Cost 1 is drawn to show the highest level of variable cost. Total Cost 2 is based on a lower level of variable cost and Total Cost 3

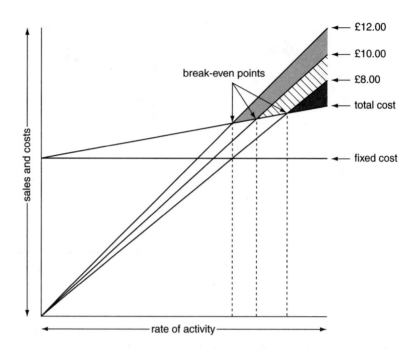

Figure 5.3 Pricing break-even chart for a market-oriented business

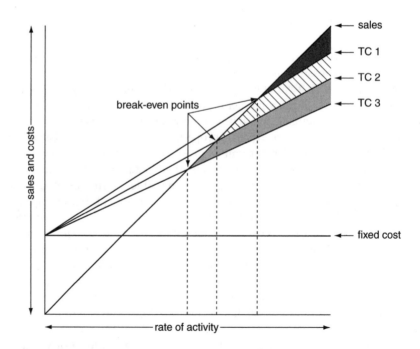

Figure 5.4 Pricing break-even chart for a cost-oriented business

on a yet lower level of variable cost. As in the previous break-even chart each possible solution results in a different profit wedge and a different margin of safety.

PROFIT APPROPRIATION BREAK-EVEN CHART

The aim of the profit appropriation break-even chart is to show what volume of sales or rate of activity has to be attained to satisfy various claims on the profits of a business. This is illustrated in Figure 5.5.

Debenture interest is a charge against profits and not an appropriation of profits. The true break-even point of the business in Figure 5.5 is, therefore, at the rate of activity which enables the payment of debenture interest. However, in a break-even chart of this kind it is desirable to show debenture interest as a separate claim rather than add it to the fixed costs.

CONTROL BREAK-EVEN CHART

The aim of the control break-even chart is to contrast the actual trading results with those budgeted. The break-even chart thus shows the main causes responsible for any difference between the budgeted and actual net profit. An example is given in Figure 5.6.

As may be seen from Figure 5.6, there were two main reasons for the difference between budgeted and actual net profit. Variable costs were higher than budgeted; also, the actual volume of sales was less than budgeted.

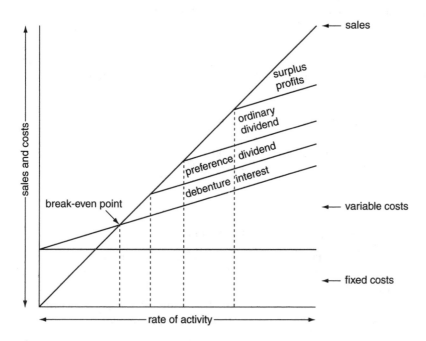

Figure 5.5 Profit appropriation break-even chart

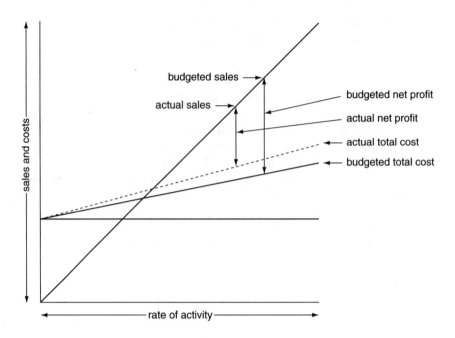

Figure 5.6 Control break-even chart

PROFIT–VOLUME GRAPH

The profit–volume graph is a device similar to the break-even chart. It differs from the latter mainly in its construction. Sales here are measured horizontally. Vertically, the axis on the left-hand side measures fixed costs. The vertical axis on the right-hand side measures net profit. A straight line from the total of fixed costs to the point denoting net profit will cut the sales line at the break-even point. The profit–volume graph shown in Figure 5.7 is based on the following figures:

Sales		£20,000
Less fixed costs	£8,000	
variable costs	8,000	16,000
Net profit		£4,000

Profit–volume graph—alternative version

There is another type of profit–volume graph, which is particularly useful where there are periodical figures of the sales volume and the resulting net profit or net loss.

Let us assume that we are given the following figures in respect of a seasonal restaurant and there is no other information available.

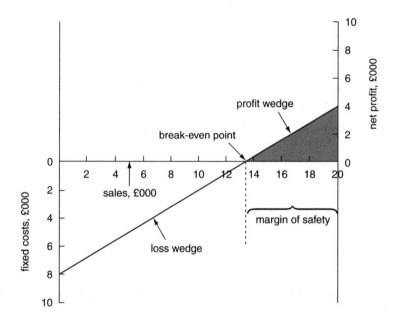

Figure 5.7 Profit–volume graph (1)

Month	Sales £	Net profit/loss £
January	10,000	(5,000)
February	30,000	5,000
March	35,000	10,000
April	40,000	10,000
May	45,000	11,000
June	50,000	15,000

The information given above would be plotted as shown in Figure 5.8.

In this version of the profit–volume graph the sales volume is measured horizontally and the vertical axis is used to measure the periodical net profit above the point of origin and, below it, net loss. The figures of net profit or net loss for each month are plotted and a line of best fit is drawn. Its intersection with the sales line indicates the break-even point.

When sales are nil, the monthly net loss is £10,000, and this indicates that the restaurant incurs fixed costs at the rate of £10,000 per month. Quite clearly, when sales are nil no variable costs are incurred, and the £10,000 must represent fixed costs only.

We may now calculate the percentage of variable costs and the C/S ratio. Let us look at the figures for June.

Sales		£50,000
Less fixed cost	£10,000	
net profit	£15,000	£25,000
Hence, variable costs		£25,000

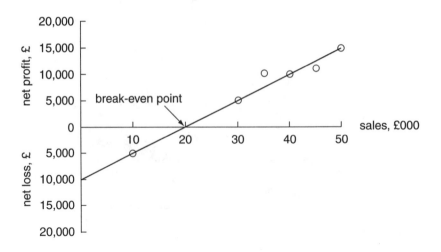

Figure 5.8 Profit–volume graph (2)

It follows, therefore, that variable costs of the restaurant are 50 per cent in relation to the sales volume. The C/S ratio is, therefore, also 50 per cent.

Departmental profit–volume graph

The departmental profit–volume graph is merely an extension of the basic profit–volume graph shown in Figure 5.7. The aim of the graph is to show, in addition to the break-even point and the margin of safety, the contribution of each department to the profits of a business.

Let us assume that a catering establishment has three revenue-producing departments, A, B and C, and that their trading results for the last quarter are as summarized below:

Department	Sales	Variable costs	Contribution
	£	£	£
A	200,000	100,000	100,000
B	200,000	50,000	150,000
C	100,000	100,000	—
	£500,000	£250,000	£250,000
Less Total fixed costs			100,000
Net profit			£150,000

The departmental profit-volume graph would be prepared as shown in Figure 5.9.

The graph in Figure 5.9 was constructed as follows. The break-even point was ascertained by drawing a straight line from the point denoting total fixed cost (£100,000) to that denoting total net profit (£150,000). The departmental contributions were then drawn by arranging the departments according to their profitability and starting with the department having the highest C/S

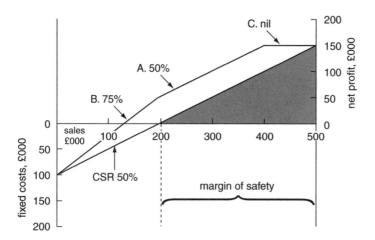

Figure 5.9 Departmental profit–volume graph

ratio, i.e. department B. The line representing the contribution of this department was drawn from the point denoting total fixed cost to the point denoting its sales (£200,000) and its contribution of £150,000. The same procedure was then followed for departments A and C.

Departmental profit–volume graphs are particularly appropriate in the case of hotels and restaurants, the vast majority of which have several revenue-producing departments.

LIMITATIONS OF BREAK-EVEN CHARTS

Break-even charts have many important advantages. They are simple to construct, create a powerful impact and give a great deal of insight into the sales–cost–profit relationships of a business. They do, however, have some important limitations.

First, let us look at the *time factor*. During inflationary periods it is unrealistic to attempt to prepare a break-even chart for more than about twelve months. Both fixed and variable costs show a substantial upward trend, which is not always easy to predict.

Secondly, let us look at *linearity*. When constructing a break-even chart we assume that the sales volume may be represented by a straight line. The same assumption is usually made in respect of variable costs and total cost. In fact this is not always true. Once a certain volume of sales has been achieved, it may be necessary to offer discounts or reduce room rates or menu prices to achieve higher occupancies. The sales line may well then look as shown in Figure 5.10.

Similar considerations apply to the cost side of the business. Where there is no effective system of food and beverage control, food and beverage costs (particularly the former) may fluctuate quite considerably from one trading period to another. The variable cost line, and hence total cost line, will not in such circumstances be a straight line.

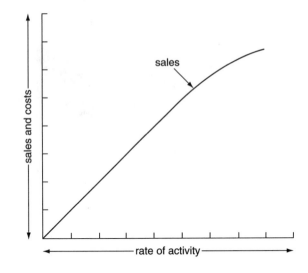

Figure 5.10 Effect of price reductions on sales volume

In some seasonal hotels it is possible to vary what are usually regarded as fixed costs by opening or closing blocks of rooms. The effect of this procedure is to vary a whole range of costs: labour, laundry and cleaning, space heating, etc. Where that is so, the effect is to produce a 'stepped' total cost line, and sometimes more than one break-even point, as shown in Figure 5.11.

Thirdly, let us look at the problem of the *sales mix*. In most hotels and restaurants the C/S ratio varies considerably from one element of the sales mix to another. A change in the sales mix will, therefore, usually result in an appreciable change in the net profit of the business. Hotel occupancies tend to be lower from September to March than from April to August. Yet it is during the former period that many hotels do a great deal of banqueting business. The general decrease in departmental profits resulting from lower room, food and beverage sales is thus partly offset by increased banqueting sales attracting a fairly high C/S ratio. It will be appreciated, therefore, that the greater the changes in the sales mix the more difficult the construction of the break-even chart.

Finally, let us consider the position of *joint costs* (sometimes referred to as common costs) in break-even analysis. Joint costs present no problem in the preparation of the break-even chart for a business as a whole. When, however, a break-even chart is being prepared for a particular revenue-producing department there are clearly two possibilities: one may attempt to apportion—on some basis—the total of joint costs to revenue-producing departments or prepare a break-even chart on the basis of direct costs only.

The subject of cost apportionment is a matter of some considerable controversy in accounting circles. It is clear, however, that the balance of informed accounting opinion is strongly against cost apportionment. Charles T. Horngren (*Cost Accounting: A Managerial Emphasis*, 3rd edn, Englewood Cliffs, NJ: Prentice-Hall, 1972, p. 576) writes under the heading 'Irrelevance of joint costs in decision making':

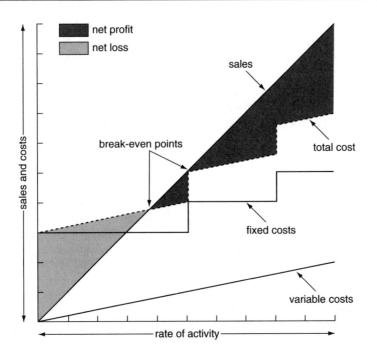

Figure 5.11 'Stepped' total cost line

the accountant must concentrate on opportunity costs rather than on how historical joint costs are to be split among various products. The only relevant costs are the additional costs as compared with additional revenue.

Quite clearly there is no scientific method of apportioning joint costs to revenue-producing departments. Let us take an example or two. Rent, rates and other occupancy costs may be apportioned on the basis of space occupied. However, a square metre of space on the ground floor is not equivalent in value to a square metre of space in the basement or the first floor of the hotel.

Sales promotion and advertising clearly benefit all the revenue-producing departments. It would be tempting, therefore, to apportion this cost in proportion to departmental sales volumes. However, each change in the sales mix of the hotel would call for an adjustment of the respective shares of the cost to the revenue-producing departments.

The cost of repairs and maintenance is almost equally difficult to apportion. Whilst a proportion of the expense may be traced to particular departments and allocated, repairs to the building and external painting can only be apportioned on some arbitrary basis.

It is suggested, therefore, that the best method to prepare a departmental break-even chart is to exclude joint costs and show direct costs only. One notable exception to this general rule is the apportionment of joint costs when a new hotel or restaurant is being planned. It is then frequently possible to vary some joint costs in accordance with the operational requirements of various departments. Thus the banqueting department may be allocated x square metres or that plus or minus *y* square metres. At this stage it is still meaningful to speak of the cost of space of a particular department. However, after a period of time, and especially after not uncommon subsequent re-allocations of space between departments, one can only regard the cost of space as a joint cost. This is particularly obvious in situations where the opportunity cost of an area is nil. A full discussion of the problems of cost apportionment and departmental profitability will be found in Chapter 17.

PRACTICAL APPLICATIONS

In the last two sections of the present chapter we shall look at some practical applications of break-even analysis. Our aim here is not only to enhance the understanding of the practical problems which exist but also to provide some additional insight into the relevant sales–cost–profit relationships, which present themselves differently in different types of operation.

Example A—Hotel operation

Set out below is a Profit and Loss Account from which we are required to produce a break-even chart of the hotel. It will be remembered that the preparation of a break-even chart requires the segregation of all the costs as between those which are fully fixed and those which are fully variable.

Meru Valley Hotel
PROFIT & LOSS A/c
for the year ended . . .

Department	Sales	Cost of sales	Dept. payroll	Dept. expenses	Dept. profit
	£000	£000	£000	£000	£000
Rooms	1,148	–	250	116	782
Food	850	322	312	64	152
Beverages	328	108	86	14	120
Others	24	10	6	2	6
	2,350	440	654	196	1,060

Less Undistributed operating expenses:		
Administration and general	210	
Marketing	64	
Energy	70	
Repairs and maintenance	105	
Rent, insurance and interest	201	
Depreciation	160	810
Net profit		£250

Our problem here is that, whilst we may assume that the cost of sales is a fully variable cost, departmental payroll and departmental expenses are both semi-fixed costs. It is essential, therefore, that we split the total semi-fixed cost of £654,000 + £196,000 = £850,000 as between fixed and variable elements. As explained in Chapter 3, four different methods may be used for this purpose. Let us assume that, having applied one of these, we obtain a division of the £850,000 as follows:

	Fixed element £000	Variable element £000	Total S-F cost £000
Departmental payroll	580	74	654
Departmental expenses	170	26	196
	£750	£100	£850

Readers will note that, typically, the fixed element is considerably larger than the variable element. We may now add the variable element to the cost of sales to obtain the total variable cost. Similarly we may add the fixed element to the undistributed operating expenses (which in most practical situations are assumed to be a fixed cost) to obtain the total fixed cost.

We now have the necessary figures, as follows:

	£000	£000
Fixed costs—Operating expenses	810	
Departmental payroll	580	
Departmental expenses	170	1,560
Variable costs—Cost of sales	440	
Departmental payroll	74	
Departmental expenses	26	540
Total cost		£2,100

We may now prepare the hotel's break-even chart as shown in Figure 5.12. From the break-even chart it may be seen that the hotel reaches its break-even point at a volume of sales of approximately £2,000,000.

We may now calculate the exact break-even point as follows:

	£000	%
Sales volume	2,350	100.0
Less variable cost	540	23.0
Contribution and C/S ratio	1,810	77.0

Therefore:

$$\frac{\text{Fixed cost}}{\text{Contribution per £1 sales}} = \frac{£1,560,000}{77p} = £2,025,974$$

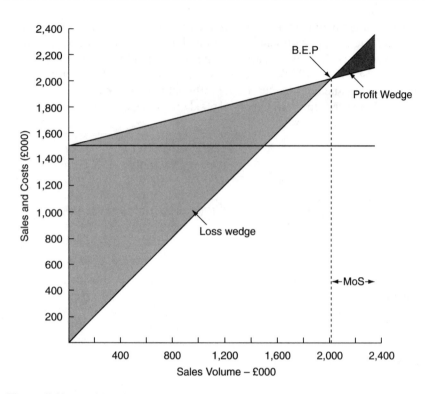

Figure 5.12 Hotel break-even chart (1)

We may express the break-even point of £2,025,974 as a percentage of the present sales volume:

$$\frac{£2,025,974}{£2,350,000} \times 100 = 86.2\%$$

Three observations should be made before the conclusion of our first example. First, it should be noted that our hotel is a typical hotel in terms of its cost structure:

	£000	%
Fixed costs	1,560	74.3
Variable costs	540	25.7
Total cost	2,100	100.0

From published statistics it is clear that the above cost structure, where fixed costs account for approximately three-quarters of total cost, is typical of the majority of good-class European hotels. Secondly, the margin of safety of our hotel is narrow. As we need to achieve 86.2 per cent of the present sales volume to break even, our margin of safety is only 13.8 per cent and is an indication that our hotel is subject to a high degree of profit instability in that relatively small changes in the volume of sales have a strong impact on profitability. Finally, we have calculated the break-even point of the hotel in terms of the sales volume—simply because we have no information relating to the hotel's number of rooms, room occupancy, etc.

Example B—Hotel operation

In this second example we show how break-even calculations are undertaken in terms of room occupancy. The Indiana Hotel has 100 rooms. The average room rate is £30.00 and the variable cost per occupied room is £4.00. Additionally we are informed that:

(a) Food sales amount to £10.00 per occupied room and beverage sales £5.00. In the minor operated departments sales amount to £1.00 per occupied room.
(b) The departmental contribution-to-sales ratios are as shown below:
    (i) Food sales   65%
    (ii) Beverage sales   60%
    (iii) Minor operated departments*   50%
(c) The fixed costs of the hotel amount to £800,000 per annum. We are required to:
    (a) Prepare a break-even chart for the hotel
    (b) Calculate the hotel's break-even point
    (c) Tell John Brown, the owner of the hotel, what room occupancy he must achieve to make a net profit of £200,000

The fixed cost is given, and our first task, therefore, is to work out the variable cost per occupied room in order to be able to calculate the contribution per occupied room.

Variable cost per occupied room

	£
Rooms department	4.00
Food department (35% of £10.00)	3.50
Beverage department (40% of £5.00)	2.00
Minor operated departments (50% of £1.00)	0.50
Total	10.00

Contribution per occupied room

	£
Sales—Rooms department	30.00
Food department	10.00
Beverage department	5.00
Minor operated departments	1.00
Total	46.00
Less Variable cost	10.00
Contribution per occupied room	36.00

* Minor operated departments (MOD) include telephone, gift shop, guest laundry, etc.

Our next task is to secure the basic data for our break-even chart. As we do not know at what level of occupancy the hotel breaks even or earns the required £200,000 net profit, it is best for us to prepare the break-even chart on the assumption of 100 per cent room occupancy

Basic data for break-even chart

		£
(a) Sales: 100 rooms × £46.00 × 365		1,679,000
(b) Variable costs: 100 rooms × £10.00 × 365		365,000
(c) Fixed costs—as given		800,000

The break-even chart of our hotel would then be drawn as shown in Figure 5.13.

Let us now examine our break-even chart. The hotel has an untypically wide margin of safety as well as a huge profit wedge. This, of course, is apparent rather than real, as we have produced the break-even chart on the assumption of 100 per cent room occupancy. We can see that the hotel breaks even when it reaches just over 60 per cent room occupancy. The exact break-even point will now be calculated using the formula with which the reader is already familiar.

$$\frac{\text{Fixed cost}}{\text{Contribution per occupied room}} = \frac{£800,000}{£36} = 22,222 \text{ (rooms)}$$

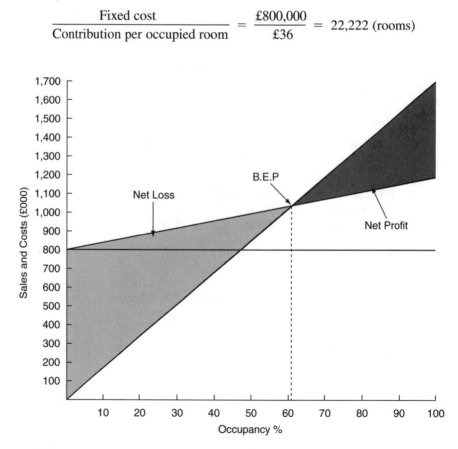

Figure 5.13 Hotel break-even chart (2)

The hotel's potential is (100 rooms × 365) = 36,500 rooms sold per annum. Of these we have to sell 22,222 rooms to break even. From this we conclude that the hotel's break-even point is reached when room occupancy is:

$$\frac{\text{Rooms to be sold}}{\text{Rooms available}} = \frac{22,222}{36,500} \times 100 = 60.9\%$$

Now, if the hotel is to earn a net profit of £200,000 it needs a total contribution of:

	£
Contribution required to break even	800,000
Contribution required for net profit	200,000
Total	1,000,000

Hence,

$$\frac{\text{(F.C. £800,000 + N.P. £200,000)}}{\text{Contribution per occupied room}} = \frac{£1,000,000}{£36} = 27,777$$

We see that 27,777 rooms would have to be sold for the hotel to earn a net profit of £200,000. This is equivalent to room occupancy of:

$$\frac{\text{Rooms to be sold (27,777)}}{\text{Rooms available (36,500)}} \times 100 = 76.1\%$$

Let us return to the questions of cost structure, margin of safety and profit stability. On the assumption that our hotel will operate at an average room occupancy of 70 per cent, its cost structure will be:

	£	%
Fixed costs	800,000	75.8
Variable costs: 70 rooms × £10 × 365	255,500	24.2
Total cost	1,055,500	100.0

Here again we have an indication of a typical hotel operation with fixed costs accounting for approximately 75 per cent of total cost. The hotel breaks even at 60.9 per cent room occupancy and, therefore, assuming an average room occupancy of 70 per cent, we have a relatively narrow margin of safety and a high degree of profit instability.

Example C—Restaurant operation

Our last example is a high-ASP (£18.00) restaurant whose Profit and Loss Account is shown below.

Serengeti Restaurant
PROFIT & LOSS A/c
for year ended . . .

	Sales		Cost of sales		Gross profit	
	£	%	£	%	£	%
Food	480,000	66.7	144,000	30.0	336,000	70.0
Beverages	240,000	33.3	108,000	45.0	132,000	55.0
Total	720,000	100.0	252,000	35.0	468,000	65.0

Less Operating expenses:

Payroll and related expenses	160,000	
Administration and general	43,200	
Gas and electricity	9,200	
Advertising and sales promotion	10,000	
Repairs and maintenance	10,000	
Rent and rates	80,000	
Depreciation	32,000	344,400	47.8
Net profit before tax		£123,600	17.2

In order to prepare a break-even chart of this restaurant we have to divide all the expenses as between those which are fixed and those which are variable. Here, again, we may use any one of the four methods available for this purpose. In many practical situations it is possible to segregate fixed and variable costs on the basis of observation. Thus wages and salaries paid to full-time employees would be regarded as a fixed cost, whilst any wages paid to part-time and casual employees would be considered as a variable cost. Expenses such as gas, electricity, repairs, maintenance are, ordinarily, a semi-fixed cost. The variable element in these costs is frequently so small as to be almost negligible: many restaurant operators will, therefore, regard such costs as fixed. Our analysis of total cost may take the following form.

Analysis of Total Cost

Expense	Fixed cost	Variable cost	Total cost
	£	£	£
Food cost		144,000	144,000
Beverage cost		108,000	108,000
Payroll & related expenses	140,000	20,000	160,000
Administration & general	43,200		43,200
Gas & electricity	9,200		9,200
Advertising & sales promotion	10,000		10,000

Repairs & maintenance	10,000		10,000
Rent & rates	80,000		80,000
Depreciation	32,000		32,000
Totals	324,400	272,000	596,400

As far as the cost structure of the restaurant is concerned the position is as follows:

	£	%
Fixed costs	324,400	54.4
Variable costs	272,000	45.6
Total cost	596,400	100.0

Our restaurant has a reasonably equal distribution of costs as between fixed and variable; and in this respect is different from both high-fixed-cost hotels and other residential establishments. The break-even chart of the restaurant is shown in Figure 5.14.

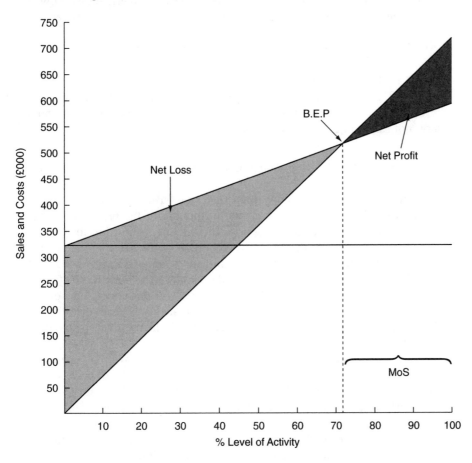

Figure 5.14 Restaurant break-even chart

We may calculate the restaurant's percentage composition of total turnover as follows:

	£	%
Fixed costs	324,400	45.0
Variable costs	272,000	37.8
Net profit	123,600	17.2
Sales volume total	720,000	100.0

We now know that the restaurant operates at a variable cost of 37.8 per cent and from this we may calculate its contribution per cover and the C/S ratio.

	£	%
Average spending power	18.00	100.0
Less variable cost	6.80	37.8
Contribution and C/S ratio	11.20	62.2

If we now divide the fixed costs of the restaurant by the contribution per cover we will have the exact break-even point in terms of the number of covers.

$$\frac{\text{Fixed costs}}{\text{Contribution per cover}} = \frac{£324,400}{£11.20} = 28,964 \text{ covers}$$

In terms of the sales volume the break-even point is 28,964 (covers) × £18.00 (ASP) £521,352. This expressed as a percentage of the total sales volume of the restaurant, (£720,000) gives a break-even point of 72.4 per cent and a margin of safety of 27.6 per cent.

ASPECTS OF PROFIT MANAGEMENT

Quite frequently—perhaps more often than not—a business executive will prepare a break-even chart, look at the positioning of the break-even point and, regrettably, take no further action. In fact, the right thing to do is to regard the completion of the break-even chart as the first step in the process of profit management. The important point here is that one should not accept the size or shape of the profit wedge or the width of the margin of safety as factors outside one's control. What is required, on the completion of the break-even chart, is a positive attempt to manipulate costs, profit margins and all the other controllable elements in order to reach the most acceptable level of profit.

With regard to variable costs and gross profit margins, we may operate at a cost of sales of x or $x + 2$ per cent, $x - 3$ per cent, etc. As will be seen later in this volume (see Chapter 10) even a small decrease in the cost of sales—particularly in restaurants and similar catering establishments—can have a significant impact on profitability.

Also it is unfortunate that fixed costs are described as fixed: frequently the effect of this term is that executives assume that nothing can be done about such costs. Yet many hotels and restaurants have recently achieved substantial improvements in profitability through the reduction of fixed costs, particularly in the area of permanent labour.

Finally, we are always able to vary to some extent the relative proportions of fixed and variable costs. A high proportion of fixed costs (as shown in Figure 5.12) implies a high C/S ratio. The latter, in turn, results in profit instability, in that relatively small changes in the volume of sales have a disproportionately large impact on net profits. If, therefore, we can maintain a fairly low level of full-time, permanent labour and make a greater use of part-time and casual labour, we will have a relatively high level of variable costs and our operation will enjoy a higher degree of profit stability.

PROBLEMS

1. 'The City of London' is a travel agency which, amongst other things, specializes in the provision of one-day sightseeing coach tours for foreign tourists. The business is to an appreciable extent seasonal and the number of passengers per tour varies substantially over the calendar year.

   The following information is available:
   (a) coach capacity: 30 passengers
   (b) price charged: £20.00
   (c) cost of coach hire per day £120.00
   (d) guide's salary per day: £40.00
   (e) other costs, e.g. passengers' meals, admission tickets, etc. amount to £8.00 per passenger.

   You are required to:
   (a)   (i) construct a break-even chart for the coach tour
        (ii) ascertain the break-even point
       (iii) calculate the margin of safety
   (b) argue the case for and against the inclusion of a proportion of the travel agency's fixed costs in the break-even chart for these sightseeing tours.

2. As newly appointed management accountant in a hotel company, you have undertaken a survey of the data available in respect of the Splendid Hotel. The data include the following:

Month	Sales £000	Profit (Loss) £000
January	80	(96)
February	120	(64)
March	160	(40)
April	200	—
May	320	96
June	360	128
July	400	160
August	360	120
September	320	104
October	240	32
November	160	(32)
December	120	(56)

You are required to prepare a profit–volume graph of the Splendid Hotel and calculate its break-even point, C/S ratio and comment generally on the profitability of this hotel.

3. The Oasis International Hotel has 100 rooms. The average room rate is £60.00 and the variable cost per occupied room is £5.00. Additionally, you have the following information.

Food sales amount to £20.00 per occupied room and beverage sales £8.00. In the minor operated departments sales amount to £2.00 per occupied room.

The departmental C/S ratios are as follows:

food sales   65%
beverage sales   60%
minor operated departments   40%

The fixed costs of the hotel amount to £1,500,000 per annum.

You are required to:

(a) prepare the hotel's break-even chart
(b) calculate the hotel's break-even point in terms of (i) sales volume and (ii) room occupancy
(c) find what room occupancy must be achieved in order for the hotel to earn a net profit of £300,000.

4. Set out below is the Profit & Loss A/c of the Lucerne International Hotel in respect of the year ended 30 June 19 . . .

PROFIT AND LOSS A/c (£000)

Operated dept.	Net sales	Cost of sales	Payroll and related expenses	Other expenses	Dept. profit
	£000	£000	£000	£000	£000
Rooms	4,140	—	730	270	3,140
Food and beverage	4,005	1,370	1,560	415	660
Telephone	235	160	35	15	25
Rentals	125	—	—	—	125
	8,505	1,530	2,325	700	3,950

Less undistributed operating expenses:

Administrative and general expenses	315	405
Marketing	90	235
Guest entertainment	45	20
Property operation, maintenance and energy costs	155	305
	605	965	1,570

Operating profit	2,380

Less fixed charges:		
Property tax and insurance	205	
Interest	415	
Depreciation	450	1,070
Net profit		£1,310

You are required to prepare a break-even chart of the hotel. Also calculate the C/S ratio and the precise break-even point.

Assume that of the total (£3,025,000) of 'payroll and related expenses' and 'other expenses', £2,860,000 is the fixed element and that the balance of £165,000 is wholly variable. Also assume that undistributed operating expenses are fixed and do not respond to changes in the level of activity.

5. Set out below are the trading results of the Torino Restaurant in respect of the third quarter of 1997.

PROFIT AND LOSS A/c

No. of covers		20,000
		£
Sales: Food		360,000
Beverages		120,000
Total		480,000
Less: Food cost	£120,000	
Beverage cost	48,000	168,000
Gross profit		312,000
Less: Semi-fixed costs	96,000	
Fixed costs	180,000	276,000
Net profit		36,000

You are required to:
(a) Prepare, in summary form, the restaurant's budget for the last quarter of 1997.
   Assume that:

   (i) the number of covers will be 15,000
   (ii) there will be no change in average spending power, the percentage of food and beverage costs or the fixed costs of the restaurant
   (iii) semi-fixed costs will behave as during the first three quarters of 1997.

You are informed that during the first two quarters the position was as follows:

	Semi-fixed cost	No. of covers
1st quarter	£106,800	26,000
2nd quarter	£114,000	30,000

(b) Prepare a break-even chart for the business in respect of 1997. Any assumptions must be stated clearly.

(c) Calculate the C/S ratio, the contribution per cover and the margin of safety, and comment on the profitability of the restaurant.

(d) Comment on the orientation of the restaurant.

6. Set out below is a summary of the operating results of the Cherry Blossom Restaurant for March 1998.

RESULTS—MARCH 1998

No. of covers			1,000
Average spending power			£20.00
Sales			£20,000
Less: Variable costs:	F & B costs	£7,000	
	Other costs	2,000	9,000
Contribution			11,000
Less: Fixed costs:	Labour	£5,000	
	Other costs	3,000	8,000
Net profit			£3,000

In April there will be no change in the operating costs or the number of covers—the only change will be a 10% increase in the menu prices.

You are required to:

(a) prepare a break-even chart for March which additionally shows the effect of the increased prices in April

(b) calculate for both months the break-even point and the margin of safety as well as the percentage increase in net profit from March to April.

7. Set out below is the Profit & Loss A/c of the Delta Hotel.

DELTA HOTEL

Profit & Loss A/c for year ended 31 Dec. 1998

Department	Net sales	Cost of sales	Dept. payroll	Dept. expenses	Dept. profit
	£000	£000	£000	£000	£000
Rooms	4,500	–	990	210	3,300
Food	3,000	1,050	1,350	300	300
Beverages	1,200	480	300	60	360
Other	300	120	60	30	90
	9,000	1,650	2,700	600	4,050

Less: Undistributed operating expenses:

Administrative and general	720	
Marketing	240	
Heat, light and power	660	
Repairs and maintenance	390	
Depreciation	780	
Interest and fixed charges	360	3,150
Net profit		900

You are required to:

(a) prepare a break-even chart of the hotel
(b) calculate the hotel's C/S ratio and the exact break-even point
(c) comment on the profitability of the four revenue-producing departments and the hotel as a whole.

Assume that all the undistributed operating expenses are fixed, and that of the total of departmental payroll and departmental expenses (£3,300,000) £2,850,000 is fixed and the rest is fully variable.

8. You are planning to open a gift shop in the main lobby of a hotel. Monthly fixed costs are estimated as follows:

	£
Wages	1,500
Other costs: electricity, stationery, etc.	300
	1,800

The estimated cost of sales (variable cost) is equal to 70 per cent, giving a contribution of 30 per cent. You are to calculate:

(a) the volume of sales to break even
(b) the volume of sales to achieve a monthly net profit of £6,000.

9. A travel agent sells weekend trips to Paris. The selling price is £320 and the variable cost (flight, hotel room, meals, etc.) £240 per person. The annual fixed cost of running the travel agency is £160,000. How many persons must they send to Paris to break even?

10. Given below is the Profit & Loss A/c of the Alice Springs Hotel.

ALICE SPRINGS HOTEL

Profit & Loss A/c for year ended 30 June 1998

Department	Net Sales	Cost of Sales	Dept. Payroll	Dept. Expenses	Dept. Profit
	£000	£000	£000	£000	£000
Rooms	4,000	—	800	300	2,900
Food	2,000	800	900	200	100
Beverages	1,000	350	250	50	350
Other	500	200	100	50	150
	7,500	1,350	2,050	600	3,500

Less: Undistributed operating expenses		
Administrative and general	800	
Marketing	200	
Utility costs	450	
Repairs and maintenance	350	
Depreciation and fixed charges	950	2,750
		750

You are required to prepare a break-even chart of the hotel. Also calculate the C/S ratio and the exact break-even point.

You are informed that all the undistributed operating expenses are fixed. Of the total of departmental payroll and departmental expenses (£2,650,000) £2,400,000 is the fixed element and the rest is fully variable.

11. Jack Lacey is the owner of Acton Coaches Ltd and specializes in running coach trips for foreign tourists. Mrs Molly O'Brien, his part-time accountant, has prepared the following forecasts for the year ended 31 December 1999.

	£	£
Sales: 200 trips @ 25 passengers @ £30.00		150,000
Fixed costs: Office and garage rent		15,000
Office salaries		45,000
Wages—Driver	18,000	
Guide	10,000	28,000
Office expenses		5,000
Gas and electricity		3,000
Insurance		2,000
Coach repairs and maintenance		2,000
Total		100,000
Variable costs: Petrol and oil (200 trips @ £40)		8,000
Meals en route, etc. (5,000 pass @ £5)		25,000
Parking fees, etc: (200 trips @ £10)		2,000
Total		35,000
Net profit		15,000

Jack Lacey is not quite satisfied with the projected net profit and is convinced that the price per passenger could be increased to £34 without any loss of business: You are required to:

(a) prepare a break-even chart incorporating Mrs O'Brien's original proposals as well as the effect of the price increase to £34
(b) calculate the exact break-even point for both alternatives
(c) explain how you would determine the break-even point for an individual trip.

6 Introduction to decision accounting

It was stated in an earlier chapter that the two principal ingredients of management accounting were control accounting and decision accounting. The aim of the present chapter is to illustrate several specific and typical applications of accounting to business decisions. In addition to the problems considered in this chapter, readers will find more relevant decision accounting material in other chapters, particularly 5, 7, 10 and 19.

BUSINESS DECISIONS

The reader will realize that most decisions made in a business context are short-run decisions. Whether we are fixing menu prices, arranging a banquet, choosing advertising media or even planning to close the business during the low season, all such decisions affect our sales and variable costs, but leave the fixed costs unchanged. Also, such decisions do not involve any capital expenditure. It is for this reason that in the majority of business decisions we keep the fixed costs very much in the background, and concentrate on sales, variable costs and the resulting contribution.

All such decisions are different from those described as 'long-run decisions'. When we are planning to build an extension to the hotel, we quite clearly have to take into account all the costs involved, including fixed costs. The additional revenue from the extension must cover additional variable and fixed costs and produce a reasonable net profit. Similarly when reallocating space between revenue-producing departments, e.g. converting a few guest rooms into a conference room, we have to take into account all the costs involved. Long-run decisions affect all costs and frequently involve considerable capital expenditure on new plant and equipment. Such long-run decisions, it will be appreciated, are rather uncommon; and the whole of this chapter is therefore devoted to short-run decisions only. Techniques for dealing with long-run decisions are discussed in Chapter 19.

Example

A hotel has one function room with sufficient capacity to accommodate a banquet for 120 persons. The daily fixed cost of the room is £300. Three clients are interested in using the room on one particular day, as follows:

Function A

This is a banquet of 120 persons. The menu required by the client is priced at £16.00 and would involve a food cost of £4.00 per cover. Beverage sales are estimated at £6.00 and beverage cost at £1.50 per cover. Twelve casual waiters would be employed at £14.00 each. Floral decorations would cost £12.00.

Function B

This is a function for 100 persons. The client is interested in a menu priced at £18.00 and involving a food cost of £6.00 per cover. It is estimated that beverage sales will average £8.00 per cover and involve a unit beverage cost of £2.00. Ten casual waiters would have to be employed at £14.00 each. Floral decorations would cost £30.00.

Function C

This is a conference for a local political organization. No food would be required by the client, but it is estimated that bar sales would amount to £2,000.00, and involve a cost of sales of 25 per cent. Additional staff would cost £50.00.

From the above information we may calculate the estimated contribution of each function as shown below:

Function A				£
Food sales:	120	@ £16.00		1,920.00
Beverage sales:	120	@ £6.00		720.00
Total				2,640.00
Less: Variable costs:				
Food cost	120	@ £4.00	£480.00	
Beverages cost	120	@ £1.50	180.00	
Wages	12	@ £14.00	168.00	
Floral decorations			12.00	840.00
Contribution				1,800.00

Function B				
Food sales	100	@ £18.00		1,800.00
Beverages sales	100	@ £8.00		800.00
Total				2,600.00
Less: Variable costs:				
Food cost	100	@ £6.00	£600.00	
Beverages cost	100	@ £2.00	200.00	

Wages	10 @ £14.00	140.00	
Floral decorations		30.00	970.00
Contribution			1,630.00

Function C

Sales		2,000.00
Less: Variable costs:		
Cost of sales	£500.00	
Wages	50.00	550.00
Contribution		1,450.00

It is quite clear that whichever function is undertaken the daily fixed cost of the banqueting room will remain unchanged. The only elements that will vary from one function to another are the respective sales volumes, the variable costs and the resulting contributions. From our calculations it is apparent that Function A will produce the highest level of contribution. The role of contribution in these decisions is illustrated in Figure 6.1.

The functions would be ranked as follows.

RANKING

	Contribution(£)
Function A	1,800
Function B	1,630
Function C	1,450

Once again it is emphasized that fixed costs, because they remain constant as between the three cases, do not feature in this kind of decision.

```
                   ┌─ A    Sales            £2,640
                   │       Variable cost       840
                   │       ─────
                   │       Contribution      1,800
                   │
                   │       Fixed cost          300
┌────────────┐     │
│ CHOICE OF  │─────┼─ B    Sales            £2,600
│ FUNCTION   │     │       Variable cost       970
└────────────┘     │       ─────
                   │       Contribution      1,630
                   │
                   │       Fixed cost          300
                   │
                   └─ C    Sales            £2,000
                           Variable cost       550
                           ─────
                           Contribution      1,450

                           Fixed cost          300
```

Figure 6.1 Role of contribution in decision making

Let us now look at some examples.

CLOSURE IN OFF-SEASON

The Four Seasons Restaurant is a seasonal establishment. At the end of 31 December 19. . the book-keeper of the restaurant prepared the following summary of trading results.

Trading, Profit & Loss A/c
for year ended 31 December 19. .

	Quarter			
	1	2	3	4
	£	£	£	£
Sales	144,000	216,000	288,000	192,000
Food and beverage costs	57,600	86,400	115,200	76,800
Wages	60,000	72,000	96,000	66,000
Rent and rates	7,200	7,200	7,200	7,200
Advertising	3,600	3,600	3,600	3,600
Depreciation—lease	19,200	19,200	19,200	19,200
Depreciation—other	8,400	8,400	8,400	8,400
Repairs and replacements	1,800	2,400	3,000	1,800
Light and heat	4,200	3,600	3,000	4,200
Miscellaneous expenses	600	600	600	600
Total expenses	162,600	203,400	256,200	187,800
Net profit (Net loss)	(18,600)	12,600	31,800	4,200

Notes

(a) The policy of the restaurant is to maintain food and beverage costs at 40 per cent of sales.
(b) Wages are allocated to each period as they actually accrue.
(c) Rent, rates and advertising are apportioned on a time basis.
(d) Depreciation of lease is also apportioned on a time basis; other depreciation is, however, regarded as 50 per cent variable.
(e) The item repairs and replacements consists of a fixed element of £1,200; the balance is fully variable.
(f) Light and heat are allocated to each period on the basis of actual metered consumption.
(g) Miscellaneous expenses: this consists of a large number of small items and is regarded as a fixed cost.

The proprietors of the restaurant expect that the trading results for the following year will not materially differ from those shown above. They are anxious to improve the profitability of the restaurant, and would like you to advise them on the desirability of closing the restaurant during the first quarter of the forthcoming year.

Solution

Basically, there are two different methods of deciding whether or not closure during the off-season should be contemplated:

(a) To compare the net loss resulting from operations with that which would result in the event of closure.
(b) To compare the gain resulting from closure (i.e. savings in variable costs) with the loss resulting from closure (i.e. loss of sales revenue).

Hence:

(a) Net loss if restaurant remains open   £18,600
(b) Net loss if restaurant closes—i.e. the sum of fixed costs for that period:

Rent and rates	£7,200	
Advertising	3,600	
Depreciation—lease	19,200	
Depreciation—other	4,200	
Repairs and replacements	1,200	
Miscellaneous expenses	600	£36,000

In closing down, the restaurant would therefore be £17,400 worse off.

Loss resulting from closure (sales)		£144,000
Gain resulting from closure (i.e. savings in variable costs)		
Food and beverage costs	£57,600	
Wages	60,000	
Depreciation	4,200	
Repairs and replacements	600	
Light and heat	4,200	£126,600

The result is again as before and, at least on the face of it, there is no sound financial reason for closing the restaurant during the first quarter of the following year.

In practice, however, the proprietors of the restaurant would have to take into account some other factors when making this kind of decision. Some of the questions they would have to ask themselves are the following: (a) How easy or difficult will it be to replace the labour force? (b) Is it desirable to offer the key staff a retainer? (c) What will be the effect of closure in the off-season on the volume of sales during the season? (d) Is it possible for the proprietor(s) to take up employment during the period of the closure? Thus the calculations shown above are only the first step.

CLOSURE OF A DEPARTMENT

Situated in the foyer of the Granada International Hotel is a kiosk, open seven days a week, from 8.00 a.m. to 8.00 p.m.

The financial director of the company insists that all departments should make a contribution to the general overheads of the hotel and show a satisfactory net profit. Each department is, therefore, charged with a proportion of: administrative and general expenses; advertising and sales promotion; rent and occupancy costs; depreciation; light and heat. The charge has been fixed at 20 per cent of departmental sales.

At 31 December 19.. the trading results of the kiosk were ascertained as shown below.

Kiosk
TRADING, PROFIT AND LOSS ACCOUNT
for year ended 31 December 19 . .

		£
Sales		500,000
Less Cost of sales		440,000
Gross Profit		60,000
Less Wages	£40,000	
Proportion of overheads	100,000	140,000
Net loss		80,000

The financial director is considering the possible closure of the kiosk; and you are asked to comment on the financial consequences of this decision.

Solution

Following the first method in the previous example, the position is this:

Net loss if kiosk remains open	£80,000
Net loss if kiosk closes—i.e. the sum of general overheads whose level would not be affected	100,000

It is clear that the hotel would be £20,000 worse off by closing the kiosk. Following the second method:

Loss resulting from closure (sales)		£500,000
Gain resulting from closure:		
cost of sales	£440,000	
wages	40,000	£480,000

Here again we see that, following closure, the hotel would be worse off to the extent of £20,000.

And now a few comments on the preparation of the above trading profit and loss account. The method of apportioning the general overheads in this case is quite arbitrary and most inaccurate. A kiosk normally occupies little space and to charge it with a uniform rate of expense for rent and occupancy costs, depreciation, light and heat is grossly unfair. The decision on the possible closure of the kiosk should be made in the light of a strong likelihood that the opportunity cost of the space occupied is nil, i.e. if the kiosk were closed down the space could not be used by another department.

Finally, the decision should be made in the light of certain service aspects. If the turnover of the kiosk is in the region of £10,000 per week it must be fulfilling an important need of hotel clients.

There seems, therefore, to be a very strong argument for not closing the kiosk. Following our arguments against the apportionment of joint costs, this example shows how difficult it is to effect a rational and fair apportionment. It also shows how such apportionment may lead to wrong conclusions and incorrect management decisions.

PRICING DECISIONS

The Metropolitan Restaurant Company is operating, amongst others, the Portofino Restaurant whose typical weekly results are given below.

	Mon.	Tues.	Wed.	Thu.	Fri.	Sat.	Total
No. of covers	20	40	50	60	80	100	350
	£	£	£	£	£	£	£
Sales	200	400	500	600	800	1,000	3,500
Variable cost	80	160	200	240	320	400	1,400
Fixed cost	300	300	300	300	300	300	1,800
Total cost	380	460	500	540	620	700	3,200
Net profit (Net loss)	(180)	(60)	—	60	180	300	300

The restaurant is subject to a pronounced weekly pattern of trading, and the sales volume on Saturday is limited by the seating capacity of the establishment. The directors are not satisfied with the profitability of this unit and are of the opinion that the restaurant should earn sufficient contribution to achieve a net profit of at least £500 per week. The following suggestions have been made to improve the profitability of the Portofino Restaurant.

(a) In view of the losses incurred at the beginning of the week, the restaurant should be closed on Mondays, or Mondays and Tuesdays.
(b) A cover charge of £1.00 should be imposed. This, it is anticipated, will result in a loss of business of 6 per cent.
(c) A minimum charge of £12.50 should be imposed on Saturdays only. It is expected that this will reduce the number of covers by 10 per cent but result in an average spending of £15.00 per head.
(d) The most far-reaching recommendation is to introduce a rather unusual method of pricing. It is suggested that there should be a cover charge of

£5.00 per customer, designed to recover the fixed costs. All food and beverages should then be priced at cost plus 25 per cent. It is anticipated that, in addition to the cover charge, average spending per head will amount to £6.00. It is claimed that this new arrangement should not affect the number of covers adversely.

State, giving reasons, which of the four suggestions should be preferred.

Solution

		£
(a) Closure on Monday		
Present contribution (£200 − £80)		120
Contribution after closure		—
Restaurant worse off		120
(a) Closure on Monday and Tuesday		
Present contribution (£600 − £240)		360
Contribution after closure		—
Restaurant worse off		360
(b) Imposition of cover charge		
Present contribution (£3,500 − £1,400)		2,100
Contribution with cover charge:		
Sales: 329 covers @ £10	£3,290	
Add cover charge	329	
	3,619	
Less variable cost (40% of £3,290)	1,316	2,303
Restaurant better off		203
(c) Imposition of minimum charge		
Present contribution (£1,000 − £400)		600
Contribution with minimum charge:		
Sales: 90 covers @ £15	£1,350	
Less variable cost (40% of £1,350)	540	810
Restaurant better off		210
(d) New method of pricing		
Present contribution (£3,500 − £1,400)		2,100
Contribution with new pricing method:		
Sales: cover charge (350 @ £5)	£1,750	
Add ASP (350 @ £6)	2,100	
	3,850	
Less variable cost (4/5 of £2,100)	1,680	2,170
Restaurant better off		70

We may now rank the four cases in terms of their respective effect on the contribution and net profit of the restaurant.

RANKING

Alternative	Contribution £	Net Profit £
(c)	2,310	510
(b)	2,303	503
(d)	2,170	370
(a) Monday	1,980	180
Monday & Tuesday	1,740	(60)

PROFIT PROJECTIONS I

Given below is the Trading, Profit and Loss Account of the Messina Restaurant for Year 1.

	Sales £	Cost of sales £	Gross profit £
Food	300,000	120,000	180,000
Beverages	200,000	100,000	100,000
Total	500,000	220,000	280,000
Less Wages and staff costs		120,000	
Linen and laundry		10,000	
Office and administration		30,000	
Repairs and maintenance		15,000	
Depreciation		10,000	
Advertising		5,000	
Music and entertainment		10,000	200,000
Net profit			£80,000

It is expected that in Year 2 the number of covers will increase by 10 per cent. No change is expected in the ASP of the restaurant.

An analysis of the cost-behaviour patterns of the operating costs of the restaurant has given the division shown in the table below as between fixed and variable costs in respect of Year 1.

You are informed that the ASP of the restaurant in Year 1 was £50.00 and that in Year 2 it is intended to operate at the same percentages of food and beverage gross profits as in Year 1. You are required to:

(a) project the net profit for Year 2
(b) prepare a break-even chart of the restaurant for Year 2
(c) ascertain the break-even point for Year 2 in terms of the number of covers.

Expense	Fixed	Variable	Total
	£	£	£
Wages and staff costs	80,000	40,000	120,000
Linen and laundry	4,000	6,000	10,000
Office and administration	30,000		30,000
Repairs and maintenance	13,000	2,000	15,000
Depreciation	8,000	2,000	10,000
Advertising	5,000		5,000
Music and entertainment	10,000		10,000
Total	£150,000	£50,000	£200,000

Solution

Net profit—Year 2

Sales—£500,000, plus 10% thereof		£550,000
Less food and beverage costs (44% of sales)		242,000
Gross profit		308,000
Less fixed costs	£150,000	
variable costs (£50,000 plus 10%)	55,000	205,000
Net profit for Year 2		103,000

The break-even chart for Year 2 is given in Figure 6.2
The exact break-even point for Year 2 may be calculated as follows.

		£
Average spending power		50.00
Less food and beverage costs (44%)	22.00	
other variable costs (£55,000 ÷ 11,000)	5.00	27.00
Contribution per cover		23.00

Therefore:

$$\frac{\text{Fixed costs}}{\text{Contribution per cover}} = \frac{£150,000}{£23.00} = 6,522 \text{ (covers)}$$

PROFIT PROJECTIONS II

During Year 1 the trading results of the Pimlico Hotel were as follows.

Quarter	Sales	Net profit (Net loss)
	£	£
1	400,000	20,000
2	600,000	180,000
3	800,000	340,000
4	200,000	(140,000)

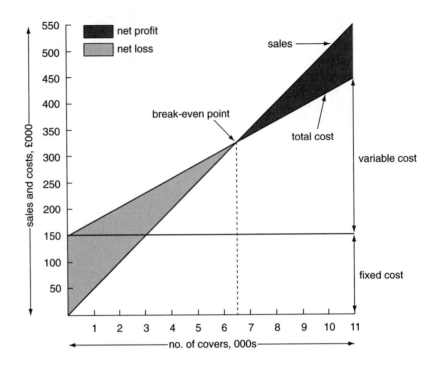

Figure 6.2 Break-even chart for Year 2

In view of current inflationary pressures it is expected that during Year 2 variable costs will increase by 20 per cent. In order to maintain the profitability of the hotel the general manager insists that the net profit for Year 2 must be at least 10 per cent more than in Year 1.

Advise the general manager what volume of sales must be reached in Year 2 to ensure adequate profitability.

Solution

The first step is to prepare a profit–volume graph as in Figure 6.3

As may be seen from Figure 6.3, the hotel incurred fixed costs in Year 1 at the rate of £300,000 per quarter. We may now calculate the variable costs for Year 1.

Sales		£2,000,000
Less Net profit	400,000	
Fixed costs	1,200,000	1,600,000
Therefore, variable costs		£400,000

It is clear that variable costs were incurred at the rate of 20 per cent in relation to the volume of sales.

With regard to Year 2, the position is as follows.

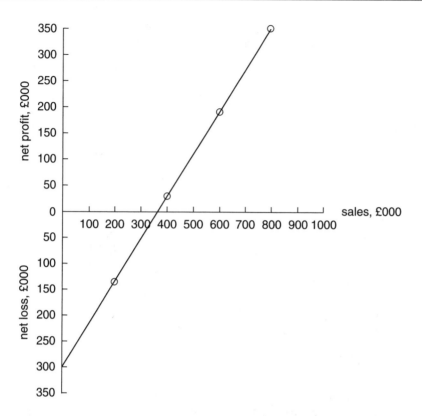

Figure 6.3 Profit–volume graph

Fixed costs	£1,200,000
Variable costs (£400,000 plus 20 per cent)	480,000
Net profit required	440,000
Sales volume	£2,120,000

It follows, therefore, that the hotel must reach a sales volume of £2,120,000 to maintain its profitability. The increase in the sales volume must be secured by increasing charges to clients. If the increase in the sales volume were to be secured through higher occupancies there would be some increase in variable costs, and quite clearly an increase of £120,000 would not be adequate.

ADVERTISING DECISIONS

Peter Jones is the owner of the Safari Travel Agency. His accountant prepared the following budget for the second half-year, 1 October 1998 to 31 March 1999.

Budgeted Profit & Loss A/c
for six months ending 31 March 1999

	Sales	Cost of sales	Commission
	£	£	£
Package tours	900,000	810,000	90,000
Rail tickets	500,000	450,000	50,000
Insurance	100,000	85,000	15,000
	1,500,000	1,345,000	155,000

Less Operating expenses:		
Salaries	55,000	
Rent and rates	10,000	
Gas and electricity	5,000	
Administrative expenses	10,000	
Depreciation	4,000	
Advertising	6,000	
Miscellaneous expenses	5,000	95,000
Net profit		60,000

Peter Jones is of the opinion that his business should produce a significantly higher level of net profit. After a number of consultations, his manager, Richard May, suggests that an advertising campaign costing £10,000 would increase total sales by 10 per cent. It is estimated that of the total operating costs, £85,000 is fixed and the remainder fully variable. You are required to re-draft the Budgeted Profit & Loss A/c on the assumption that Richard May's recommendation is accepted; and decide whether the expenditure on advertising would be justified.

Solution

Budgeted Profit & Loss A/c
for six months ending 31 March 1999

	Sales	Cost of sales	Commission
	£	£	£
Package tours	990,000	891,000	99,000
Rail tickets	550,000	495,000	55,000
Insurance	110,000	93,500	16,500
	1,650,000	1,479,500	170,500

Less	Operating expenses:		
	Salaries	55,000	
	Rent and rates	10,000	
	Gas and electricity	5,000	
	Administrative expenses	10,000	
	Depreciation	4,000	
	Advertising	16,000	
	Miscellaneous expenses	5,000	
	Additional variable costs	1,000	106,000
	Net profit		64,500

From the above Budgeted Profit & Loss A/c it appears that the expenditure on advertising is justified. It would raise the net profit for the half-year by £4,500.

BUSINESS DECISIONS: BASIC TECHNIQUES OF PROFIT MANAGEMENT

Business decisions relate to a large number of operational, financial, marketing and other matters. From the point of view of profitability such decisions may affect operating costs, the sales volume or both. Ultimately, however, every business decision has, what is sometimes described as, 'bottom-line consequences', i.e. they may all be traced—in terms of their impact—to the net profit of the business.

The purpose of this last section of the present chapter is to illustrate how some of the concepts already explained (e.g. contribution, C/S ratio, break-even point) may be used to aid a variety of business decisions. We will illustrate the relevant techniques by reference to the Serengeti Restaurant. The Profit & Loss A/c of the restaurant, already shown in Chapter 5, has been re-written and is now presented in the form of a 'Contribution Profit & Loss A/c'. From the point of view of decision making this method of presentation is more appropriate in that one can see immediately the division of all costs into fixed and variable. Also, the relevant percentages, including the C/S ratio, are shown against the principal elements of the Profit & Loss A/c. You are reminded, for the purpose of the calculations which follow, that the ASP of the restaurant is £18.00.

Serengeti Restaurant
CONTRIBUTION PROFIT & LOSS A/c
for year ended . . .

		£	£	%
Sales:	Food	480,000		
	Beverages	240,000	720,000	100.0

Less Variable costs:

Food cost	144,000		
Beverage cost	108,000		
Payroll and related expenses	20,000	272,000	37.8
Contribution		448,000	62.2

Less Fixed costs:

Payroll and related expenses	140,000		
Administration and general	43,200		
Gas and electricity	9,200		
Advertising and sales promotion	10,000		
Repairs and maintenance	10,000		
Rent and rates	80,000		
Depreciation	32,000	324,400	45.0
Net profit		£123,600	17.2

Reduction in permanent labour

Let us assume that the restaurant manager has decided to reduce his permanent labour and, in this way, secure an annual saving of £11,000. This reduction in labour costs lowers the total fixed cost and, in effect, means that a lower volume of contribution (and hence fewer covers) need now be secured to break even. The original break-even number of covers was 28,964 and this is now reduced to:

$$\frac{\text{Fixed costs} = (£324,400 - £11,000) = £313,400}{\text{Contribution per cover} = £11.20} = 27,982 \text{ covers}$$

In terms of the number of covers the effect of this decision is as follows:

	Annual	*Weekly*
Original NoC required to break even	28,964	557
New NoC required to break even	27,982	538
Resulting improvement	982	19

The effect of the above improvement on the net profit of the restaurant is quite obvious. Total cost is now £11,000 less and this means a corresponding increase in net profit, which will now be £134,600 and represent 18.7 per cent of the sales volume.

Increase in food and beverage prices

The restaurant manager is planning to increase all his food and beverage prices by 5 per cent, and wants to know the effect of this decision on the break-even point and net profit of the restaurant. On the assumption that we have no other changes, the whole of the price increase will materialize as additional net profit, as shown below.

	Composition of sales volume			
	Present		Proposed	
	£	%	£	%
Fixed costs	324,400	45.0	324,400	42.9
Variable costs	272,000	37.8	272,000	36.0
Net profit	123,600	17.2	159,600	21.1
Sales volume	720,000	100.0	756,000	100.0

The effect of the 5 per cent price increase is to decrease variable costs from 37.8 per cent to 36.0 per cent. The new contribution per cover will, therefore, be:

	£	%
Average spending power (£18.00 + 5%)	18.90	100.0
Less variable cost	6.80	36.0
Contribution and C/S ratio	12.10	64.0

We may now calculate the new break-even point, which will be as follows:

$$\frac{\text{Fixed costs}}{\text{Contribution per cover}} = \frac{£324,400}{£12.10} = 26,810 \text{ covers}$$

In terms of the number of covers, the improvement achieved through the 5 per cent price increase may be summarized as follows:

	Annual	Weekly
Original NoC required to break even	28,964	557
New NoC required to break even	26,810	516
Resulting improvement	2,154	41

From the point of view of the overall profitability of the restaurant the effect of the price increase is very powerful indeed. The new level of net profit, £159,600, is 29.1 per cent higher than the original figure of £123,600.

Increase in overall gross profit percentage

The restaurant manager is planning a complete revision of his menus and wine lists with the aim of increasing his gross profit margin from 65 per cent to 68 per cent. In terms of the cost of sales this means that the latter will decrease from 35 per cent to 32 per cent. The new level of variable costs may be calculated as follows:

	£	%
Present variable cost	272,000	37.8
Less saving in cost of sales	21,600	3.0
New variable cost	250,400	34.8

The new level of variable costs means a change in the restaurant's contribution to 65.2 per cent. The contribution per cover will now be:

	£	%
Average spending power	18.00	100.0
Less variable cost	6.26	34.8
Contribution and C/S ratio	11.74	65.2

Our break-even point is now:

$$\frac{\text{Fixed costs}}{\text{Contribution per cover}} = \frac{£324,400}{£11.74} = 27,632 \text{ covers}$$

From the point of view of the number of covers the improvement due to the higher gross profit is:

	Annual	*Weekly*
Original NoC required to break even	28,964	557
New NoC required to break even	27,632	531
Resulting improvement	1,332	26

Finally, the 3 per cent improvement in the gross profit level will show itself in the net profit of the restaurant as follows:

	Composition of sales volume			
	Present		*Planned*	
	£	%	£	%
Fixed costs	324,400	45.0	324,400	45.0
Variable costs	272,000	37.8	250,400	34.8
Net profit	123,600	17.2	145,200	20.2
Total	720,000	100.0	720,000	100.0

As the above percentages of net profit suggest, the whole of the saving in the cost of sales (3.0 per cent) is an addition to the net profit of the restaurant.

Multiple changes

We have so far considered the effect on the break-even point and profitability of one single change. The same technique may, however, be used when several changes are to take place.

Let us imagine that the employees of the Serengeti Restaurant are to be given a 5 per cent rise and that this will increase our payroll and related expenses by £8,000. Let us also assume that, in spite of this increase in operating expenses, the owners require us to improve the net profit of the restaurant by £15,000.

And so, in order for us to achieve the above aims we will have to secure total contribution as follows:

		£
(a)	Contribution to cover existing fixed costs	324,400
(b)	Contribution to cover additional labour costs	8,000
(c)	Contribution to cover existing N. profit	123,600
(d)	Contribution to cover additional N. profit	15,000
	Total contribution required	471,000

The above total contribution will necessitate:

$$\frac{\text{Total contribution} = £471,000}{\text{Contribution per cover} = £11.20} = 42,053 \text{ covers}$$

In order to secure the original level of net profit the number of covers required was:

$$\frac{(\text{F.C. } £324,400 + \text{N.P. } £123,600) = £448,000}{\text{Contribution per cover} = £11.20} = 40,000 \text{ covers}$$

Hence it is clear that if we are to give the employees a 5 per cent rise and improve our net profit we will have to increase the total annual number of covers by 2,053 and the weekly number of covers by approximately 39.

PROBLEMS

1. Thomas Jones is the owner of the Colwyn Bay Restaurant. The establishment is seasonal and each year, during the low season, incurs a net loss. The part-time accountant of the restaurant, Mrs Tick, has prepared the following budgeted Profit & Loss A/c for 1998/99.

Budgeted Profit & Loss A/c for 1998/99

	Spring	Summer	Autumn	Winter	Total
	£	£	£	£	£
Sales	192,000	288,000	384,000	256,000	1,120,000
Less Cost of sales	76,800	115,200	153,600	102,400	448,000
Gross profit	115,200	172,800	230,400	153,600	672,000
Fixed costs	70,000	70,000	70,000	70,000	280,000
Variable costs	60,000	90,000	110,000	80,000	340,000
Total cost	130,000	160,000	180,000	150,000	620,000
Net profit/loss	(14,800)	12,800	50,400	3,600	52,000

Thomas Jones is anxious to explore ways and means of improving the profitability of the restaurant. He has, therefore, asked all members of the family to attend a meeting. The following comments/suggestions are made by members of the family.

Daughter Helen: Our annual turnover is in excess of £1 million and the net profit only £52,000, which is 4.6 per cent. I myself would be inclined to cut all portions by 10 per cent, which, I'm sure, would result in a worthwhile addition to profits.

Son Phillip: The best solution is to cut costs. Our chef is costing us £30,000. Why don't we find someone cheaper?

Mrs Jones: From the accounts it is clear that the net profit for the autumn is just about equal to the profit for the whole year. Let's close the restaurant for nine months and open in the autumn only. For a fraction of the effort we're putting in now we'll have the same profit.

Thomas Jones: Well, I don't know about closing for nine months, but I'm sure we could close in winter and spring each year and still earn a good profit. Let me speak to Mrs Tick before any final decisions are made.

Assess critically each of the four suggestions. Is there, in your opinion, another—a more fruitful—solution?

2. The Riviera Restaurant Co. is operating, amongst others, the San Remo Restaurant. Its typical weekly results are shown below:

Day	Mon.	Tue.	Wed.	Thur.	Fri.	Sat.	Total
No. of covers	40	80	100	120	160	200	700
	£	£	£	£	£	£	£
Sales	400	800	1,000	1,200	1,600	2,000	7,000
Variable costs	160	320	400	480	640	800	2,800
Fixed costs	600	600	600	600	600	600	3,600
Total cost	760	920	1,000	1,080	1,240	1,400	6,400
N. profit/(N. loss)	(360)	(120)	—	120	360	600	600

The directors of the company are not satisfied with the profitability of this restaurant, and are determined to take immediate steps to raise the weekly profit of the restaurant to approximately £1,000. The following suggestions are made.

(a) The restaurant should be closed each Monday and Tuesday to avoid the losses incurred during the early part of the week.
(b) A cover charge of £0.50 should be imposed. This, it is estimated, will result in a decrease in the number of covers of 5 per cent.
(c) A minimum charge of £12.00 should be imposed on Fridays and Saturdays only. It is expected that this will reduce the number of covers by 10 per cent but result in an average spending power of £13.00.

State, giving reasons, which of the three suggestions you find most acceptable.

3. Given below are the summarized trading results of the Eastbourne Restaurant in respect of the year ended 31 December 19 . .

Department	Sales	Cost of Sales	Gross Profit
	£	£	£
Food	1,000,000	400,000	600,000
Beverages	400,000	200,000	200,000
Sundries	200,000	160,000	40,000
	1,600,000	760,000	840,000
Less fixed costs			600,000
Net profit			£240,000

   The number of covers served during the above period was 80,000. The general manager of the restaurant is not satisfied with the profitability of this unit. At an *ad hoc* meeting called to discuss this problem two suggestions are made:

   (a) to increase all food and beverage prices by 5 per cent which, it is confidently expected, will have no adverse effect on the number of covers
   (b) to reduce the cost of food from the present 40 per cent to 37 per cent and beverage cost from the present 50 per cent to 45 per cent. These changes are not expected to have any impact on the volume of sales.

   State, giving reasons, which suggestion you prefer.

4. John Fenech is the owner of the 200-bedroomed four-star Melita Sun Hotel, situated in a prime location of Floriana, Malta. The daily variable costs per room (linen, toiletries, flowers, etc.), amount to £2.00. In the food and beverage department variable cost averages 40 per cent. The hotel's average room rate is £21.00 and the guests' average spending power on food and beverages is £10.00 per day.

   In September 1998 John undertook a review of the availability of rooms in the first quarter of 1999. He found that all the rooms had been sold, with the exception of 100 rooms which were still available for the first two weeks of March. He had just received three requests for hotel accommodation and these are summarized below.

   Request A—from the Scottish Countrydancers Assn, who would like 80 rooms over 14 days. They would require additionally breakfast and dinner at an inclusive price of £6.00. The Association is offering £21.00 per person per room. John knows from previous experience that members of the Association are likely to spend an additional £5.00 a day on food and beverages. Of the remaining 20 rooms only 25 per cent would be sold to 'walk-in' customers.

   Request B—from Senior Citizens Travel Ltd, who would like all the 100 rooms over 14 days and are offering £17.00 per person per room; and would like the hotel to provide a full buffet breakfast at £3.00 per head.

Additional spending on food and beverages is likely to average £7.00 per day.

Request C—a French travel company, Soleil Touristique SA, who require 70 rooms for 12 days and are offering £26.00 per room. They would additionally require breakfast, lunch and dinner at a total price of £13.00. John remembers that (as in the case of Request A) only 25 per cent of the rooms not taken up by Soleil Touristique would be sold to 'walk-in' guests.

Advise John Fenech on which of the three proposals he should accept. State clearly any assumptions you have made.

Introduction to pricing | 7

A business enterprise is like a living organism, and each company, firm and establishment is in some ways unique, differing from all others in many important respects.

A brief examination of the firms in any industry will show that they all differ in the amount of capital investment, the turnover they achieve, sales mix, cost structure, composition of the labour force, style of management; and that they all pursue rather different policies on purchasing, personnel, cost control, marketing, profitability and pricing.

What applies to other industries equally applies to the hospitality industry: hotels, motels, restaurants, cafés, canteens, snack-bars, etc. All those types of operation are highly individualized. With few exceptions they all aim at a rather different market, provide a varying type and extent of service, offer a different quality of food, provide a different kind of atmosphere and solve their business problems in a manner which is quite dissimilar.

Yet there is at least one thing which most hotels and restaurants have in common. This is a high degree of dependence on the market, a pronounced market orientation which pervades almost all hotel and catering operations and has far-reaching consequences on the financial well-being of each establishment. It is this high degree of market orientation which places pricing in hospitality establishments at the forefront of business problems and operating policies.

IMPORTANCE OF PRICING

There is some relationship between the price level of a hotel or catering establishment and its volume of sales. Although the volume of sales will, in the majority of cases, fluctuate from one day to another and, often, show a seasonal trend, the volume of sales in respect of a longer period will generally be higher when the price level of the establishment is lower, and vice versa. Over a longer period, therefore, the lower the price level of the establishment the higher usually its volume of sales and, conversely, the higher the level of charges the lower the volume of sales. This appears to be true in the majority of market situations.

Quite clearly then in an industry which operates at a high proportion of fixed costs and at relatively high profit margins the volume of sales is a most important determinant of profitability. Hence, unless the price level of the establishment is correct it will be impossible for it to achieve the volume of sales which results in the most desirable level of profitability. There is no doubt, therefore, that the price policy of hospitality establishments is one of the most critical factors determining their profitability.

If, as has been suggested, the price level affects the volume of sales and profitability then it must also have some considerable effect on the general financial position of the establishment and, ultimately, influence the dividends paid, the remuneration of the directors and managers, the degree of plough-back, working capital, cash position and capital expenditure.

The last decade or so has witnessed an unprecedented trend in the hotel and catering industry towards mergers, amalgamations and absorptions. The large hospitality organizations tend to expand over a period of time and thus present an increasing challenge to the owner-managed hospitality unit. As competition becomes more intensive the fight for survival through effective competition makes pricing a more indispensable and valuable weapon. Many of the newly formed types of operation are highly standardized, operating efficient control systems and employing the most up-to-date methods of marketing and sales promotion. In such circumstances the continued existence of the owner-managed hospitality unit operated on conventional lines must necessarily be dependent on the employment of more sophisticated methods of cost control on the one hand and more effective marketing and rational pricing on the other.

Another relatively new development in the hospitality industry is a faster tempo of technological change. Much progress has recently been made in microwave cookery, deep freezing and convenience foods. Information technology (IT) is now very much in evidence not only in large hospitality units but also medium-sized and smaller establishments. One of the main effects of these developments is to alter well-established cost structures by shifting the emphasis from one type of cost to another. The newly emerging patterns of cost force the caterer to re-examine his sales–cost–profit relationships and reappraise his methods of pricing.

Finally, hospitality establishments are an important element in the tourist industry of the country. Just as the volume of sales of the individual catering establishment depends to some extent on the level of prices charged so does the demand of foreign tourists depend to some extent on the level of prices they pay on arrival here. Clearly then, if the hospitality industry is to continue making a substantial contribution to the earnings of foreign currency it must be conscious of the effect which its price level has on tourism as an invisible export. It is suggested, therefore, that the pricing policies of hospitality, establishments are of considerable importance to the national economy via their effect on the balance of payments.

From what has been said it is possible to draw the following conclusions:

(a) In view of the high degree of market orientation of hospitality establishments their pricing policies are of particular importance with regard to competition, profitability and the general financial well-being of each establishment.

(b) Faster technological progress affects cost patterns and necessitates a continual review of the price structure of each establishment.

(c) As the price level has a key role in the financial affairs of the hospitality establishment, price-level decisions should be the responsibility of the senior management and not be delegated to lower levels of management, where the implications of price-level decisions are not usually fully appreciated.

PRICING IN TOURISM

An important characteristic of the package tour industry is its price sensitivity. Tour operators publish their brochures well in advance of the relevant holiday season; and intending travellers have ample opportunity to compare the offerings and prices of the companies concerned. In a situation like this differences in prices charged from one tour operator to another are bound to be negligible.

As far as the individual tour operator is concerned, therefore, price competition offers little scope for securing adequate profitability. The right approach is to concentrate on product competition and service competition (discussed later in this chapter) in order to secure customer loyalty and thus the right volume of business.

The operating costs of a tour operator are reasonably easy to arrange (with airlines, hotels, etc.) well in advance. What is less controllable and predictable is market demand. This is influenced by many factors—both in the tourist-generating countries (unemployment, government fiscal policy, etc.) and in tourist destinations (political instability, terrorism, etc). In this respect, therefore, tour operators are in the same situation as hotels; and need to recognize that the main threats to profitability flow from the demand side of the business. As in the case of hotels, seasonality in tourism brings its own specific problems. During off-peak periods many departures will not be fully booked; and the resulting spare capacity has to be converted into sales revenues by offering sizeable discounts to persons prepared to travel at short notice. Pricing tactics are, therefore, as important for tour operators as they are for hotels.

The retail travel agent makes no pricing decisions. The prices charged are determined by tour operators, railways and insurance companies. As most of the travel agent's costs are fixed, profits are determined—first and foremost—by the volume of business. Travel agents are not able to influence the quality of the product they sell. They can, however, offer a satisfactory level of service and, in this way, attract sufficient business. Service competition should, therefore, lie at the forefront of the travel agent's business strategy.

CONVENTIONAL PRICING METHODS

In the section which now follows we examine critically the most common pricing methods in use in various industries. All of these have been used—though some more extensively than others—in hospitality establishments. It is important that we should be familiar with these methods as, inevitably, some of them are more relevant to hospitality operations than others.

The cost-plus method

The cost-plus method is applied almost universally in the pricing of food and beverages and works as follows: one ascertains the food cost per unit and, to arrive at the selling price, adds a given percentage of gross profit. The percentage of gross profit should be such as to cover the cost of labour and overheads and leave a satisfactory margin of net profit. Frequent references to 'food costing', 'food cost plus kitchen profit' and 'food cost control' suggest that the conventional approach to pricing is very much food cost-oriented and that other factors which should properly influence price fixing are taken into account only to a limited extent.

There is no doubt that this generally accepted approach to pricing has its advantages. The cost-plus method is easy to understand and simple in application; and it is presumably its simplicity that is responsible for its wide use in the hospitality industry.

Yet it is clear that this conventional approach to pricing suffers from a number of disadvantages. One of the strongest objections to this method is that the gross profit margin added to food cost, and hence the resulting net profit, is not related to the capital invested in the business. The net profit achieved with the cost-plus method of pricing is largely a function of sales turnover: the higher the volume of sales the higher the net profit, and vice versa. However, what matters ultimately in almost any business enterprise is the net profit in relation to the capital invested in the business. In the cost-plus method this vital relationship between capital and profit is ignored.

Secondly, this method of pricing places too much stress on one single element of cost, i.e. food cost. The method does not take the cost of labour and overheads into account. Yet in high ASP establishments the provision of the right atmosphere, necessitating a relatively high cost of labour and overheads, is of great importance. It may be claimed, therefore, that a method of pricing based on one single element of cost cannot possibly result in a correct price structure.

Finally, as its name implies, the cost-plus method of pricing is based on cost, and does not take the demand for the product/service into account. Whilst in cost-oriented industries there is generally more justification for this method, its indiscriminate application in a market-oriented industry is wholly irrational. It will be appreciated that there is even less justification for the application for the cost-plus method to hotel room rates. A room selling for £50 may well have a direct cost of under £3. The link between cost and selling price is thus very vague and indirect—even more so than in the case of food and beverages.

The above critical comments on the cost-plus method may appear to be at variance with general pricing practice in hotel and restaurants, where this particular method enjoys wide and undoubted popularity. The explanation of the apparent paradox is this: the cost-plus method may be used in food and beverage pricing—and indeed used successfully—provided it is applied within strict marketing constraints. The application of the method within the right market-oriented context is explained in detail in Chapter 8.

Rate of return pricing

The fundamental objective of a business enterprise is to earn a satisfactory return on its capital. And it is this fundamental objective that is responsible for the underlying philosophy of rate of return pricing.

To quote from a well-known American text (S. A. Tucker, *Pricing for Higher Profit*, New York: McGraw-Hill, 1966, p. 159):

> The ultimate objective of a business enterprise is to earn a satisfactory return on all capital employed in its operations. This objective is the basic reason for the formation of the enterprise and for the confidence which creditors place in its management. Stated goals of a return on sales or a profit on total costs are not significant until the profit has been compared with the amount of capital resources that is required to generate it. While profit on sales may be considered high, it cannot be accepted as satisfactory unless the profit percentage on total capital is adequate and at least higher than what management could get if it invested its capital in another enterprise.

Thus whilst the cost-plus method is cost-oriented the rate of return method is profit-oriented. Its basic aim is to ensure the correct relationship between capital invested and the resulting net profit. The exact procedure adopted in this method will be apparent from the example given below.

Example

A catering company is planning to establish a large restaurant. The capital required for this venture is £400,000, and the estimated annual turnover of this unit is £800,000. The directors of the company insist that all newly established units must show a return on capital of 20 per cent. It is assumed that food and beverage costs will have to be maintained within 35–45 per cent of turnover. Other costs (labour and overheads) should account for about 50 per cent of the sales volume.

From the data given above it would then be necessary to evolve a basic cost structure and determine appropriate gross profit margins to ensure that the restaurant can reach its profit target of 20 per cent.

Let us first determine the overall level of food and beverage costs for this new operation.

	Food and beverage costs as % of sales		
	35%	40%	45%
	£	£	£
Sales	800,000	800,000	800,000
Less Food and beverage costs	280,000	320,000	360,000
Gross profit	520,000	480,000	440,000
Less Other costs	400,000	400,000	400,000
Net profit	120,000	80,000	40,000
Return on capital	30%	20%	10%

From the above preliminary calculations it may be seen that the restaurant should operate at a food and beverage cost of 40 per cent, and therefore price its food and beverages so as to achieve an overall gross profit of 60 per cent.

The next step would be to predict the sales mix and evolve the necessary pattern of differential profit margins. These, as explained in Chapter 8, provide for a different gross profit loading for each element of the sales mix. Thus, assuming a particular sales mix, the respective contributions to the total gross profit required of £480,000 could be as follows.

	Sales mix	Sales	DPM	Gross profit
	%	£	%	£
A la carte	37.5	300,000	70.0	210,000
Table d'hôte	25.0	200,000	55.0	110,000
Beverages	32.5	260,000	60.0	156,000
Sundries	5.0	40,000	10.0	4,000
Total	100.0	£800,000	60.0	£480,000

From the point of view of the profitability of the business, the advantages of rate of return pricing are readily apparent. The method provides a direct link between prices, profit margins and the capital of the business. Provided that the estimated sales volume is achieved and the differential profit margins adhered to, net profit at the end of the year is more than likely to be pretty close to the profit target.

Rate of return pricing has, however, its disadvantages. It is mechanistic, rigid and unduly profit-oriented. It ignores more factors influencing pricing policy than it takes into account. Its approach to pricing problems is therefore too simple to be realistic. Its greatest failure is that it loses sight of the customer and market demand generally. Thus, in a market-oriented business, it cannot be wholly acceptable—at least in its crude form.

A diagrammatic representation of the application of the rate of return pricing method is shown in Figure 7.1.

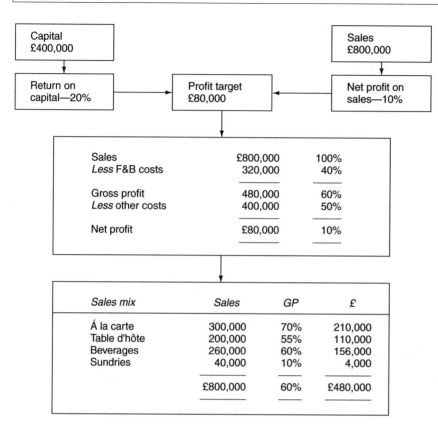

Figure 7.1 Rate of return pricing

Absorption pricing

Absorption pricing is known as such because each 'unit of output' absorbs, in addition to its rightful direct cost, a proportion of indirect costs. To be more specific the procedure, with this pricing method, is as follows:

(a) We ascertain the direct cost (usually the cost of direct materials, direct labour and direct expenses, if any) per unit.
(b) We then add a proportion of indirect costs (e.g. office and administration expenses, marketing, repairs and maintenance, depreciation, financial charges, etc.) to arrive at the 'total cost per unit of output'.
(c) Finally, we add the required margin of net profit to arrive at selling price.

The example that follows will make the procedure clear.

PRODUCT 'A'

	£	£
Direct costs:		
Materials	10	
Labour	15	
Expenses	5	30
Overhead expenses		10
Total cost per unit		40
Add Mark-up (Net profit)		10
Selling price		50

Absorption pricing is widely practised in the manufacturing industries. Its proponents claim two major advantages for it. First, it is argued, the method allows all costs to be charged against output—as each product sold carries a proportion of overhead expenses. Secondly, it is claimed that the method facilitates the recovery of overheads. Both these considerations are important but are not central to the problem of pricing.

There is no logical, nor even wholly satisfactory, method of apportioning costs; and different accountants will choose different methods of apportionment in very similar sets of circumstances. Absorption pricing is cost-oriented and ignores the demand for the product/service.

To revert to our example of Product A, there is no guarantee that £50 is the right price. Our competitors may be producing a similar product and selling it at £75. If so then we should pay rather less attention to our costs and, possibly, charge about £70 which will give us considerably more profit—and will still keep us price competitive. If, on the other hand, our competitors are selling a similar product for £45, then again the 'total cost per unit of output' is a poor guide to the price we should charge. Several attempts have been made in recent years to apply absorption pricing to food and beverage operations. There is, as yet, no evidence that the method can provide a sensible pricing approach in hotels or restaurants.

Contribution pricing

This is a more recent, but increasingly popular, method of pricing. Its essential features are as follows:

(a) All costs are divided as between those which are variable and those which are fixed
(b) The variable cost per unit is increased by an appropriate amount of contribution to arrive at the selling price
(c) No attempt is made to apportion fixed, indirect costs to individual products or departments.

Contribution pricing has several advantages over absorption pricing. As far as short-run, tactical pricing is concerned the variable cost per unit is the lowest acceptable price—though in most practical pricing situations price reductions are not normally such as to take the selling price to the variable cost level. During the last decade many London hotels have offered substantial price reductions to foreign tour operators as well as other clients, frequently up to 50 per cent of the published tariff. As the variable cost per occupied room is normally very low in relation to the average room rate, even a 50 per cent reduction in the selling price leaves a handsome amount of contribution per occupied room.

There is a great deal of scope for the application of contribution pricing in banqueting operations, where the variable cost per unit (cover) is quite easy to identify: in most cases it will consist of food and beverage costs plus the additional part-time and casual labour. During a relatively slack period (as indeed during the early part of the week throughout the year when the demand for functions is relatively low) as long as the sales revenue is in excess of the additional cost, the business is worth having in that some additional contribution is earned. Also a further benefit is employment for the (frequently permanent) part-time staff of the hotel.

Backward pricing

What is described as 'backward pricing' is not really a method of pricing: it is a method of adjusting operating costs to a fixed price. The method works as follows.

(a) A national or local trade association or professional body recommends a price to its members. For instance, a local hotel and restaurant association may recommend that members should charge £200 a week for bed, breakfast and evening meal.
(b) Hopefully, most members of the association accept the recommended price.
(c) As price is now fixed, the task that the members of the association face is how to adjust costs in order to secure a sufficient level of profit.

Backward pricing is a fairly common phenomenon throughout the international hospitality industry. Whilst in some situations the initiative will come from a trade association, quite frequently it is a national government or a local tourist board that will set maximum selling prices (for rooms rather than meals or beverages). Examples of this practice may be seen in several European countries. Whoever is responsible for fixing such prices, it is clear that this practice reflects a large measure of market orientation as, inevitably, maximum selling prices must—in the long run—be based on what the customer is able to pay, as indeed it is on what the market sees as the 'right' and 'reasonable' price.

DETERMINANTS OF PRICE POLICY

After a brief examination of the conventional pricing methods and their relevance to hotel and restaurant operations, let us look at some of the wider aspects of pricing and some of the specific determinants of price policy.

Figure 7.2 shows some of the factors that have a direct bearing on price policy. In addition to those listed one could think of many more. However, let us look at a few and see what relevance they have to pricing decisions.

Elasticity of demand (see p. 112–3) is one of the most important factors influencing price policy as well as actual pricing decisions. Yet most of the conventional pricing methods ignore this factor. Each hotel and restaurant should have at least a general appreciation of the elasticity of demand for their facilities. This is particularly relevant to their pricing tactics: off-season rates, price reductions on banquets and special functions, mini-weekends, etc. The more elastic the demand the greater the scope for an imaginative pricing policy in general and price discrimination and similar devices in particular.

Some products are homogeneous or identical: a particular make of pen or brand of vermouth will not vary in size or quality from one shop to another. Other products are heterogeneous or differentiated: a Wimpy bar lunch is a considerably different product (and experience) from a lunch at the Savoy; a room at a seaside private hotel is a different 'product' from a room at the London Hilton. The greater the homogeneity of the product the less scope for price competition. The room at the London Hilton may well cost five times the price of the room at the seaside private hotel. Yet we are unlikely to come across one wine shop asking five times the price of another shop for a bottle of vermouth.

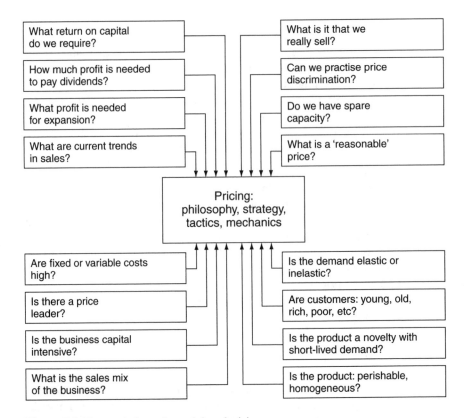

Figure 7.2 Factors influencing pricing decisions

The cost structure of the business is most certainly one of the principal factors which influence pricing policy directly and decisively. The higher the proportion of fixed costs, the narrower the margin of safety, the greater the degree of profit instability and finally, the greater the degree of market orientation. Where fixed costs are high, therefore, cost-based methods of pricing tend to lose their relevance, and we must look to the revenue side of the business for guidance in pricing decisions.

The question 'do we have spare capacity?' is equally important. Spare capacity, together with high cost fixity, presents one of the most serious threats to profitability in hospitality operations, and demands an imaginative and flexible approach to pricing policies.

To sum up, pricing is a most complex matter and one that cannot be resolved by a simple formula. A purposeful approach to pricing must take into account all the variables and influencing factors and determine the right starting point (the pricing situation) for price policy. We must then develop the pricing strategy, pricing tactics and finally develop the machinery for producing the right pricing decisions in the business.

THE PRICING SITUATION

In spite of the multiplicity of the influencing factors, it is possible to put them all under three headings. Some of them relate to the objectives of the business; some operate, so to speak, on the revenue side of the enterprise; others influence the operating costs.

Thus in spite of the complexity of the pricing problem, we may categorize all the influencing factors and reduce what is a complex problem into one which is essentially three-dimensional. That done, it is possible to identify the pricing situation of the business (Figure 7.3)

It will be appreciated that because of the highly individualistic nature of hospitality establishments, each of the three dimensions will present itself differently from one establishment to another. It follows, therefore, that one cannot legislate for all hospitality establishments. Each establishment will pursue a rather different policy on profitability, have a different cost structure and operate in somewhat different market conditions. Hence, although all the three dimensions must be taken into account in evolving a rational approach to pricing for a particular business, there will always be shifts of emphasis from one dimension to another depending on the circumstances of each individual business. Let us now examine the three dimensions in some detail.

PROFITABILITY AND OTHER OBJECTIVES

As mentioned earlier in this chapter, profitability, i.e. adequate return on capital invested, is the most important single objective of the business enterprise. Whilst most accountants would not disagree with this proposition, it does require certain qualifications.

Textbooks of accounting and economics contain numerous references to

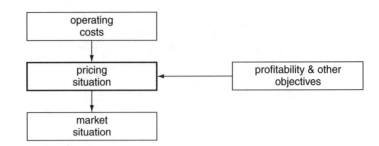

Figure 7.3 The pricing situation

'maximum profitability', 'maximum efficiency' and 'profit maximization', and tend to give the impression that the objective of the business enterprise is, purely and simply, to maximize profits. This is not so.

A professional accountant may find that he can secure a great deal of work in addition to what he is doing currently. If he starts accepting more and more clients, he may soon find that there is a point after which leisure is preferable to extra profit. A hotel manager may be in a position to attract a fair amount of business over Christmas. Yet he may prefer to give his staff an extra day or two off, because in his view good staff relations may, in the long run, be preferable to a marginal addition to the total of annual profits. Hence in each case it is not the immediate profit but long-run profitability that really matters. It is, therefore, more appropriate to speak of *profit optimization* rather than profit maximization. The former recognizes the obvious constraints and places profitability in the proper context of the long run; the latter is crude, simplistic and misleading.

Secondly, it has to be realized that in addition to profitability there are other objectives which, sometimes, are almost equally important. A new hotel or catering establishment may in the first two years or so concentrate on building up its volume of sales. In such circumstances it will set its prices at a relatively low level: *rate of growth* may then take precedence over profitability. Similarly an old-established business may face increasingly acute competition, in the face of which retention of its *share of the market* may be as important as current profitability. A well thought out price policy will, therefore, stem from the objectives of the business and, indeed, recognize that these may well change over a period of time.

MARKET SITUATION

Competitive situations

Hospitality operators find themselves in many types of competitive situation. Whilst some are virtually monopolistic, others are situated in areas of intensive competition. And it is clear that the type of competitive situation a business finds itself in will have an important bearing on its price policy.

Where there are many similar establishments concentrated in a particular area, the price charged by any one establishment is a most critical factor. In such circumstances demand will be very sensitive to the price level of the establishment: even a modest rise in room rates or menu prices of, say, 10 per cent may well result in a substantial decrease in demand. Conversely, the establishment which lowers its price level by 10 per cent may well gain over 20 per cent more customers. In a situation like this the more similar the hotel and catering establishments (in terms of the facilities they provide) the greater the effect of a change in price on hotel and restaurant occupancies. The usual reaction of the hospitality establishment to this problem is to stress the special, distinctive features of its operation. The more successful the establishment in differentiating its 'product' from all the competitors the greater its ability to pursue a reasonably independent price policy.

Hospitality establishments enjoying an almost completely monopolistic situation are few and far between. However, the greater the element of monopoly in any given situation, the greater the freedom of the establishment to determine its own price level. It must be remembered, however, that though the monopolist may charge any price he likes, it is for the customers to decide how many meals they purchase or how many nights they spend in the hotel at that price. Where there is virtual monopoly it is sometimes tempting for an establishment to 'cash in' on the situation by charging unreasonably high prices. However, the higher the monopolist's price level the greater the likelihood of a competitive business being established in the locality.

In between the two competitive situations described above there is often what is described as *oligopoly*, i.e. a situation where several businesses offer an identical or similar product. In oligopolistic situations there is often one major business and several smaller ones. When that is so there tends to be a condition of *price leadership*. The dominant business will set the basic price level; the others then follow the leader. There is some evidence of price leadership in the British hotel industry, particularly in the large cities. Hotels of a particular grade wait for the price leader to make the first move. If the price leader raises tariffs by 10 per cent, they—for good or evil—do likewise. It should be appreciated that the greater the degree of market orientation the stronger the inclination to follow the leader. The leader may, and sometimes does, make mistakes; and the followers should, therefore, guard against automatic price adjustments as these need not always be the right pricing decisions.

Kinds of competition

Hospitality and tourism establishments may compete with one another in different ways. Traditionally, the economist distinguishes three kinds of competition:

(a) price competition
(b) product competition
(c) service competition.

It is important to be quite clear about these forms of competition, as what is appropriate and effective in one situation may prove disastrous in another.

From observation it is obvious that in some situations the price level of the establishment has a greater effect on demand than in others. The general principle here is this: the higher the price level the less responsive demand to changes in price, and vice versa. If follows that demand will be most responsive to changes in price in low-ASP catering establishments and the cheaper end of the accommodation market. Thus a restaurant with an ASP of £6 will, as a result of a 10 per cent price decrease, gain much more in terms of new custom than an internationally famous West End restaurant. The most effective competitive weapon in the case of the latter is a high standard of cuisine and service. To revert to the problem of the pricing situation, the higher the price level of the establishment, the greater the emphasis required on the excellence of food and service and the greater the influence of the market situation on price policy. In the case of low-priced hospitality establishments, on the other hand, there will naturally be relatively more stress on cost control procedures to maintain competitive prices and thus ensure long-run profitability. The pricing situation of such establishments will, therefore, be less market-oriented, i.e. more influenced by operating costs.

Elasticity of demand

Several references have already been made to the responsiveness of demand to changes in price. When a small change in price has a substantial effect on the quantity demand we speak of *elastic demand*. Conversely, when an appreciable change in price results in a negligible change in the quantity demanded, we speak of *inelastic demand*. Diagrammatically this may be illustrated as shown in Figure 7.4.

There are a number of factors influencing elasticity of demand. The most important of these is the availability of substitutes. There are very imperfect substitutes for bread. Hence, within reason, whatever the price charged we are going to purchase the same number of loaves each week. Our demand for bread is therefore price-inelastic.

There are many makes of medium-priced family cars, and one is probably a fairly good substitute for another. The demand for such cars is, therefore, likely to be elastic. There is only one Savoy Hotel in London, and the London

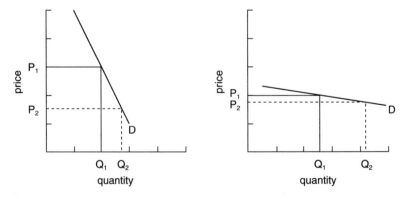

Figure 7.4 Elasticity of demand

Hilton is not necessarily a good substitute for it, and vice versa. The demand for the services offered by these hotels is therefore likely to be fairly inelastic.

However, there are numerous low-ASP restaurants in many parts of central London. Given adequate geographical proximity, one is certainly a good substitute for almost any other such establishment. Thus the better the substitutes the more elastic the demand.

Another factor influencing elasticity of demand is the degree of necessity. Hence necessities tend to have inelastic rather than elastic demand. The opposite, naturally, applies to luxuries. To extend this to catering operations, the demand for banqueting facilities is likely to be more inelastic than the demand for low-priced meals in cafés, snack-bars, etc. The consumer's income is also important. The higher his income, the less elastic his demand. Upward price adjustments in high-ASP establishments will, therefore, result in less consumer resistance than such adjustments in low-ASP establishments.

The lower the price of an item the more inelastic the demand. In terms of menu prices, a rise in the price of a cup of tea of 20 per cent will often be found by customers less objectionable than a rise of 10 per cent in the price of a T-bone steak. Finally, habit plays an important part here, too. The stronger the habit the more inelastic the demand. From the point of view of pricing policy, the advantage of regular and loyal customers can hardly be over-emphasized.

Nature of product

As already mentioned, some products are homogeneous, others are heterogeneous. The more homogeneous the product the less scope for price competition between the sellers. Sellers of homogeneous products must, therefore, take the price as given and compete on the basis of the quality of service provided to the customers.

Hospitality establishments offer 'products' which are essentially heterogeneous: dinner at restaurant A may be a considerably different gastronomic experience from dinner at restaurant B, even if the price paid is quite similar. The greater the heterogeneity of catering facilities provided by establishments in a particular location, the greater the measure of freedom that they have in their pricing policies.

The same applies to hotels. Hotel X and hotel Y may both charge £60 for a single room. The quality of service, the atmosphere and the catering facilities may in both cases be quite dissimilar, yet in total quite comparable in terms of what one might describe as value for money considerations. Here again the greater the distinctiveness or differentiation in the style, atmosphere, decor and catering facilities of the hotel the greater the price fixing discretion of the hotel concerned.

Products may also be classified as durable or perishable. The more durable the product the less dependent the seller on the whims of the market. Where the product is perishable there is inevitably a degree of market orientation. Hospitality establishments sell 'products' which are essentially perishable which, in addition to the widespread sales instability, makes for a high degree of dependence on consumer demand. The more perishable the product the greater, therefore, the influence of the market situation on the pricing situation of the establishment.

OPERATING COSTS

Cost structure

The cost structure of the business is one of the most important factors determining its pricing situation. The higher the proportion of fixed costs, the more market-oriented the approach to pricing, and vice versa. This is illustrated in Figure 7.5.

It is also the cost structure that determines the nature of the link between cost and selling price. Where a retailer buys an article for 50p and sells it for 60p, the link between cost and selling price is direct, real and quite obvious. In a situation like this the case for cost-plus pricing is strong. When a room is sold for £50 and has a variable cost of £3, the link between cost and selling price is very vague, indirect and unreal. Cost cannot, in such circumstances, constitute a meaningful basis for pricing and the approach to price policy must then flow from the market situation rather than be based on operating costs.

Range of price discretion

The concept of the range of price discretion flows directly from the type of cost structure of the establishment. In the short run fixed costs are fixed and

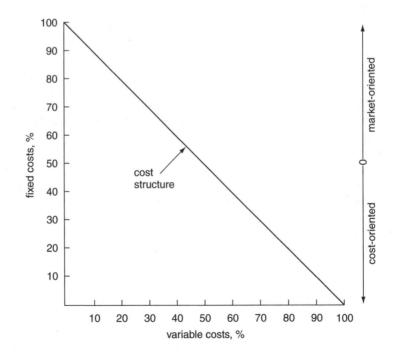

Figure 7.5 Effect of cost structure on pricing

any price in excess of variable cost is bound to produce some contribution to fixed costs/net profit. The lower the variable costs the wider the range of prices which will, in the short run, produce some contribution and the wider, therefore, the range of price discretion. This is illustrated in Figure 7.6.

To revert to our last example the position is this. The retailer, having paid 50p for the article himself, could not possibly charge any less than 50p. If the current market price is 60p then, in the short run any price between 50p and 60p will produce some contribution and be worthwhile. His range of price discretion is, therefore, quite narrow. Our hotelier, on the other hand, may in the short run charge any price between £3 and £50 and secure some contribution. His range of price discretion is very wide.

The wider the range of price discretion the wider the range of prices that may profitably be charged, and the more difficult the pricing problem. A wide range of price discretion has, however, certain advantages. It offers much scope for imaginative pricing in general and the introduction of various pricing devices (reduced rates, off-season charges, mini-weekends, etc.) designed to optimize profits in particular.

It is because of the wide range of price discretion that industries with high fixed costs tend to have more complex pricing policies than those industries with high variable costs. In the field of public transport there is no single price for carrying a passenger from A to B. The price he pays depends on whether he is an occasional passenger, whether he commences his journey before or after 10 a.m., whether he holds a monthly ticket, quarterly ticket, etc. It is for the same reasons that the local hairdresser will offer to serve old-age pensioners at a reduced price during slack periods of the week and refuse to serve schoolboys on Saturday mornings.

It is emphasized that the range of price discretion is a short-run concept and is, therefore, relevant to pricing tactics rather than pricing strategy. In the long run it is not enough to recover variable costs: the revenue resulting from the multiplicity of the individual prices must be adequate to cover all costs—variable and fixed—and leave an adequate net profit.

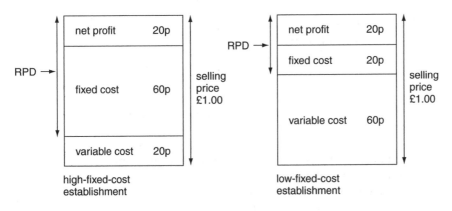

Figure 7.6 The range of price discretion

PROBLEMS

1. Explain what is meant by cost-plus pricing. Enumerate its advantages and disadvantages.
2. 'Price is determined by supply and demand.' If this is so, comment on the hotel manager's role in pricing decisions.
3. Give a brief outline of the rate of return method of pricing. Comment on its applicability in a market-oriented industry.
4. Enumerate the main determinants of pricing policy and explain how they may be categorized to ascertain the 'pricing situation' of a business.
5. 'In market-oriented industries the role of costs in pricing is secondary. Only in the long run is it necessary to cover all costs.' Explain, relating your arguments to short-run and long-run pricing.
6. 'A business firm is an organization designed to make profits and profits are the primary measure of its success. Social criteria of business performance usually relate to quality of products, rate of progress, and behaviour of prices. But these are tests of the desirability of the whole profit system. Within that system, profits are the acid test of the individual firm's performance' (Joel Dean, *Managerial Economics*, Englewood Cliffs, NJ: Prentice-Hall, 1951, p. 3). Discuss.
7. Distinguish clearly between the concepts of profit maximization and profit optimization. Illustrate the distinction by references to hotels and restaurants.
8. 'The firm should continue in production as long as price is in excess of marginal cost.' What is the time scale implicit in the above quotation?
9. Explain the concept of elasticity of demand. State in which sectors of hospitality and tourism you would expect to find: (a) elastic demand; (b) inelastic demand.
10. Explain the effect of (a) product homogeneity; and (b) product perishability on the pricing situation of a business.
11. Given below is a summary of the trading results of two businesses, A and B.

	A £	B £
Sales	100,000	100,000
Fixed costs	60,000	20,000
Variable costs	20,000	60,000
Total cost	80,000	80,000
Net profit	20,000	20,000
	100,000	100,000

(a) By reference to the figures given above comment on the link there is in the two businesses between cost and selling price.
(b) In which of the two businesses would you say there is more justification for cost-plus pricing?

12. Explain what you understand by the concept of the 'range of price discretion'. How relevant is the concept to pricing strategy?

13. Given below are some of the determinants of the pricing situation of a business:

wide margin of safety
narrow margin of safety
high C/S ratio
low C/S ratio
perishable product
durable product
stable demand
unstable demand
high fixed costs
high variable costs
elastic demand
inelastic demand.

State which of the above you associate with a market-oriented and which with a cost-oriented pricing situation.

15. Compare and contrast cost-plus pricing and contribution pricing.
16. Suggest possible applications of contribution pricing in the hotel industry.
17. Explain what you understand by 'absorption pricing' and comment on its suitability for the determination of hotel room rates.
18. Give a brief outline of 'backward pricing' and suggest what benefits it may offer to (a) hotel operators and (b) hotel guests.
19. Evaluate and describe the three principal kinds of competition and explain their respective importance to:
    (a) travel agents
    (b) tour operators
    (c) museums
    (d) theatres.
20. Explain how the three determinants of the pricing situation, i.e. operating costs, market situation and business objectives, determine the pricing strategy and pricing tactics of (a) tour operators and (b) travel agents.

Pricing: some practical applications

DETERMINING ROOM RATES

Introduction

The aim of the section which now follows is to describe the price fixing process in an existing hotel and throw sufficient light on the main methods of pricing rooms. This, it will be appreciated, is wholly different from the development of a basic price strategy for a new hotel which can only be attempted on the basis of a market feasibility study.

The essential aim of a market feasibility study is to identify and quantify the potential demand for a particular hotel or catering facility. This entails the examination and interpretation of a large number of factors such as: the nature and extent of existing facilities in a particular location; socio-economic structures of local population; potential business to be had from local industries, government departments and other sources; existing and proposed transport networks, and numerous other factors.

An investigation of this kind will often disclose a 'market gap' and point to a particular need which is not currently satisfied. When the market feasibility study has been completed, it is essential to quantify the data and produce a forecast of potential sales. This would include particulars of sales mix, ASP, NoC, trends in occupancies, etc. That, briefly, is the first step and the correct approach to the development of a pricing strategy for a market-oriented business. It is next necessary to look at the cost side of the proposed venture and determine what costs would be involved in satisfying the demand identified in the market feasibility study. Finally, it would be necessary to produce a projection of the profitability of the proposed business. A detailed description of market feasibility studies cannot be attempted in this chapter. Readers will, however, find a competent treatment of this subject in a contribution by Edward J. G. Davies (Chapter 3 in R. Kotas, *Market Orientation in the Hotel and Catering Industry*, London: Surrey University Press, 1975).

Old 'rule-of-thumb' method

For several decades and until quite recently hotel operators were using a simple, yet apparently quite accurate, method of fixing room rates. This method was developed over many years of experience during which it became apparent that there was a direct relationship between the cost of investment in hotel property and the average room rate (i.e. room sales divided by rooms occupied—for a full explanation see Chapter 15). It was found that whether a hotel was built in London, Paris or Cairo, it was necessary to charge £1.00 for every £1,000 investment cost per bedroom.

Consequently, if a hotel was built with 100 rooms at a cost of £5,000,000, to achieve satisfactory profitability the average room rate would have to be:

(a) $\dfrac{\text{Total cost of investment}}{\text{No. of rooms}} = \dfrac{£5,000,000}{100} = £50,000 \text{ per room}$

(b) $\dfrac{\text{Cost per room}}{1,000} = \dfrac{£50,000}{1,000} = £50 \text{ average room rate}$

This rule-of-thumb method was based on certain assumptions:

(a) that the hotel was fairly large
(b) that it had an average annual occupancy of approximately 70 per cent
(c) that the hotel had sufficient additional income from food and beverage operations and other sources such as store rentals, etc.

It will be readily appreciated that the above three operating characteristics are not always present in modern hotel/motel operations. Both in the UK and throughout Western Europe room occupancies have fluctuated considerably in recent years; and there must be few hotels with consistent room occupancies of about 70 per cent from one year to another. The income stability which characterized hotel operations for many decades is no longer present. Similarly, many of the new operations—motels in particular—have a very modest income from their food and beverage outlets. It is for these reasons that this old rule-of-thumb is no longer relied upon as an adequate guide in the fixing of room rates.

The bottom-up approach to pricing

The bottom-up approach to the fixing of hotel tariffs is now extensively used throughout the American hotel industry. It has, in recent years, also been used in the UK and several European countries. It is known as the 'bottom-up' approach for the following reason. If we produce a Profit & Loss A/c in what is described as vertical form, we read it from the top down, as illustrated in the example below.

PROFIT & LOSS A/c FOR . . .

	£	£
Sales		10,000
Less cost of sales		4,000
Gross profit		6,000
Less Operating expenses:		
Wages and salaries	2,500	
Office expenses	800	
Gas and electricity	500	

Marketing	500	
Repairs and maintenance	400	
Depreciation	300	
Other expenses	200	5,200
Net profit		£800

In other words we start with the sales volume, deduct all the expenses and arrive at net profit. With the bottom-up approach we reverse the procedure; we start with the profit required, project the expenses and arrive at the desired sales volume. Consequently, the procedure used in this pricing method consists of three essential steps.

(a) First, we must determine how much profit we should aim at. This, in practice, would be determined by reference to profits achieved in recent years, current trends in hotel occupancies, patterns of cost behaviour, etc.

(b) Secondly, we must determine our operating costs for the next period (usually, next year). This, in an existing hotel, should not present undue difficulties, as particulars of operating expenses are available for several past years. Our projection of operating costs should, therefore, be reasonably accurate.

(c) Finally, having determined the required level of profit and the total of operating expenses we arrive at the required volume of room sales. Given the estimated percentage of room occupancy we can then calculate the desired average room rate.

Example

A hotel company operates, amongst others, the 200-bedroomed Kariba Lake Motel. The investment in the motel amounts to £3,000,000 and the company expects a profit of 10 per cent after tax on that figure. The company pays tax at the rate of 50 per cent.

The hotel accountant has made the following projections of costs, etc., for the forthcoming year.

	£	£
Depreciation: Building	300,000	
Furniture	150,000	450,000
Rates and insurance		140,000
Administrative and general expenses		220,000
Advertising and sales promotion		130,000
Gas and electricity		80,000
Repairs and maintenance		160,000
Mortgage interest		340,000
Rooms department—operating costs (wages, linen, laundry and supplies—assuming 70 per cent room occupancy)		680,000
Coffee shop: departmental profit (at 70 per cent room occupancy)		80,000

(a) Assume that the motel will operate at 70 per cent room occupancy, and calculate the average room rate which will enable it to reach its profit target.

(b) Assuming that the motel's double rate is approximately 35–40 per cent more than the single rate and that the projected double occupancy is 30 per cent, calculate the motel's single and double rates for the forthcoming year.

Solution

(1) Average room rate calculation

	£
Net profit after tax	300,000
Tax	300,000
Depreciation	450,000
Rates and insurance	140,000
Administrative and general expenses	220,000
Advertising and sales promotion	130,000
Gas and electricity	80,000
Repairs and maintenance	160,000
Mortgage interest	340,000
Rooms dept—operating expenses	680,000
	2,800,000
Less Coffee shop departmental profit	80,000
Volume of room sales required	2,720,000

We next calculate how many rooms will be sold (irrespective of whether they are sold as singles or doubles) at the projected level of 70 per cent room occupancy.

200 rooms × 365 days = 73,000 rooms = 100% occupancy
therefore 51,100 rooms = 70% occupancy

Hence:

$$\frac{\text{Rooms sales required}}{\text{Projected rooms sold}} = \frac{£2,720,000}{51,100} = £53.23 \text{ (average room rate)}$$

(2) Calculation of single and double rates

We now calculate the single and double room rates by reference to the projected double occupancy of 30 per cent. Double occupancy, as explained in Chapter 15, refers to the percentage of rooms sold as doubles rather than singles. Thus if we sell 80 rooms and of these 60 as singles and 20 doubles, our double occupancy will be 25 per cent.

As the projected average room rate is £53.23, it is clear that the single rate will be less than £53.23 and the double rate more than £53.23. There is no formula available for calculating single and double rates from an average room rate. One has, therefore, to proceed by trial and error; let us assume a single rate of £44.00 and a double rate of £60.00.

		£
Singles	= 70%, i.e. 35,770 rooms @ £44.00 =	1,573,880
Doubles	= 30%, i.e. 15,330 rooms @ £60.00 =	919,800
Projected room sales revenue		£2,493,680

Quite clearly the above rates are too low and will not result in the right level of room sales. Let us try again on the assumption that we charge £48.00 as a single and £66.00 as a double rate.

		£
Singles	= 70%, i.e. 35,770 rooms @ £48.00 =	1,716,960
Doubles	= 30%, i.e. 15,330 rooms @ £66.00 =	1,011,780
Projected room sales revenue		£2,728,740

Our second attempt is evidently satisfactory, as the projected room sales revenue is only £8,740 in excess of the volume of room sales required.

The bottom-up approach to pricing is, clearly, profit-oriented. Consequently, whenever it is applied it is essential to ensure that we seek adequate profitability within the right marketing context. Our proposed single and double rates should, therefore, be compared to the relevant rates charged by similarly placed motels. In our example we assumed a departmental profit of £80,000 from the coffee shop operation. The volume of departmental profit secured from food and beverage operations depends, amongst others, on the room rates charged; and in this respect the bottom-up approach is not wholly satisfactory, as we have to assume a particular level of food and beverage departmental profit before actually deciding on the level of room rates to be charged.

Finally, we were instructed that the differential between the single rate and the double rate should be about 35–40 per cent. As already mentioned, there is no generally accepted formula for determining such differentials. Each hotel company should, therefore, develop its own policy on room rate differentials within the general framework of its corporate pricing strategy.

YIELD MANAGEMENT

Yield management (YM) is a relatively new development, although its underlying principles have been generally recognized for quite some time. The fundamental and most important idea behind YM is to maximize rooms revenue. Whilst until recently hotel managers were aiming to achieve this through the highest possible room occupancy, with YM the aim is to maximize rooms revenue by adjusting room rates in response to current demand.

This approach to pricing, though quite new in the hospitality industry, has been practised in many industries for quite a long time. Industries that practise demand-oriented pricing are basically those that have:

(a) a perishable product
(b) fixed product capacity
(c) unstable demand
(d) high fixed costs
(e) ability to divide the market into distinct segments.

Industries such as public transport, electricity supply and airlines have all the above characteristics and have practised some form of YM for a long time. The price of a rail ticket from London to Manchester will vary considerably, depending on the number of journeys covered, day of the week, etc.

Hotel managers who operate YM aim to maximize their 'yield'. This may be defined as actual room sales in relation to potential room sales. Let us take an example. A hotel has 200 rooms, all of which may be sold as doubles or singles. If the published double-room rate is £90, then the potential room sales are £18,000 per day. If, one day, actual room sales amount to £11,700 then the yield is:

$$\frac{\text{Actual room sales £11,700}}{\text{Potential room sales £18,000}} \times 100 = 65 \text{ per cent}$$

What we are trying to achieve here, from one day to another, is the highest possible rooms revenue inflow in relation to the room sales potential. This, clearly, is more logical than trying to achieve the best room or guest occupancy, which—in some circumstances—is a poor indicator of the profitability of room operations. Let us assume that a hotel company operates three hotels, A, B and C. Each hotel has 200 rooms and all rooms may be sold as doubles or singles. The published double rate is £80. One day the results are as follows:

	% room occupancy	Rooms sold	Average room rate(£)	Rooms revenue(£)	% yield
Hotel A	50	100	65	6,500	40.6
Hotel B	60	120	54	6,480	40.5
Hotel C	70	140	46	6,440	40.3

From the above table we see that, although each hotel achieved a very different percentage room occupancy, all three hotels have practically the same rooms revenue and the same yield. One important conclusion from this example is that if we want to achieve sound profitability in the rooms department, we must control not only room occupancy but also the average room rate. It is this approach that is clearly evident in the operation of YM.

The basic approach in the operation of YM is to: (a) predict, over a period of 6–9 months, the demand for rooms of each market segment and (b) respond to such demand by adjusting, day by day, the rates offered to different market segments. With this arrangement a given room will have a different price from one day to another. Also on any given day different rates will be quoted to different market segments for the same room. As a general rule lowest rates are offered to senior citizens, and the rates then rise for government employees, business travellers and 'walk-ins' (guests who arrive without prior booking). When demand is high, and we know that we can sell practically all the rooms at published rates, we do not offer any discounts and aim at the highest possible average room rate. When business is slack, we still want to achieve a high average room rate. We are, however, quite happy to offer discounted rates, and welcome senior citizens, groups and other business to fill as many rooms as possible. A YM system is invariably fully computerized. Also the full benefits of YM can only be secured in larger hotels which cater for several distinct market segments.

As a pricing method YM represents a radical departure from the pricing methods described earlier in this chapter. The most important pricing characteristic of YM is that it is demand-oriented: we are not interested in the investment cost per room or the cost of servicing rooms. What is important is the intensity of demand. Secondly, with traditional pricing methods we fix room rates for six to twelve months. With YM pricing decisions are made on a daily basis. Finally, it should be noted that, invariably, where YM has been in operation for some time, there is always a significant improvement in the average room rate. From our discussion of profit sensitivity analysis in Chapter 10, it will be realized that this must necessarily lead—through the appropriate profit multiplier—to an appreciable increase in overall hotel profitability.

FOOD AND BEVERAGE PRICING

As shown in Figure 8.1 the development of a comprehensive pricing policy for a food and beverage operation consists of five main stages.

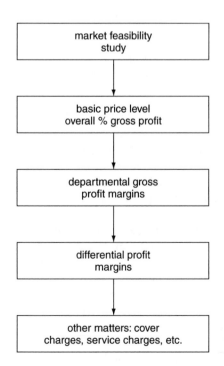

Figure 8.1 Development of pricing strategy

Market feasibility study

A market feasibility study is normally only required in the case of a new operation and, therefore, this first stage of the pricing process would not feature in periodic, routine pricing calculations of already established hotels, restaurants and similar operations. An important point to note at this stage is that, amongst others, a market feasibility study must:

(a) produce a customer profile—this will describe, in some considerable detail, the intended customers in terms of their nationality, age, sex, socio-economic status, etc.
(b) determine the customers' average spending power.

Thus the principal benefit of a market feasibility study is, as far as actual operations are concerned, that we know who our customers will be and how much spending power they will have available. It is only with this vital information that we may begin to plan our menus, decide on portion sizes, choose an appropriate type of service and, indeed, select the necessary kitchen plant and equipment. It should be realized that the customer profile has a most comprehensive and all-pervasive effect on all food and beverage operations.

Basic price level and overall percentage gross profit

It is from the customer profile and the projected ASP that we determine our basic price level and decide on the overall percentages of food and beverage gross profits. We may, therefore, decide that we should charge £12–£16 for lunch and £15–£20 for dinner. Following these decisions our executive chef will have to produce appropriate menus so that, in the case of lunch, after one has added together the price of the starter, the main dish, the sweet and coffee, the total falls somewhere within the projected price range of £12–£16. In the case of dinner, all the individual components of the meal would have to add up to at least £15 but not more than £20.

Similar considerations apply to beverage sales. We have to decide, in relation to the customer profile, what wines should be featured on the wine list. We may, as a result, come to the conclusion that our table wines should be priced at between £10 and £15 per bottle. We should also decide how much to charge for spirits, fortified wines, beers, minerals, etc.

The second major decision we have to make at this stage of the pricing process relates to the overall percentages of food and beverage gross profit. Whether the combined overall intended percentage is 60 per cent, 65 per cent or 70 per cent depends on both the customer profile and financial considerations such as projected sales revenues and operating costs. It is stressed that this is one of the most critical decisions as it has a direct and most profound effect on overall profitability. As a general principle, we associate a high percentage of overall gross profit with high-ASP operations and, conversely, a rather lower percentage of gross profit with low-ASP, popular establishments. Thus, restaurants with an ASP of £25–£40 will tend to aim at an overall gross profit of approximately 70 per cent, whilst those with an ASP of £10–£15 will probably be satisfied with 55–60 per cent.

Departmental gross profit margins

A larger hotel will, within its total food and beverage operation, operate several selling outlets and each of these may be expected to achieve a rather different percentage of food gross profit. For example, if a hotel has a food and beverage operation consisting of four selling outlets (grill room, coffee shop, banqueting department and room service)—it could expect all the four selling outlets to produce overall gross profits as follows. The grill room table d'hôte menu could be priced to produce a gross profit of 60 per cent, whilst at the same time the à la carte menu could be priced to achieve a gross profit of 70 per cent. The coffee shop, usually a cheaper and more popular operation, could be expected to produce a gross profit of 60 per cent. Banqueting sales are, traditionally, a high gross profit activity and one often expects the gross profit here to be approximately 75 per cent. Finally, room service food sales comprise a high percentage of high gross profit items (e.g. breakfasts) and an above-average gross profit of 70–75 per cent is often expected in this area of operations. Similar decisions would, of course, be made in respect of beverage sales in all the four selling outlets.

Departmental gross profit margins should also be determined in larger restaurants where, in addition to beverage sales, we frequently have an à la carte and a table d'hôte menu, both of which would be priced to produce significantly different overall gross profit results.

Differential profit margins

Within a given selling outlet different food and beverage items will attract different rates of gross profit. Thus starters may be priced at an above-average gross profit simply because—in relation to what appears to be a reasonable price—the food cost per portion is low. Many popular restaurants, for instance, use soup mixes quite extensively and are thus able to secure considerably high gross profit margins on this section of the food sales mix. On the other hand meat and fish prices are frequently quite high, and if we priced meat and fish items at 60–70 per cent our prices might appear too high. In such circumstances many restaurant operators will accept significantly lower rates of gross profit on all meat and fish items. Finally, it is generally found that tea and coffee produce a considerably higher percentage of gross profit than all the other elements of the food sales mix. A restaurant with food sales of £450,000 may operate at differential profit margins as follows.

	Sales mix		Differential profit margins	
	£	%	£	%
Starters	45,000	10.0	33,750	75.0
Meat, fish, poultry	225,000	50.0	123,750	55.0
Vegetables	67,500	15.0	47,250	70.0
Sweets	67,500	15.0	47,250	70.0
Teas and coffees	45,000	10.0	36,000	80.0
Total	450,000	100.0	288,000	64.0

If the restaurant's beverage sales amount to £140,000, its differential profit margins might look as suggested below.

	Sales mix		Differential profit margins	
	£	%	£	%
Beers	10,000	7.1	4,000	40.0
Minerals	30,000	21.4	18,000	60.0
Table wines	40,000	28.6	20,000	50.0
Fortified wines	20,000	14.3	11,000	55.0
Spirits	40,000	28.6	28,000	70.0
Total	140,000	100.0	81,000	57.9

Quite clearly, once the differential profit margins have been developed, pricing is a simple routine. As explained in Chapter 7 most food and beverage operators use the cost-plus method of pricing, where the selling price is obtained by adding so much gross profit to the cost per portion. The basic formula, then, is:

FOOD/BEVERAGE COST PER PORTION +
GROSS PROFIT = SELLING PRICE

Portion costs are readily available in most hotels and restaurants. As may be seen in Chapter 14, standard recipes are the best instrument for ascertaining portion costs of menu items. In the case of beverages, we sell many items by the can (beers, minerals, etc.) or by the bottle (beers, minerals, wines, etc.): in all these cases portion costs are always available by reference to suppliers' invoices. Other beverages are sold by the measure, and for each beverage a standard portion is determined. Here again the calculation of portion costs presents no problems.

Other relevant matters

Finally we should consider several other matters such as the desirability of a cover charge, the imposition of a service charge and possibly—where there is a high degree of sales instability—a minimum charge.

Additions to the customer's bill such as the cover charge or service charge may be justified differently in different situations but—in all cases—have the effect of increasing the operator's immediate sales volume. Hospitality establishments are all heterogeneous and it is impossible to argue the case for or against these charges except by reference to the specific circumstances of each business.

A minimum charge is—at least in the UK—somewhat less common; and is usually imposed to exclude low spenders during peak periods. Whilst the logic behind the minimum charge is unassailable it is, in practice, quite difficult to decide on the optimum level of the minimum charge. If it is too high it excludes too many customers and creates spare capacity. If it if fixed at too low a level it results in a relatively low ASP for the day concerned.

Example

A catering company proposes to establish a low-ASP restaurant in a large provincial city. A preliminary market feasibility study has been carried out and the following information is available.

(a) Capital investment required—£200,000
(b) Annual operating costs—other than food and beverage costs—£200,000
(c) Annual number of covers—100,000
(d) Average spending power—£4.00.

The directors of the company insist on a minimum return on capital of 25 per cent before tax. From experience in similar operations it is assumed that the new restaurant would have to operate at an overall gross profit of about 60 per cent. In order to ensure adequate profitability the directors would be pre-pared to allow the imposition of a cover charge of 20p which in their opinion, would not result in an adverse NoC effect.

Now if the restaurant were to operate at a gross profit of 60 per cent and without a cover charge, the position would be as follows.

	£	%
Sales	400,000	100.0
Less food and beverage costs	160,000	40.0
Gross profit	240,000	60.0
Less operating costs	200,000	50.0
Net profit	£40,000	10.0

As may be seen net profit on sales would be 10 per cent and the return on capital invested 20 per cent. Both figures are below those expected by the directors. The alternative solution is to impose the cover charge, the effect of which would be to increase the net profit by (100,000 covers @ 20p) = £20,000 to £60,000. The return on capital would thus be 30 per cent and net profit on sales 14.3 per cent. The development of the whole pattern of profit margins would then follow as shown in Figure 8.2.

In addition to the estimate of the total turnover of the restaurant it is essen-tial to predict the respective shares of à la carte and table d'hôte sales, bever-age sales and sundries. Similarly, it is essential to predict the sales mix within each menu. The determination of departmental profit margins and differential profit margins is then a matter of experience.

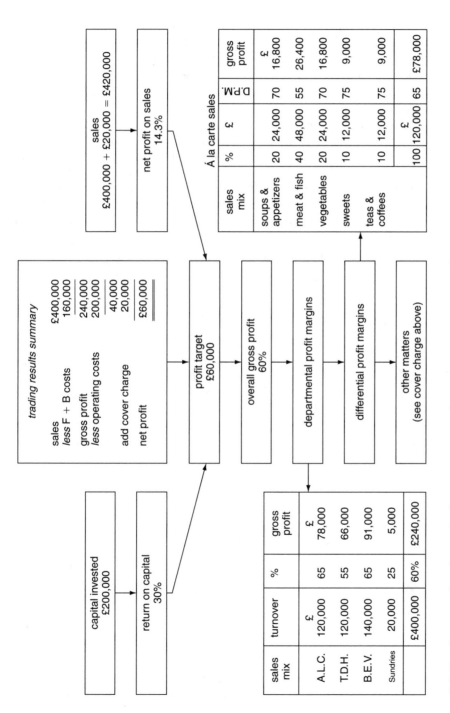

Figure 8.2 Development of profit margins in restaurant operation—the same procedure would be adopted in respect of table d'hôte sales and the sales of beverages and sundries

MENU ENGINEERING

Introduction

The use of percentages in menu pricing and gross profit control is now a well-established tradition. For many decades now hospitality operators in all parts of the world have used percentages, and no one—until recently—ever questioned this approach. The percentage method of pricing and gross profit control is simple and, as illustrated earlier in this chapter, superficially effective as a control instrument.

On reflection, however, it will be realized that the method suffers from several disadvantages. First, we are in business to earn a profit and not produce percentages; and hence an undue emphasis on percentages results in poor orientation: we are, so to speak, 'barking up the wrong tree'. We cannot bank percentages; and it is cash gross profit and actual money in the bank that enable us to pay wages and salaries, purchase equipment, pay creditors, etc. Secondly, a high percentage of gross profit is no guarantee of satisfactory profitability. The example that follows makes this clear.

Month	Sales volume (£)	Cost of sales (£)	Cash GP (£)	% GP
Jan.	100,000	35,000	65,000	65.0
Feb.	120,000	48,000	72,000	60.0
Mar.	110,000	41,800	68,200	62.0

As may be seen from the above examples, the month that gave the highest percentage of gross profit (January) contributed the lowest amount of cash gross profit. Also, the month that produced the lowest percentage of gross profit (February) made the highest contribution in terms of cash gross profit. What applies to the results for the business as a whole applies equally to individual food items. Let us assume that a snack bar operator sells three kinds of sandwiches, as follows:

Description	Selling price (£)	Food cost (£)	Cash GP (£)	% GP
Chicken sandwich	1.10	0.35	0.75	68.2
Ham sandwich	1.30	0.45	0.85	65.4
Cheese sandwich	1.00	0.30	0.70	70.0

From the above figures we may see that the sandwich that produces the highest percentage of gross profit is, in terms of cash gross profit, the least profitable, and vice versa.

Menu engineering: the basic method

It is the imperfections of the percentage method that have prompted hospitality managers to re-examine their approach to pricing and gross profit control. During the 1980s a completely new approach was formulated by two American experts, Michael L. Kasavana and Donald I. Smith (*Menu*

Engineering: A Practical Guide, Lansing, Mich.: Hospitality Publications, 1982). This new approach represents an important departure from the traditional approach. Its main features may be summarized as follows.

The first and most important point to note is that in menu engineering we reject the use of percentages in the price fixing process. We arrive at menu prices by adding to portion costs lumps or amounts of gross profit.

In the traditional approach to pricing and gross profit control the emphasis is on total results, and so at the end of each period we calculate the total gross profit earned by the establishment as a whole. In the menu engineering method we are more analytical; and in addition to total gross profit we control the popularity (number of portions sold) and profitability (cash gross profit per portion or menu item) of each individual menu item. Controlling popularity and profitability means, in effect, controlling the contribution to total cash gross profit of each individual menu item.

We undertake a continual review of all menu items. Those which are unpopular and unprofitable tend to be removed from the menu and replaced by items that are more effective in generating cash gross profit. Menu items which are not, for some reason, popular may be renamed or repositioned on the menu. In other cases it may be necessary to upgrade the ingredients or composition of the food item. What is important is that we should have an ongoing, continual and regular reappraisal of the performance of all individual menu items.

Finally—as menu engineering is essentially about menu pricing—we should ensure a continual review of all menu prices. Where the analysis (see Menu Engineering Worksheet on p. 133) is undertaken weekly, the review of menu prices should also be on a weekly basis. It is certainly not suggested that we should change all menu prices once a week. We should, however, review such prices on a weekly basis in the light of the popularity and profitability of the food items concerned.

Menu items: performance and corrective action

The analysis of the performance of menu items necessitates an appropriate terminology, and the following terms are now in general use in hospitality operations.

- A 'star' is a menu item which is both popular and profitable. Popularity is measured in terms of the number of menu items sold. Profitability is measured in terms of cash gross profit.
- A 'plough horse' is a menu item which is popular but does not attract a high level of cash gross profit per item sold.
- A 'puzzle' is a menu item which is profitable but, for some reason (which is a puzzle!) is not popular.
- Finally, a 'dog' is a menu item which is neither popular nor profitable.

Diagramatically we may represent the four categories as shown in Figure 8.3.

The above terminology is useful for two reasons. First, the labels summarize, quickly and effectively, the two critical performance characteristics of a food item (where 'dog' is used in the American sense of something poor or a

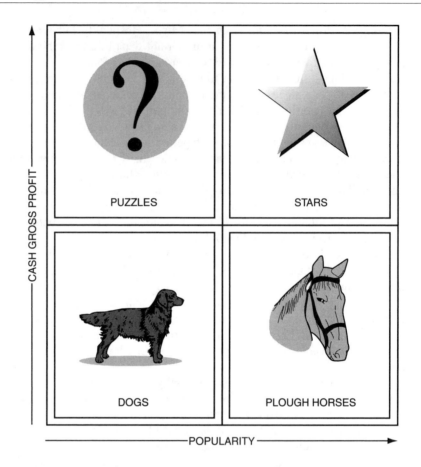

Figure 8.3 Menu engineering categories

failure). Secondly, the four categories defined above are useful in that they suggest what kind of corrective action may be required in any given set of circumstances.

Menu items described as 'stars' are our most successful food items, and we should take care of them by ensuring the best possible ingredients and attractive presentation as well as a prominent place on the menu. Most certainly we should refrain from precipitate action such as frequent changes in price which may well prejudice their success.

'Plough horses' are items that sell well, though the cash gross profit per portion is low. Examples of such menu items are salads and pasta dishes. It should be remembered that such items, though on a per portion basis not very profitable, frequently make a very respectable contribution to total cash gross profit. Both the Sirloin Steak and Mixed Grill in our example in Figure 8.4 are in this category.

'Puzzles', on the other hand, are profitable but do not sell well; and our first task is to discover why they are not popular. It is only then that the right corrective action may become possible. In some cases the presentation of the menu item may not be satisfactory. Sometimes an attractive menu item is not

Menu Item	1 No. of Items	2 Menu Mix %	3 Item Fd Cost	4 Item S.P.	5 Item C.G.P.	6 Total Fd Cost	7 Total Sales	8 Total Cash G.P. Amt	8 Total Cash G.P. %	Rnk	9 C.G.P. Cat.	10 M.M. Cat.	Notes
1. Salmon salad	240	12.0	1.50	6.75	5.25	360.00	1,620.00	1,260.00	9.0	7	L	H	Plough horse Raise price 20p
2. Grilled mullet	230	11.5	1.90	8.15	6.25	437.00	1,874.50	1,437.50	10.3	6	L	H	Plough horse no action
3. Poulet en cocotte	220	11.0	2.25	9.50	7.25	495.00	2,090.00	1,595.00	11.4	4	H	H	Star No action
4. Caneton bigarde	110	5.5	2.45	12.15	9.70	269.50	1,336.50	1,067.00	7.7	8	H	L	Puzzle Lower price £1.00
5. Escalope de veau	240	12.0	2.15	10.25	8.10	515.00	2,460.00	1,945.00	13.9	2	H	H	Star No action
6. Lamb cutlets	270	13.5	2.10	11.50	9.40	567.00	3,105.00	2,538.00	18.2	1	H	H	Star No action
7. Sirloin steak	260	13.0	2.30	9.25	6.95	598.00	2,405.00	1,807.00	12.9	3	L	H	Plough horse No action
8. Mixed grill	250	12.5	1.85	8.20	6.35	462.50	2,050.00	1,587.50	11.4	5	L	H	Plough horse Raise price 25p
9. Irish stew	100	5.0	0.95	5.15	4.20	95.00	515.00	420.00	3.0	9	L	L	Dog Eliminate, replace
10. Club sandwich	80	4.0	0.90	4.75	3.85	72.00	380.00	308.00	2.2	10	L	L	Dog Eliminate, replace
Total	2,000	100.0				3,871.00	17,836.00	13,965.00	100.0				

Figure 8.4 Menu engineering worksheet

given an appropriately attractive description. Also, the price may be too high. There are situations in which the hospitality operator is quite happy to have a few puzzles on the menu, e.g. flambée items which do not contribute much gross profit, but tend to create an amiable atmosphere in the restaurant.

Finally, 'dogs' are menu items that present us with a dual problem: both their popularity and their profitability are unsatisfactory. Our usual reaction, on finding a 'dog' is to remove it and replace it with a hopefully more cash-gross-profit-effective menu item.

Menu engineering worksheet

We have now discussed the operation of menu engineering and let us now look at a full example of a menu engineering worksheet. This is given in Figure 8.4. We will explain the compilation of the worksheet by reference to one menu item, Grilled Mullet.

During the period under review we sold 230 portions of mullet and this represents 11.5 per cent of the menu mix as shown in Col. 2. The item food cost (cost per portion) is £1.90, and with a selling price of £8.15 our cash gross profit is £6.25, which we show in Col. 5. In Col. 6 we have the total food cost of the 230 portions of mullet (230 @ £1.90 = £437.00). In the next column we show the sales volume generated by this menu item (230 @ £8.15 = £1,874.50). If we deduct the figure in Col. 6 from that in Col. 7, we will arrive at the total cash gross profit earned by the sale of Grilled Mullet. The latter, £1,437.50, represents 10.3 per cent of the total cash gross profit for the period under review. Of the ten items on the menu Grilled Mullet is no. 6 in terms of its contribution to cash gross profit.

Our classification of menu items into stars, puzzles, etc. is dependent on two criteria, i.e. profitability and popularity. In Col. 9 we state that the cash gross profit on the mullet is low (L), because it is below the average for all the menu items (£13,965.00 ÷ 2,000 = £6.98). In Col. 10 we state that the popularity of this menu item is high (H). When there are ten menu items one would expect them to average about 10 per cent of the total of all items sold. Grilled Mullet achieved 11.5 per cent of the menu mix, and this is clearly above-average performance. With below-average cash gross profit and above-average popularity this menu item is a plough horse. We should, perhaps, at this stage, explain that American hospitality managers define popularity rather differently. They take the view that a menu item that has reached 70 per cent of its 'rightful share' should be regarded as sufficiently popular to fall into the 'high' category of menu mix.

Application to beverages

Menu engineering has now gained widespread acceptance in the international hospitality industry. This, one should add, has been made possible by the general use of computers which facilitates the preparation of menu engineering worksheets. Weekly analyses of menu performance are now a routine task in many establishments.

Whilst the technique of menu engineering has had a great impact on hospitality food operations, beverage operations have not yet benefited from

Description	No. of Bottles	Sales Mix	Cost/ Bottle	S.P./ Bottle	Cash G.P.	Bev. Cost	Bev. Sales	Total Cash G.P. £	Total Cash G.P. %	Rank	C.G.P. Cat.	S.M. Cat.	Notes
White wines													
1. Château Elisa	85	17.0	2.45	6.95	4.50	208.25	590.75	382.50	13.0	4	L	H	Plough horse
2. Provence Blanc	24	4.8	3.75	9.75	6.00	90.00	234.00	144.00	4.9	9	H	L	No action Puzzle Lower price 25p
3. Castello Pisa	89	17.8	3.35	9.45	6.10	298.15	841.05	542.90	18.5	1	H	H	Star
4. Bianco Forte	47	9.4	4.65	11.25	6.60	218.55	528.75	310.20	10.5	5	H	H	Incr. price 20p Star
5. Riesling Dijon	15	3.0	8.45	19.35	10.90	126.75	290.25	163.50	5.6	7	H	L	No action Puzzle No action
Red wines													
6. Côtes Toulon	92	18.4	2.50	7.15	4.65	230.00	657.80	427.80	14.6	3	L	H	Plough horse Incr. price 20p
7. Sauvignon Roi	35	7.0	2.95	8.45	5.50	103.25	295.75	192.50	6.5	6	L	H	Plough horse No action
8. Ambassador Special	19	3.8	3.15	9.15	6.00	59.85	173.85	114.00	3.9	10	H	L	Puzzle Lower price 20p
9. Château Diana	77	15.4	4.25	10.75	6.50	327.25	827.75	500.50	17.0	2	H	H	Star No action
10. Bordeaux Rouge	17	3.4	6.35	15.95	9.60	107.95	271.15	163.20	5.5	8	H	L	Puzzle No action
Total	500	100.0				1,770.00	4,711.10	2,941.10	100.0				

Figure 8.5 Beverage engineering worksheet

this technique. On reflection it will be appreciated that there is no reason why the technique should not be used to control the cash gross profit effectiveness of beverages. The most obvious opportunity to apply the technique is in dispense bars, where we tend to sell bottles rather than glasses of wine and where, frequently, the choice of wines is limited. In a situation like this we are able to use the technique in the same manner as in the case of food operations. An example is given in Figure 8.5.

From the beverage engineering worksheet we can see clearly which wines are more successful than others. Also, a periodic analysis of this nature facilitates the pricing of wines by reference to their popularity as well as their potential contribution to cash gross profit. Although, in this particular case, our offerings are limited (we have only ten wines here), it is clear that most of our customers are interested in only four of them. The most popular four wines account for 68.6 per cent of our wine sales.

PRICING PACKAGE TOURS

In Chapter 7 we examined the main factors that influence pricing in tourism. Also we discussed the importance to the tour operator of the revenue side of the business. A closer look at package tour operations would indicate, however, that, to succeed in business, the package tour company must be both revenue- and cost-oriented.

Running package tours is like an assembly operation: buying all the required elements—air transport, hotels, meals, excursions, etc.—and offering to the client a complete package at an inclusive price. A critical aspect here is the bulk buying of all these elements at the lowest possible price to secure a low level of unit costs (air transport, hotel accommodation, etc. per traveller). It is only in this way that the tour operator can compete successfully. The imperative to secure low input prices places cost management and cost control at the forefront of package tour operation. The pricing of package tours (see example below) is, therefore, an essentially cost-oriented procedure.

Traditionally package tour companies operate at modest profit margins. Frequently the break-even point is reached when the aircraft is 80–90 per cent full. And this means an extremely narrow margin of safety and a high degree of profit instability. However, there is always some additional revenue that helps to ensure reasonable profitability. Cancellation charges imposed by tour operators are quite severe, and more than offset any losses the tour companies incur as a result of cancelled holidays (most of which tend to be sold to other clients). Some unsold packages that would ordinarily result in empty seats tend to be sold at a reduced price to holiday-makers prepared to travel at short notice. Others tend to be sold as flight-only packages. Duty-free sales are an important source of revenue and add significantly to the profits of tour companies (however, at the time of writing the future of this source of revenue is uncertain). Finally, tour operators have the use of clients' deposits many months before the commencement of the relevant holidays. The same applies to the payment of the remaining sum due which, frequently, is payable eight weeks before departure. Such arrangements place tour operators in an advantageous situation and enable them to invest the money at interest.

Example

The example given below illustrates the pricing process; it should be noted that the approach to pricing here is similar to the cost-plus pricing method generally used in catering operations.

Package Tour X

	£
Flight costs—including air passenger duty, in-flight meals, etc.	120.00
Hotel accommodation: 14 nights' half-board	145.00
Transfers—to and from hotel	10.00
Excursions, including meals *en route*	18.00
Gratuities, etc.	2.00
Total direct costs	295.00
Add Mark-up	95.00
Selling price	£390.00

Readers should note that the mark-up is quite substantial and amounts to about one-third of the total of direct costs. Its function is to cover all administrative and marketing costs as well as agency commissions and, of course, the tour operator's net profit.

PROBLEMS

1. Write a short essay explaining how you would develop a pricing strategy for a new restaurant. State clearly any assumptions you have to make.
2. Explain the bottom-up approach to pricing. What are its advantages and disadvantages?
3. What is the practical importance of differential profit margins in food and beverage operations?
4. Compare and contrast the pricing of food and the pricing of beverages.
5. Give a brief outline of the aims and operation of yield management. Compare and contrast it with the conventional methods of pricing hotel rooms.
6. Explain the role of the average room rate in the operation of a yield management system.
7. The Yellow River Hotel has 200 rooms all of which may be sold as doubles or singles. The published double room rate is £80. From the information given below you are required to calculate the percentage yield for the three days: Monday to Wednesday.

	% room occup.	Rooms sold	Average room rate (£)	Room sales (£)	% yield
Monday	50		55		
Tuesday	75		65		
Wednesday	85		45		

8. Given below is the budgeted beverage sales mix of a restaurant for May 19 . . .

Sales	£	DPM (%)	GP(£)
Minerals	2,000	61	1,220
Beers	10,000	42	4,200
Table wines	12,000	53	6,360
Fortified wines	6,000	57	3,420
Spirits	10,000	68	6,800
Total	£40,000		£22,000

At the end of May it was found that actual differential profit margins were as budgeted but that the actual sales mix for May was as follows:

Sales	£
Minerals	2,400
Beers	9,200
Table wines	11,400
Fortified wines	6,800
Spirit	10,200
Total	£40,000

Calculate the budgeted and actual gross profit on beverage sales and explain how the difference between the two has arisen.

9. Jack Vivaldi is proprietor of the Four Seasons motel. The capital invested in the motel is £4,400,000 and Vivaldi expects a profit of 10 per cent after tax, on that figure. He pays tax at the rate of 50 per cent. The motel has 200 rooms.

　　The hotel accountant has made the following projections of costs, etc. for the forthcoming year.

		£	
Depreciation:	Building	280,000	
	Furniture	120,000	400,000
Rates and insurance			240,000
Administrative and general expenses			376,000
Advertising and sales promotion			200,000
Gas and electricity			136,000

Repairs and maintenance		256,000
Mortgage interest		140,000
Rooms dept—operating cost (wages, linen, laundry, etc.—assuming 70 per cent occupancy)		1,096,000
Coffee shop—departmental profit (at 70 per cent occupancy)		124,000

You are required to:

(a) assume that the motel will operate at 70 per cent occupancy and calculate the average room rate which will enable it to reach its profit target;
(b) assume that the motel's double rate is approximately 45 per cent more than its single rate and that the projected double occupancy is 30 per cent, and calculate the motel's single and double rates for the forthcoming year.

10. The following information is available in respect of Week 27 of a London restaurant.

	Portions sold	Cash GP £
Club Sandwich	280	2.15
Chicken Salad	320	2.50
Grilled Trout	130	4.75
Chicken Kiev	90	2.35
Roast Turkey	110	4.15
Rognons de Veau	80	2.45
Lamb Cutlets	270	4.85
Gratin of Chops	140	4.10
Roast Beef	250	5.15
Mixed Grill	230	4.95
	2,000	

You are required to categorize the above menu items into stars, puzzles, plough horses and dogs. Explain the characteristics and significance of each category.

11. Figure 8.6 shows a menu engineering worksheet which you are required to complete. Also suggest what action is appropriate in relation to each of the ten menu items.

12. The Sarmatia Hotel Co. operates amongst others the Vistula International Hotel. The hotel has 100 rooms and the estimated room occupancy for the forthcoming year is 75 per cent. The management accountant of the hotel company has made the following projections of operating costs, etc.

Menu Item	1 No. of Items	2 Menu Mix %	3 Item Fd Cost	4 Item S.P.	5 Item C.G.P.	6 Total Fd Cost	7 Total Sales	8 Total Cash G.P. Amt	%	Rnk	9 C.G.P. Cat.	10 M.M. Cat.	Notes
1. Lemon sole	190		1.85	6.75									
2. Lobster thermidor	120		2.75	10.94									
3. Chicken brochette	210		1.05	5.95									
4. Calves liver	120		0.85	4.95									
5. Veal cutlet	190		1.60	7.50									
6. Roast pheasant	150		2.60	8.95									
7. Lamb chops	230		1.80	8.50									
8. Beef stroganoff	280		1.55	6.95									
9. Roast turkey	220		1.75	7.25									
10. Mixed grill	290		1.85	8.25									
Total	2,000												

Figure 8.6 Menu engineering worksheet for completion

Operating expenses	*£*
Rooms department	880,000
Telephone department	30,000
Administrative and general	540,000
Training department	70,000
Advertising and promotion	92,000
Heat, light and power	344,000
Repairs and maintenance	330,000
Taxes, insurance, etc.	
Rates	190,000
Insurance	26,000
Depreciation	
Building	170,000
Contents	128,000
Return on present value of property	
Calculated at	800,000
Income from sources other than rooms;	
Store rentals	120,000
Food and beverage operations	480,000
Minor operated depts	150,000

You are required to:

(a) calculate the average room rate the hotel requires to achieve adequate profitability— expressed in this case as 'return on the present value of property' (£800,000);

(b) assume that: (i) the hotel's projected double occupancy is 20 per cent, and (ii) its double rate is approximately 40 per cent more than its single rate, and suggest what single and double rates should be charged during the forthcoming year.

13. The Bridge Restaurant offers the following desserts on its à la carte menu.

	Portions sold	*Portion cost £*	*Selling price £*
Fruit salad	270	0.75	2.35
Bread pudding	65	0.55	1.90
Charlotte russe	210	0.65	2.20
Apple tart	90	0.70	1.65
Crêpes aux figues	115	0.95	2.10
Ice cream	250	0.45	1.70

From the information given above you are required to divide all the menu items into the four menu engineering categories. Suggest what action, if any, is appropriate following your analysis.

14. Nick Owen is the owner of Southern Excursions Ltd; each year he arranges a trip to Stratford-on-Avon for members of the Pacific Eco-

tourism Society. In 1998 a total of thirty members booked the trip, and some were of the opinion that a rather higher standard of comfort could have been provided than that offered by the three-star Macbeth Hotel (normally used by Nick Owen). A choice of two hotels is, therefore, to be offered in 1999: 15 rooms at the Macbeth Hotel and 15 rooms at the four-star Macduff Hotel—on the assumption that all the thirty places on the coach will be taken up. The following information is available.

(a) The Macbeth Hotel will charge £45.00 per person which includes a pre-theatre dinner and a full breakfast the following day. As on previous occasions, the hotel will accommodate the guide free of charge and offer her or him the meals available to members of the group. The corresponding charge by the Macduff Hotel is £55.00.

(b) Coach hire will cost £240.00; and the coach company will be responsible for the driver's board and lodging. The guide, who works for Southern Excursions Ltd on a casual basis, charges £75.00 per trip. Theatre tickets, always booked well in advance, will cost £25.00 per person.

Nick Owen has asked you to calculate how much he should charge in 1999, assuming that:

(i) thirty persons will book the trip and the party will be divided equally between the two hotels;

(ii) each passenger is expected to contribute £10.00 to the overheads of the company;

(iii) in 1998, when all members of the party stayed at the Macbeth Hotel, the charge was £110.00. It is considered that those who choose the Macduff Hotel should pay 10–15 per cent more than the others.

State clearly any assumptions you have to make in the development of your pricing proposals.

15. It has been said that the 'pricing of package tours is a cost-oriented procedure'. Do you agree?

16. 'Package tour companies, to succeed in business, must be both revenue- and cost-oriented.' Discuss.

Profitability $\boxed{9}$

The role of profits has been referred to earlier in this volume, particularly in Chapters 7 and 8. The aim of the present chapter is to explain certain specific aspects of profitability and relate these to the special circumstances of the international hospitality industry.

CONCEPTS OF PROFITABILITY

The profitability of a business may be measured and expressed in several different ways. The method actually employed depends on what aspects of profitability one wants to measure.

Return on capital

This is the *most fundamental measure of profitability*. As already mentioned, the basic objective of a business enterprise is to earn a satisfactory return on the capital employed. Return on capital is the best single measure of the extent to which this basic objective has been achieved. The formula to be used is:

$$\frac{\text{Net profit}}{\text{Capital employed}} \times 100 = \text{return on capital}$$

Thus where the capital employed is £200,000 and the annual net profit £40,000, the return on capital is 20 per cent. The figure of net profit may be shown either before or after tax.

Net profit on sales

Whilst return on capital measures the fundamental aspect of profitability, net profit on sales or net profit ratio measures the *relative operating efficiency of the business* from one trading period to another.

The formula to be used is:

$$\frac{\text{Net profit}}{\text{Net sales}} \times 100 = \text{net profit ratio}$$

Let us take an example.

	Year 1 £	Year 2 £	Year 3 £
Capital employed	400,000	400,000	400,000
Net sales	200,000	200,000	200,000
Less total cost	180,000	170,000	160,000
Net profit	£20,000	£30,000	£40,000
% Net profit on sales	10.0%	15.0%	20.0%
% Return on capital	5.0%	7.5%	10.0%

As may be seen from the above example, the two concepts of profitability measure different things. Net profit on sales is increasing throughout this period of three years, thus indicating some improvement in the operating efficiency of the business. On the other hand, return on capital is in this case very unsatisfactory, even in Year 3. It will be appreciated that the greater the disparity between the capital employed and the volume of sales the greater the difference between the percentage return on capital and the net profit ratio. This is discussed later in this chapter.

GROSS PROFIT: PERCENTAGE V. CASH

We have already referred to various aspects of gross profit. In particular, in Chapter 8 we mentioned the importance of the concept of cash gross profit; and in the section which now follows let us examine the main practical aspects of gross profit control.

The percentage of gross profit is an indication of how efficiently we operate from one trading period to another. The higher the gross profit percentage the lower the food/beverage cost percentage and—other things being equal— the more efficient the operation. The gross profit percentage is thus an immediate and clear indication of the relative efficiency of the business over a period of time.

A great deal of attention has been paid to the concept of cash gross profit in recent years. As already mentioned in the previous chapter (in connection with menu engineering), cash gross profit is in many situations a more appropriate profit concept. Thus, we said, in managing menu profitability we should concentrate on the cash gross profit of each menu item rather than the relevant gross profit percentages. Let us now look at a few examples.

In self-service operations it is desirable to arrange the display of food items in a manner that promotes their cash gross profit effectiveness. Fruit juices, sandwiches, salads, etc. which attract the highest cash gross profit per item should be given more prominence and/or greater exposure. If the cash gross profit on orange juice is £0.75 and that on mango juice £0.65, then orange juice should be placed nearer to the customer flow. In banqueting sales, when negotiating the menu with the client, it is essential for the banqueting manager to be aware of the relevant cash gross profit margins of all the menu items. Any suggestions made to the client should take these into account to ensure a satisfactory overall result. In many situations the waiting staff are asked by customers for advice on menu items. Here again it is essential that such advice should be given in the light of the relevant cash gross profit margins. This calls for the right sequencing of food items on the menu—one where the waiting staff can identify the more profitable items and recommend them accordingly. Finally there is a lot of scope for cash gross profit improvement in the area of wine sales. Wines that carry the highest cash gross profit loading per bottle—whatever the gross profit percentages—should be recommended and sold in preference to others.

Most certainly, we want to keep an eye on the percentage gross profit earned by the establishment. We must remember, however, that the overall gross profit is unlikely to be satisfactory unless we pay sufficient attention to cash gross profit margins of individual food and beverage items. Readers will appreciate that what is being advocated here is a more analytical approach to gross profit control—a shift from preoccupation with total results to the gross profit performance of individual food and beverage items.

GROSS PROFIT: SOME SPECIFIC MEASURES

If we are to secure a sufficient overall gross profit, it is desirable to develop appropriate measures of gross profit. These facilitate the control of the actual gross profit earned from one period to another. The measures actually selected will vary from one establishment to another, depending on the special circumstances of each case. A number of such measures are discussed below.

Cash gross profit per cover

This may be defined as total cash gross profit divided by the number of covers. The aim of this measure is to stress the importance of achieving the highest possible level of cash gross profit from each guest. This will not be achieved unless the waiting staff make the effort to sell not only the main course but also starters, desserts and beverages.

Cash gross profit per waiter

This may be defined as total cash gross profit divided by the number of waiters. The main aim of this measure is to encourage the individual members of the waiting staff to secure the best results in terms of cash gross profit. Generally the best results will be obtained by waiters who take the trouble to recommend starters, desserts and beverages. Some—regretfully not many—hospitality establishments control the daily and weekly ASP of individual waiters. It should be noted that the control of cash gross profit per waiter is more purposeful, as high sales volumes do not in all circumstances imply correspondingly high volumes of cash gross profit. Where the food and beverage control system is computerized, and this applies to the majority of larger hospitality establishments, the cash gross profit margins of all food and beverage items are always known. We also know the number of food and beverage items sold by each waiter. In such circumstances the control of each waiter's cash gross profit performance is relatively easy.

Cash gross profit per available seat

This may be defined as total cash gross profit divided by the seating capacity of a given sales outlet. Where an establishment operates a number of sales outlets, it is essential to ensure that each outlet makes the right contribution to overall profits. And the cash gross profit per available seat in each sales outlet will give a good indication of its contribution to the overall profitability of the total operation.

MEANING OF RETURN ON CAPITAL

In the previous section we referred to the concept of return on capital without considering the different methods of calculating it. The capital of a business, particularly a larger one, does not usually come from one single source. There are, typically, several sources of capital, represented by ordinary shares, preference shares, debentures and finance made available by trade and expense creditors, overdrafts and other current liabilities. The balance sheet of a larger business may have a structure such as the following.

Balance sheet

(a)	Ordinary shares	xxx		
(b)	Preference shares	xxx	Fixed assets	xxx
(c)	Debentures	xxx		
(d)	Current liabilities	xxx	Current assets	xxx

The left-hand side of the balance sheet shows where the finance has come from. The right-hand side shows how such finance has been invested in the fixed and current assets of the business. Quite clearly, where there are four sources of capital as in the above example, one could have four different definitions of return on capital, *viz.*:

(a) return on ordinary shareholders' (equity) capital
(b) return on total shareholders' capital
(c) return on long-term capital
(d) return on total capital.

If we define capital as ordinary share capital (plus any reserves) the relevant definition of profit is the sum of ordinary dividends plus undistributed profits. In other words we must exclude preference dividends and any debenture interest.

If we define capital as the total of shareholders' (ordinary and preference) capital we must define profit as the total of dividends paid plus undistributed profits.

If we define capital as long-term capital (i.e. the total of all shareholders' capital plus reserves and debentures) then the correct definition of profit is the sum of all dividends, undistributed profits and debenture interest.

Finally, we may define capital as total capital (i.e. the total of fixed and current assets, plus any investments). In that case the definition of profit will be the same as in the case of long-term capital simply because the funds made available to the business through the existence of current liabilities do not attract a separate reward or payment. Thus the four possibilities may be shown as in Figure 9.1.

It is difficult to say which of the four definitions should normally be used. One thing is, however, quite clear: whichever definition is chosen it should be applied consistently from one year to another. Otherwise comparisons over a period of time will prove difficult.

Let us take another look at the four definitions. Many smaller businesses have only ordinary shares and a certain amount of current liabilities. In such circumstances the capital base may be taken as ordinary shareholders' capital or total capital.

A business which has both ordinary and preference shares will, of course, have three possible ways of measuring its return on capital. If, however, the business is highly geared (i.e. has a small amount of ordinary share capital in relation to its preference capital) to define capital as ordinary shareholders' capital would tend to result in a misleadingly high return on capital.

It seems that most larger companies tend to favour the third definition and regard long-term capital as their capital base. One could, however, argue equally strongly in favour of the last definition on economic grounds. Total capital is the sum total of resources employed in a business. Current liabilities, though described as 'current', tend to be a permanent element in most business situations. In any case, in the majority of hospitality establishments current liabilities constitute a very small percentage of total capital. For practical purposes, therefore, in the market-oriented sector of the hospitality industry, both long-term capital and total capital appear quite acceptable bases for the calculation of return on capital.

To sum up, the choice of the appropriate concept of return on capital can only be attempted in the light of the special circumstances of each business. Once the choice has been made, the same definition of capital should be used from one accounting period to another, and until such time as there is a material change in the capital structure or other relevant circumstances.

Capital base	Definition of profits
(a) Ordinary shareholders' capital	Ordinary dividends plus undistributed profits
(b) Total shareholders' capital	All dividends plus undistributed profits
(c) Long-term capital	All dividends plus undistributed profits plus debenture interest
(d) Total capital (total assets)	Total net profit

Figure 9.1 Alternative definitions of return on capital

Example

Given below is a summary of the Profit and Loss A/c and Balance Sheet for two accounting periods. You are required to calculate:

(a) return on ordinary shareholders' capital
(b) return on total shareholders' capital
(c) return on long-term capital
(d) return on total capital.

P. and L. A/c Summary	(£000s)		Balance Sheet Summary	(£000s)		
	Year 1	Year 2		Year 0	Year 1	Year 2
Net sales	120	135	Fixed assets	100	105	108
Less cost of sales	50	55	Current assets	20	20	22
Gross profit	70	80	Current liabilities	10	9	5
Less operating			Working capital	10	11	17
expenses	55	60				
Net profit	15	20				
Debenture interest	1	1	Ordinary shares			
Preference			and reserves	60	66	75
dividends	2	2	Preference shares	30	30	30
Ordinary dividends						
and reserves	12	17	Debentures	20	20	20

Solution

Part	Year 1		Year 2	
(a)	$\dfrac{£12,000}{\frac{1}{2}(£60,000 + £66,000)}$	= 19.0%	$\dfrac{£17,000}{\frac{1}{2}(£66,000 + £75,000)}$	= 24.1%
(b)	$\dfrac{£14,000}{\frac{1}{2}(£90,000 + £96,000)}$	= 15.1%	$\dfrac{£19,000}{\frac{1}{2}(£96,000 + £105,000)}$	= 18.9%
(c)	$\dfrac{£15,000}{\frac{1}{2}(£110,000 + £116,000)}$	= 13.3%	$\dfrac{£20,000}{\frac{1}{2}(£116,000 + £125,000)}$	= 16.6%
(d)	$\dfrac{£15,000}{\frac{1}{2}(£120,000 + £125,000)}$	= 12.3%	$\dfrac{£20,000}{\frac{1}{2}(£125,000 + £130,000)}$	= 15.6%

As may be seen from the answer shown above, the percentage return on capital will vary, and quite considerably so, depending on the capital base actually chosen. It will have been observed that in each calculation the average of the opening and closing capital is taken as the capital for a particular accounting period. Thus in part (a) the capital is £63,000, i.e. the average of £60,000 and £66,000.

This procedure is more accurate than taking the opening capital as the base.

ASSET TURNOVER

The term 'asset turnover' refers to the relationship between the capital employed and the volume of sales. Capital employed is, in this context, normally defined as total capital or long-term capital.

Where the capital employed is £100,000 and the annual volume of sales £200,000, each £1 invested in the business generates sales revenue of £2. Where the capital is £100,000 and the volume of sales £50,000, each £1 invested in the assets of the business generates sales revenue of £0.50. The term asset turnover is used to show the relationship which obtains between capital and sales. Thus in the case of the first example asset turnover is 2.0; in the second example it is 0.5.

It will be appreciated that the concept of asset turnover does not merely have accounting applications. Quite clearly, the higher the asset turnover, the greater the volume of goods and services made available to society through the investment of each £1.00.

Return on capital is determined by a combination of two factors: asset turnover and the percentage net profit on sales. A particular profit target or return on capital employed may be achieved by a variety of percentages of net profit on sales and asset turnover figures.

This is illustrated in Figure 9.2.

As may be seen from Figure 9.2, a particular return on capital depends on (a) asset turnover and (b) the percentage net profit on sales. Thus, in the case of Business A, asset turnover of 2.50 and a net profit margin of 8 per cent give the same net profit as asset turnover of 1.00 and a net profit margin of 20 per cent.

A business will naturally wish to attain the highest possible asset turnover,

	Business A Capital—£100,000 Profit target—20%				Business B Captial—£100,000 Profit target—30%		
Sales	Asset turnover	%N.P. on sales	Net profit	Sales	Asset turnover	%N.P. on sales	Net profit
£300,000	3.00	6.7	£20,000	£300,000	3.00	10.0	£30,000
250,000	2.50	8.0	20,000	250,000	2.50	12.0	30,000
200,000	2.00	10.0	20,000	200,000	2.00	15.0	30,000
150,000	1.50	13.3	20,000	150,000	1.50	20.0	30,000
100,000	1.00	20.0	20,000	100,000	1.00	30.0	30,000
50,000	0.50	40.0	20,000	75,000	0.75	40.0	30,000
25,000	0.25	80.0	20,000	50,000	0.50	60.0	30,000

Figure 9.2 Asset turnover and % net profit on sales as determinants of return on capital

as this, coupled with an even modest net profit margin, will tend to produce a high return on capital. It should be appreciated, however, that high asset turnover may result in too low a net profit margin being aimed at, and thus result in a condition of profit instability.

Let us look at the following example.

Business	Capital employed	Asset turnover	% NP on sales	Net profit
X	£100,000	3.00	6.7	£20,000
Y	100,000	1.00	20.0	20,000

Both businesses have the same amount of capital and earn the same return on capital. However, Business X operates at a very modest net profit margin which, by definition, means a narrow margin of safety. It must necessarily be subject to a greater degree of profit instability than Business Y.

The relationship between asset turnover and the net profit margin has important implications for profit planning, budgeting and generally the profitability of a business. It is certainly not good enough simply to look at capital employed and return on capital. What is almost equally important is how the return on capital is produced by these two determinants.

Iso-profit curves

Iso-profit curves (Figure 9.3) are curves denoting the same figure of net profit resulting from different combinations of asset turnover and percentage net

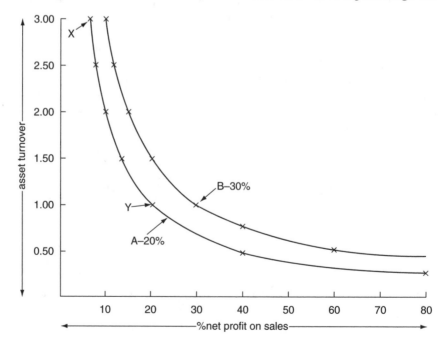

Figure 9.3 Iso-profit curves

profit on sales. Curve A—20 per cent refers to Business A in Figure 9.2. Any point on that curve denotes a net profit of £20,000. Curve B—30 per cent refers to Business B in Figure 9.2. Any point on that curve denotes a net profit of £30,000. We have indicated the positioning of the two businesses from the last example X and Y. Business X is very close to the vertical axis and operates at a very modest profit margin. Quite clearly it is subject to a high degree of profit instability.

PROBLEMS

1. Explain what is meant by each of the following:

   (a) return on capital
   (b) net profit on sales.

2. State what interpretations could be placed on the term 'return on capital'.
3. What do you understand by 'asset turnover'? How does it affect return on capital?
4. Using assumed figures, prepare a graph showing iso-profit curves for two businesses having different profit targets.
5. Explain the circumstances in which it is appropriate to use the concept of cash gross profit rather than percentage net profit.
6. Write explanatory notes on:

   (a) cash gross profit per cover
   (b) cash gross profit per waiter
   (c) cash gross profit per available seat.

10 Profit sensitivity analysis

Profit sensitivity analysis (PSA) is a relatively new technique, but one which has already had numerous applications in hotels, restaurants, outdoor catering and other types of hospitality operation both in this country and abroad.

The aim of profit sensitivity analysis is to determine how various 'key factors' (e.g. average room rate, average spending power, food and beverage costs, prices charged, etc.) influence the net profit of a business. Most practising managers will know from experience that, for instance, a 10 per cent change in the price level will have a very different impact on net profit from a 10 per cent change in labour costs. Similarly, a 10 per cent change in the average spending power will have a different effect on net profit from a 10 per cent change in food and beverage costs. Although the shrewd manager will have a pretty good idea which changes affect his profits more than others, he will, nevertheless, find it difficult to quantify these changes or arrange them in some order of magnitude.

PSA: BASIC PROCEDURE

The most important, indeed central, concept in the theory of profit sensitivity analysis is that of the 'profit multiplier', which measures the impact on net profit of a given change in the relevant key factor. The essential procedure for the calculation of profit multipliers is as follows:

(a) *Determine key factors.* First, by reference to the Profit & Loss A/c we determine the key factors. In the example which follows we have six key factors: number of covers and price level (on the revenue side) and food and beverage costs, casual labour, permanent labour and fixed overheads (on the cost side). In all practical applications of profit sensitivity analysis it is important to ensure that we do not have too many key factors, as this complicates the analysis quite unnecessarily.

(b) *Trace effect of key factors on net profit.* Having determined the key factors we calculate, in respect of each of them, a profit multiplier. This we do as follows: we assume a small change (10 per cent for ease of calculations) in one key factor at a time and, holding all other factors constant, we trace the impact of the 10 per cent change on net profit. Quite obviously we have to allow for consequential changes. Thus a change in the number of covers will cause a proportional change in food and beverage costs, variable labour and other variable costs. The profit multiplier is obtained by dividing the percentage change in net profit by the percentage change in the key factor.

(c) Having calculated the profit multipliers we *arrange the key factors in order of magnitude*, i.e. according to the strength of the impact they have on the net profit of the business. We then examine the shape of the profit multipliers—the PM profile of the business—and draw appropriate conclusions.

Example

Set out below is the Profit and Loss A/c of a restaurant in respect of the quarter ended 30 June 19.

Profit and Loss A/c

	£	£	
No. of covers			10,000
Average price			£10.00
Sales			£100,000
Less Variable costs:			
F&B costs	40,000		
Casual labour	10,000	50,000	
Fixed costs:			
Permanent labour	10,000		
Fixed overheads	30,000	40,000	90,000
Net profit			£10,000

The profit multipliers for the six key factors would be calculated as follows.

No. of covers:

Sales	£110,000
Less total cost	95,000
Net profit	£15,000

We assumed a 10 per cent increase in the number of covers, which gives us sales of £110,000. Total cost is now £95,000, which is the original £90,000 plus the consequential 10 per cent increase in the variable costs. The increase in the net profit is (from £ 10,000 to £15,000) 50 per cent following a 10 per cent increase in the number of covers. Our profit multiplier is therefore 5.0.

Price level:

Sales	£110,000
Less total cost	90,000
Net profit	£20,000

Only the price level has changed here and there is no change on the cost side. Total cost is, therefore, unchanged at £90,000. The net profit has increased (from £ 10,000 to £20,000) by 100 per cent and this, following the 10 per cent increase in the price level, gives us a profit multiplier of 10.0.

F&B costs:

Sales	£100,000
Less total cost	94,000
Net profit	£6,000

In this calculation there is an assumed change of 10 per cent in food and beverage costs, which increases our total cost by £4,000. As a result of this change we lose £4,000 of the net profit. Consequently, we have lost 40 per cent of the original net profit following a 10 per cent increase in food and beverage costs. Our profit multiplier is, therefore, 4.0. Strictly speaking it is −4.0, as we have divided a negative figure by a positive figure. The minus sign, however, is of no consequence here and is therefore ignored.

Casual labour:

Sales	£100,000
Less total cost	91,000
Net profit	£9,000

Our total cost here consists of the original £90,000 plus the assumed 10 per cent increase in the cost of casual labour. We have lost 10 per cent of the original net profit and, as the change in the key factor was also 10 per cent, we have a profit multiplier of 1.0.

Permanent labour:

Sales	£100,000
Less total cost	91,000
Net profit	£9,000

Our figures here are exactly as in the case of casual labour and, again, the profit multiplier is 1.0.

Fixed overheads:

Sales	£100,000
Less total cost	93,000
Net profit	£7,000

The assumed 10 per cent increase in fixed overheads has increased the total cost to £93,000 and resulted in a loss of 30 per cent of our original profit. Our profit multiplier is, therefore, 3.0.

As may now be seen different key factors operate through different profit multipliers, some of which are considerably more powerful than others. This is illustrated in Figure 10.1.

We may now rank our profit multipliers according to their PM values and draw appropriate conclusions.

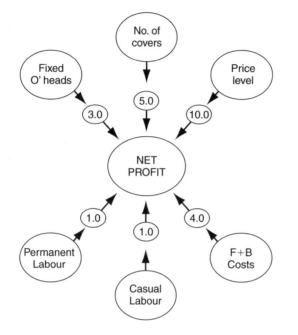

Figure 10.1 Key factors and net profit

Key factor	PM
Price level	10.0
No. of covers	5.0
F&B costs	4.0
Fixed overheads	3.0
Permanent labour	1.0
Casual labour	1.0

Conclusions

As may be seen from our ranking of key factors the two revenue-based profit multipliers have the highest values. They are then followed by the considerably lower cost-based profit multipliers. This is a clear indication that the revenue side of the business is more powerful than the cost side in influencing net profit. A 5 per cent change in the price level will, other things being equal, increase/decrease net profit by 50 per cent. A 5 per cent change in the number of covers will, again assuming that other things remain constant, increase/decrease net profit by 25 per cent. Changes on the cost side, in this restaurant, still influence the net profit quite significantly, but evidently not nearly to the same degree as those which originate from the revenue side of the business.

Our main conclusion is therefore as follows. Having regard to the PM profile, it is clear that the restaurant is a revenue-sensitive operation because it is the revenue side of the business—through the high PM values—that has a dominant influence on net profit. The obvious implication here is that we need what may be described as a 'revenue accounting' approach in our efforts to secure adequate profitability. Briefly, this means that whilst exercising adequate control over food and beverage costs, we should principally concentrate on revenue control. This, in practice, means paying particular attention to our sales volume, sales mix, gross profit margins, pricing methods and price level reviews. If we fail to review our prices and, as a result, lose 3 per cent of our sales volume then the negative effect on net profit is $(3 \times 10.0) = 30$ per cent. If, on the other hand, we fail to control our casual labour and this cost increases by 3 per cent, the negative effect on net profit is $(3 \times 1.0) = 3$ per cent. There is, in consequence, no doubt that from the point of profitability our business is revenue-sensitive rather than cost-sensitive. Let us look at one or two practical examples.

Example I: Hotel

Set out below is the Profit & Loss A/c of York City Hotel in respect of the year ended 30 September 19 . . .

You are required to

(a) calculate profit multipliers for the following key factors:
    (i) price level
    (ii) sales volume
    (iii) cost of sales
    (iv) departmental payroll
    (v) departmental expenses
    (vi) undistributed expenses;
(b) comment on the profit multiplier profile of the hotel.

    For the purpose of your answer assume that

(a) undistributed operating expenses are fully fixed and do not respond to changes in the sales volume
(b) of the total of departmental payroll and departmental expenses (£1,140,000), £890,000 is the fixed element and the balance is wholly variable.

Profit & Loss A/c

Department	Sales	Cost of sales	Dept. payroll	Dept. expenses	Dept. profit
	£000	£000	£000	£000	£000
Rooms	1,420	—	270	110	1,040
Food & beverages	1,280	450	570	120	140
MOD	300	150	60	10	80
Total	3,000	600	900	240	1,260

Less:	Undistributed operating expenses:		
	Administrative and general	330	
	Marketing	105	
	Energy	95	
	Property operation and maintenance	180	
	Depreciation and fixed charges	310	1,020
Net profit			£240

Solution

We would calculate the profit multipliers assuming, in each case, a change of 10 per cent. It should be noted, for the purpose of some of the calculations which follow, that the costs of the hotel are as follows:

		£000
Fixed cost:		
	Undistributed operating expenses	1,020
	Ppn. of departmental payroll and expenses	890
	Total fixed cost	£1,910
Variable cost:		
	Cost of sales	600
	Ppn. of departmental payroll and expenses, i.e. £1,140,000 − £890,000	250
	Total variable cost	£850

Price level:	*£000*
Sales	£3,300
Less total cost	2,760
Net profit	£540

The increase in net profit (from £240,000 to £540,000) is 125 per cent. Our profit multiplier is, therefore, 12.5.

Sales volume:	*£000*
Sales	£3,300
Less total cost	2,845
Net profit	£455

Total cost here consists of the original £2,760,000 plus 10 per cent of the consequential increase in the total variable cost of £850,000. The increase in net profit is (from £240,000 to £455,000) 89.6 per cent. Our profit multiplier is, therefore, 9.0.

Cost of sales:	*£000*
Sales	£3,000
Less total cost	2,820
Net profit	£180

Total cost here consists of the original £2,760,000 plus the assumed 10 per cent change in the cost of sales of £600,000. We have lost (£240,000 – £180,000) £60,000 (i.e. 25 per cent) of the original net profit. Our profit multiplier is, therefore, 2.5.

Departmental payroll:	*£000*
Sales	£3,000
Less total cost	2,850
Net profit	£150

The above total cost consists of the original £2,760,000 plus the assumed 10 per cent change in the cost of payroll. The loss of net profit (from £240,000 to £150,000) is equivalent to 37.5 per cent which results in a profit multiplier of 3.8.

Departmental expenses:	*£000*
Sales	£3,000
Less total cost	2,784
Net profit	£216

The total cost of £2,784,000 consists of the original amount of £2,760,000 plus the assumed 10 per cent change in departmental expenses. The decrease in net profit (from £240,000 to £216,000) is equivalent to 10.0 per cent and our profit multiplier is, therefore, 1.0.

Undistributed operating expenses: £000	
Sales	£3,000
Less total cost	2,862
Net profit	£138

The original total cost of £2,760,000 is increased here by £102,000, i.e. 10 per cent of the undistributed operating expenses. The resulting loss of net profit (from £240,000 to £138,000) is equal to 42.5 per cent, which gives us a profit multiplier of 4.3.

We may now rank the key factors as follows:

Key factor	*PM*
Price level	12.5
Sales volume	9.0
Undistributed operating expenses	4.3
Departmental payroll	3.8
Cost of sales	2.5
Departmental expenses	1.0

The PM profile of this hotel is fairly typical of the pattern of profit multipliers generally associated with larger, good-class hotels. We have the two revenue-based profit multipliers at the top; then there is quite a big gap, in terms of the magnitude of PM values, after which follow the considerably lower cost-based profit multipliers. From the point of view of the profitability of the hotel the message of the PM profile is loud and clear. The revenue side of the business exerts here considerably more influence than the cost side (see Figures 10.2 and 10.3).

In consequence there is a great deal of scope for profit improvement through the skilful manipulation of the price level of the hotel, as indeed through additions to the sales volume. Undistributed operating expenses, though represented by a fairly high profit multiplier, consist very largely of fixed, uncontrollable costs; and savings in this area are not normally easy to secure. Departmental payroll which, as already discussed, is usually a semi-fixed cost, contains an element (part-time and casual labour) which is variable and, quite clearly, there is scope for some profit improvement here, though not nearly as much as in the case of the revenue-based profit multipliers. Cost of sales, though a variable and controllable cost, offers only a limited scope for raising overall profits in that substantial savings in this cost may have a detrimental effect on food quality standards. Finally, departmental expenses are represented by a modest profit multiplier of 1.0 and, in consequence, whilst we should strive to monitor these costs as a matter of sound domestic management, one should not overestimate the effect that this may have on overall hotel profitability.

The right strategy for ensuring adequate profitability in the case of this hotel is, therefore, quite evident. Whilst controlling the hotel's costs (particularly departmental labour and the cost of sales), our greatest efforts should be concentrated on the management of the revenue side of the business.

Example II: Outdoor catering

Set out below is a summary of the Profit & Loss A/c of an outdoor catering company in respect of the year ended 31 December, 19 . . .

		£000
Profit & Loss A/c		
Food & beverage sales		1,000
Less Operating expenditure:		
Food and beverage costs	£400	
Fixed costs: wages and overheads	250	
Variable costs: casual labour	50	
Concession rent	100	800
Net profit		£200

You are required to:

(a) calculate the relevant profit multipliers and rank the key factors in the order of magnitude
(b) comment on the PM profile of the company, its profit stability and

suggest the appropriate accounting and control strategy for the maintenance of adequate profitability.

Solution

It should first of all be noted that the outdoor catering company, unlike the hotel in Example I, has a relatively high percentage of variable costs. Its total cost is made up as follows:

		£000
Fixed costs:		250
Wages and overheads	£250	
Variable costs:		
F&B costs	£400	
Casual labour	50	
Concession rent	100	550
Total cost		800

The profit multipliers may be calculated as set out in the table which follows.

	Base figs	Price	Sales volume	F & B costs	Fixed costs	Casual labour	Concession rent
	£000	£000	£000	£000	£000	£000	£000
Sales	1,000	1,100	1,100	1,000	1,000	1,000	1,000
Food and beverage	400	400	440	440	400	400	400
Fixed costs	250	250	250	250	275	250	250
Variable costs	50	50	55	50	50	55	50
Concession rent	100	110	110	100	100	100	110
Total cost	800	810	855	840	825	805	810
Net profit	200	290	245	160	175	195	190
% Change in net profit	—	45.0%	22.5%	20.0%	12.5%	2.5%	5.0%
Profit multiplier	—	4.5	2.3	2.0	1.3	0.3	0.5

We may now rank the key factors as follows:

Key factor	PM
Price level	4.5
Sales volume	2.3
F&B costs	2.0
Fixed costs	1.3
Concession rent	0.5
Casual labour	0.3

The PM profile of this company is considerably different from that of the York City Hotel in Example I. Although the price level profit multiplier is still at the top of our ranking, the sales volume profit multiplier is relatively lower due to the high percentage of variable costs. Indeed, it is only marginally higher than the profit multiplier for food and beverage costs.

Generally the profit multipliers of this company are low and this indicates a high degree of profit stability. The low PM values here are due to the high proportion of variable costs and, additionally, the high net profit margin.

Low variable-cost companies (e.g. hotels) operate at high C/S ratios, as a result of which small changes in the sales volume have a powerful impact on net profit. Where there is a relatively high percentage of variable costs—as in this case—we have a low C/S ratio and, therefore, a greater degree of profit stability. Similarly, when the net profit margin is wide, changes in key factors will have a relatively small effect on total net profit. Where, on the other hand, the net profit margin is low, e.g. 5 per cent, every small change in any key factor will tend to have a powerful impact on total profits. In this particular example the net profit margin is very substantial, 20 per cent, and this produces a high degree of profit stability.

Finally, as far as accounting and control strategy is concerned our conclusion is this. The outdoor catering company is certainly not as market-oriented as the York City Hotel and its profits are not as revenue-sensitive. In order to maintain satisfactory profitability we should pay particular attention to our price level, after which the volume of sales and food and beverage costs need almost equal attention. Both the fixed costs and the concession rent are largely uncontrollable. Casual labour (atypically low here for an outdoor catering company) offers only a marginal scope for profit improvement.

USE OF PMS IN PROFIT PLANNING

Profit multipliers may conveniently be used as an aid to profit planning. This application of PSA is particularly useful in connection with annual budgeting, at which stage price-level decisions are of critical importance. Let us look at an example.

Example

The accountant of the Dragon Restaurant has prepared the following budgeted profit and loss account for submission to the owner of the restaurant. The latter, having examined the document, decided that the level of the budgeted net profit was insufficient. He insists that appropriate price-level adjustments be effected to achieve an increase in the budgeted net profit of 10 per cent, i.e. from £120,000 to £132,000.

Budgeted Profit & Loss A/c—Draft
Year to 31 Dec. 1998

	Sales mix %	Sales value £	Gross profit %	Gross profit £
Starters	13	130,000	75	97,500
Main course	45	450,000	55	247,500
Vegetables	17	170,000	75	127,500
Desserts	15	150,000	70	105,000
Teas and coffees	10	100,000	80	80,000
Total	100	1,000,000		657,500

Less Operating expenses:	£	
Payroll	270,000	
Administrative expenses	70,000	
Marketing	40,000	
Gas and electricity	40,000	
Repairs	24,000	
Depreciation	48,000	
Laundry and dry cleaning	12,000	
Sundries	33,500	537,500
Budgeted net profit		£120,000

In order to decide on the most effective price-level revisions, it is first necessary to calculate the price-level profit multiplier for each element of the sales mix. This we will do by assuming a 10 per cent increase in the value of each element of the sales mix. The resulting addition to net profit will then enable us to calculate each profit multiplier. The procedure is as shown in the table below.

	N. profit base £	S. mix value £	10% of s. mix value £	Increased net profit £	PM £	% increase to raise net profit by 10% %
Starters	120,000	130,000	13,000	133,000	1.08	9.26
Main courses	120,000	450,000	45,000	165,000	3.75	2.67
Vegetables	120,000	170,000	17,000	137,000	1.42	7.04
Desserts	120,000	150,000	15,000	135,000	1.25	8.00
Teas and coffees	120,000	100,000	10,000	130,000	0.83	12.05
Total	120,000	1,000,000	100,000	220,000	8.33	1.20

From the above table it is clear that several different pricing strategies are possible. We now look at three alternatives:

(a) We may raise all prices by 1.20 per cent. This, through the PM of 8.33, will result in an addition to net profit of 10.00 per cent.

(b) We may increase the prices of all desserts by 5.00 per cent. This, through the PM of 1.25 will raise the net profit by 6.25 per cent. If additionally we raise the prices of main courses by 1.00 per cent, this will, through the PM of 3.75, result in a total addition to net profit of 10.00 per cent.

(c) We may raise the prices of all main courses by 2.00 per cent. This, through the PM of 3.75, will add 7.50 per cent to net profit. If we also increase the prices of desserts by 2.00 per cent then this will additionally give an increase in net profit of 2.50 per cent and result in a total increase in profit of 10.00 per cent.

One could go on and suggest a large number of different pricing strategies each of which would produce the desired level of net profit. The reader will note that the above percentage price increases are very modest in relation to the increase in net profit. It should also be noted that in all hospitality establishments the price level offers a great deal of scope for periodic adjustments to net profit.

More about profit multipliers

From our consideration of PSA it will have been gathered that the profit multiplier is a catalyst which determines the quantitative effect on net profit of a change in any given key factor. Diagrammatically we may represent the role of the profit multiplier as follows.

To revert to the York City Hotel, 5 per cent changes in the key factors would, other things being equal, produce the following changes in the net profit of the hotel.

Key factor	Profit multiplier	Change in net profit
Price level	12.5	62.5%
Sales volume	9.0	45.0%
Undistributed operating expenses	4.3	21.5%
Departmental payroll	3.8	19.0%
Cost of sales	2.5	12.5%
Departmental expenses	1.0	5.0%

From the above table it is clear that the impact at least of the revenue-based profit multipliers is very powerful indeed. This is now illustrated in Figures 10.2 and 10.3. Figure 10.2 shows the effect of changes in the sales volume on the net profit of the York City Hotel. From Month 1 to Month 2 the increase in the sales volume is 5 per cent and the resulting increase in net profit is 45 per cent. During Month 5 we lose 10 per cent of the sales volume and this results in a loss of net profit of 90 per cent.

These are, of course, the consequences on net profit on the assumption that there is no other change. In practice, however, a decrease in the sales volume

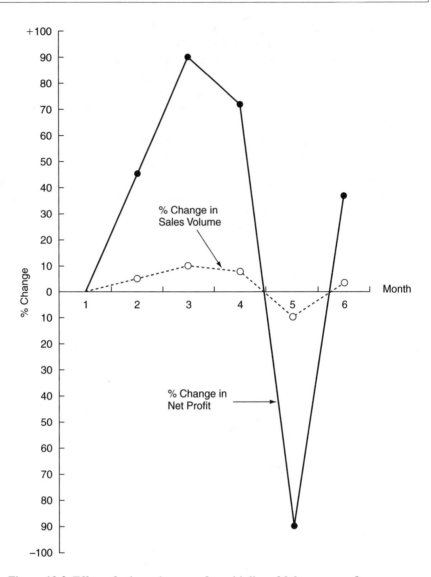

Figure 10.2 Effect of sales volume profit multiplier of 9.0 on net profit

of 10 per cent will often be accompanied by some savings in part-time and casual labour and other variable costs. The loss of net profit might not, therefore, be as much as 90 per cent but, most certainly, it would still be pretty close to this percentage. Similarly an increase in the sales volume of 10 per cent would often be accompanied by a rise in the variable costs of the hotel. The resulting addition to net profit might thus be rather less than 90 per cent. It should be remembered, however, that such variable costs are, typically, represented by small PM values. Any adjustments in respect of such marginal changes in variable costs could therefore be small and would not affect the validity of our conclusions.

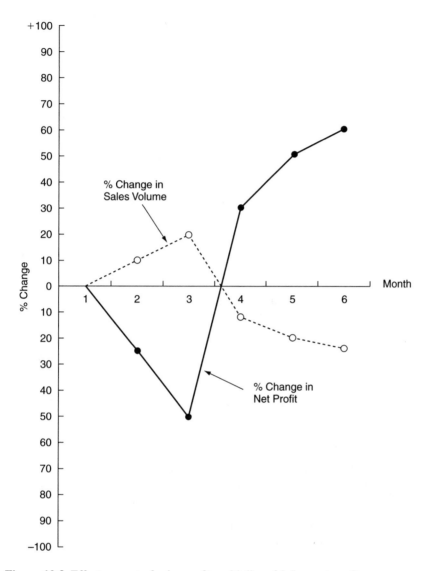

Figure 10.3 Effect on cost of sales profit multiplier of 2.5 on net profit

Figure 10.3 shows the effect of changes in the cost of sales and the impact of such changes on the net profit of the hotel. The cost of sales profit multiplier here is 2.5 and the resulting impact on net profit is quite significant.

PROBLEMS

1. Given below is the Profit & Loss A/c of the Brig Provincial Hotel in respect of the year ended 30 September 19 . . .

Profit & Loss A/c

Department	Sales	Cost of sales	Dept. payroll & expenses	Dept. profit
	£000	£000	£000	£000
Rooms	800	—	200	600
Food and beverages	700	250	400	50
MOD	100	70	20	10
	1,600	320	620	660

Less Undistributed operating expenses:			
Administrative and general		140	
Marketing		40	
Energy		60	
Property operation and maintenance		90	
Rent, depreciation and fixed charges		170	500
Net profit			£160

You are required to:

(a) calculate the profit multipliers of the hotel
(b) rank the PM values in order of magnitude.

Please assume that:

(a) all 'Undistributed Operating Expenses' are a fixed cost
(b) 'Departmental Payroll and Expenses' consist of a fixed element of £540,000; the balance of £80,000 is wholly variable.

2. Set out below is the Profit & Loss A/c of the Old Stafford Hotel in respect of the year ended 31 December 1998.

Profit & Loss A/c

Department	Net sales	Cost of sales	Payroll & rel. exps.	Dept. expenses	Dept. profit
	£	£	£	£	£
Rooms	2,500,000	—	500,000	100,000	1,900,000
Food	1,400,000	550,000	600,000	50,000	200,000
Beverages	800,000	350,000	150,000	30,000	270,000
Sundries	300,000	100,000	50,000	20,000	130,000
	5,000,000	1,000,000	1,300,000	200,000	2,500,000

Less Operating expenses

Administration & general	750,000	
Marketing	350,000	
Energy	250,000	
Repairs & maintenance	150,000	
Fixed charges	50,000	
Other expenses	50,000	1,600,000

Net profit   900,000

Payroll & related expenses and departmental expenses are semi-fixed costs. Of the combined total of £1,500,000 the fixed element is £1,200,000 and the variable element is £300,000. You are required to:

(a) calculate the appropriate profit multipliers
(b) rank the profit multipliers in the order of magnitude
(c) comment on the PM profile of the hotel.

3. Set out below is the profit and loss account of the Serendipity Restaurant.

Profit & Loss A/c
for year ended 30 June 19 . .

Sales	*Sales mix* %	*Sales volume* £	*Gross profit* %	*profit* £
Starters	10	40,000	60	24,000
Main dishes	50	200,000	55	110,000
Vegetables	15	60,000	70	42,000
Desserts	15	60,000	60	36,000
Teas and coffees	10	40,000	70	28,000
	100%	£400,000	60%	240,000

Less Fixed operating expenses   180,000

Net profit   £60,000

(a) From the information given above calculate the price-level profit multipliers for the five elements of the sales mix.
(b) Assuming that small changes (of up to 5 per cent) in the price level have no effect on the number of covers, find the separate effect on net profit of each of the following:
   (i) increasing the prices of all main dishes by 3 per cent
   (ii) increasing the prices of vegetables by 5 per cent and the prices of desserts by 5 per cent
   (iii) increasing the prices of the main dishes by 2 per cent and the prices of teas and coffees by 5 per cent
   (iv) increasing all menu prices by 3 per cent.

4. Set out below is the Profit & Loss A/c of a large hotel in respect of the year ended 30 September 19 . . .

Profit & Loss A/c

Department	Sales	Cost of sales	Dept payroll & expenses	Total dept. expenses	Dept profit
	£000	£000	£000	£000	£000
Rooms	3,080	—	864	864	2,216
Food and beverages	2,720	868	1,364	2,232	488
MOD	600	228	300	528	72
Total	6,400	1,096	2,528	3,624	2,776

Less Undistributed operating expenses:

Administrative and general	640	
Marketing	192	
Energy	260	
Property operation and maintenance	400	
Rent, depreciation and fixed charges	860	2,352

Net profit £424

You are required to:

(a) Calculate the hotel's profit multipliers in respect of
   (i) price level
   (ii) sales volume
   (iii) cost of sales
   (iv) departmental payroll and expenses
   (v) undistributed operating expenses
(b) Compare the hotel's PM profile with those of other operations in any two sectors of the hotel and catering industry.

For the purpose of your answer assume that:

(a) undistributed operating expenses are fully fixed and do not respond to changes in the sales volume
(b) departmental payroll and expenses are 80 per cent fixed and 20 per cent variable.

Responsibility accounting

11

INTRODUCTION

The concept of responsibility accounting has recently found general acceptance as an integral part of management accounting. Responsibility accounting provides guidance on the division of responsibility for operating results as well as cost and profit levels. Also it provides a sound theoretical foundation for systems of budgetary control, where the notion of individual responsibility features quite prominently. In Chapter 12 we will look at the principles of budgetary control and these should be seen as an extension of the concept of responsibility accounting.

Effective control of business operations necessitates the development of a sound and streamlined organizational framework within which each executive's role is defined in a clear and unambiguous manner. This can only be achieved by establishing what are known as *responsibility centres* and defining, in relation to each centre, the responsibility of each executive concerned.

A responsibility centre is a segment of the organization which may consist of a large department employing dozens or even hundreds of individuals (e.g. housekeeping department, or kitchen of a large hotel) or a small section or department employing a few individuals (eg. hotel kiosk, foreign currency desk). In practice responsibility centres are easy to establish. Thus in a large hotel we may regard tennis, golf and the swimming pool as one single responsibility centre. At the same time we may view the gift shop, the hairdressing salon and the pharmacy as separate responsibility centres. The exact division of the total operation will depend primarily on the size of each individual component. Other departments such as accounts, marketing and personnel and training, would also constitute separate responsibility centres, for which responsibility would have to be accepted by the chief accountant, marketing director and personnel and training manager respectively. Responsibility centres may be of three different types and these are discussed below.

COST CENTRES

A cost centre is a responsibility centre where costs are incurred but where the manager has no control over revenue. In practice departments such as the accounts department, personnel and training department and maintenance department would be regarded as cost centres: they incur costs but, however important their contribution to the success of the business operation, they have no control over its sales revenue.

PROFIT CENTRES

A profit centre is a responsibility centre where the manager has responsibility for controlling costs and revenue. Profit centres are of two types. In the majority of profit centres the revenue is earned by competing with other firms or establishments in the market place. Almost all revenue of hospitality establishments (revenue from room sales, food and beverage operations, telephone, guest laundry, etc.) falls into this category; and the relevant profit centres are described as *natural profit centres*. In other cases a profit centre may earn its revenue by 'selling' its output within the organization, e.g. to another department. This kind of profit centre is described as an *artificial profit centre*, and the price at which it sells its output within the organization is known as a *transfer price*. Let us look at two examples of artificial profit centres.

A restaurant company operating a chain of steak houses may decide that, instead of allowing the individual units to purchase their own meat, it would be cheaper to set up a central butchering department, buy the meat in bulk and then 'sell' it in smaller quantities—say at cost plus 15 per cent—to the individual steak houses. A large hotel chain may set up a print shop with the aim of producing all stationery and publicity material for the individual hotels within the chain. The print shop would charge for each job a transfer price to cover the cost of materials, labour and overheads. Students should note that, with artificial profit centres, the profits earned are somewhat unreal in that the revenue of the profit centre is the result of an assumed formula (agreed transfer price) rather than exposure to the realities of the market place.

INVESTMENT CENTRES

An investment centre is a type of responsibility centre in which the manager has the role of a chief executive and is responsible not only for his or her costs and revenue but also for the return on capital employed. An investment centre is, therefore, treated as if it were a separate autonomous business enterprise. The criterion most commonly employed in assessing the performance of an investment centre is return on capital employed—already explained in Chapter 9.

Example 1

We have now described the three types of responsibility centre; it would be useful, at this stage, to relate these concepts to a practical situation. Let us assume that the Trident Hotel Co. operates three large hotels situated in London, Leeds and Glasgow, and that the organization chart of the company is as illustrated in Figure 11.1. We may divide the total operation into responsibility centres as follows.

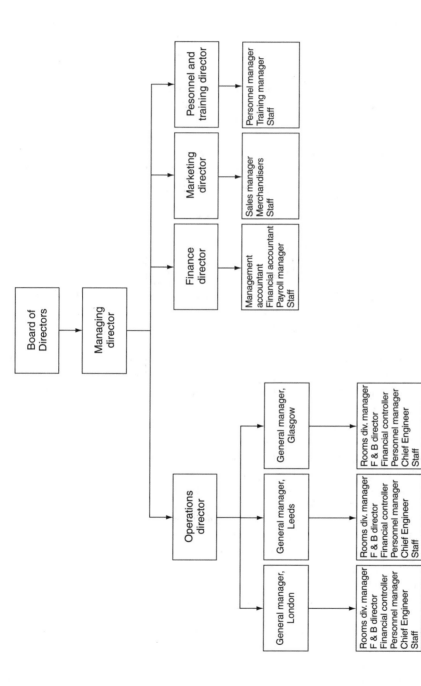

Figure 11.1 Organization chart

The managing director is the chief executive of the company. He or she interprets the major aspects of policy as laid down by the board of directors and provides the link between the board and all divisions or departments of the business. As chief executive, the managing director would be expected to accept responsibility for all costs, revenues and, indeed, the return on capital employed. The managing director would, therefore, accept responsibility for the total operation of the company as an investment centre.

The operations director would normally have responsibility for all costs and revenue; and his or her performance would be assessed by reference to the net profit margin earned by the hotels. It should be added, however, that there are situations in which each individual hotel may be regarded as a separate investment centre and expected to earn a satisfactory return on its capital employed. This would, generally, apply in the case of large hotels; and responsibility for the return on capital employed would, in such circumstances, be given to the general manager of the hotel.

The general managers of the three hotels would, ordinarily, be responsible for all costs and revenues. Each hotel would be regarded as a major profit centre. Within each hotel there would be a number of departments each of which would be regarded as a distinctly separate responsibility centre. The rooms department and the food and beverage department are invariably the principal profit centres; and responsibility for the operating results as well as the relevant cost and profit levels would be given to the rooms division manager and the food and beverage manager respectively. There are always a number of smaller profit centres such as telephone, kiosk, hairdresser, golf, etc.; and responsibility for each of these would be assigned to an appropriate manager or supervisor. Department heads such as the financial controller, personnel manager and chief engineer would be in charge of their own cost centres and be responsible to the general manager of the hotel.

The finance director would have responsibility for the operating costs for his or her department. This particular department would normally be divided into appropriate smaller cost centres for both budgeting and cost control purposes.

The marketing director would share responsibility for the total sales volume of the hotels with the general managers. Otherwise, for all practical purposes, the marketing department would be regarded as a cost centre.

The personnel and training director would, quite clearly, have responsibility for a cost centre. There is normally no revenue received by this department, except when the training courses and seminars run by a company are open to other organizations who would pay so much for each person attending. Such situations are, however, uncommon.

Let us now look at some other aspects of responsibility accounting. All budgets, reports and accounting documents should reflect the precepts of responsibility accounting and be drawn up in a manner that recognizes the existence of the relevant responsibility centres.

Example 2

The profit and loss account of the Trident Hotel Co. would probably be drawn up as shown below.

The profit and loss account consists of three parts. The top portion shows the operating results of the three natural profit centres. From the net sales of each hotel we deduct the cost of sales, payroll and related expenses as well as all those operating expenses that are capable of being controlled by the hotel general manager. The resulting figure is a surplus which we may describe as 'controllable profit'.

The middle portion of the profit and loss account shows the expenses of the three cost centres (finance, marketing, and personnel and training). In each case we show separately the cost-centre payroll and the relevant operating expenses. For example, the £450,000 of operating expenses of the marketing department would presumably consist of the cost of producing promotional material, press and television advertising, etc.

Finally, in the third part of the profit and loss account we deduct various fixed charges that are incurred on behalf of the company as a whole and not for the benefit of any one cost or profit centre.

TRIDENT HOTEL CO.
Profit & Loss A/c for year ended . . .

Profit centre	Net sales	Cost of sales	Payroll and related expenses	Operating expenses	Controllable profit
	£000	£000	£000	£000	£000
London hotel	10,000	4,000	3,000	900	2,100
Leeds hotel	6,000	2,200	1,950	550	1,300
Glasgow hotel	4,000	1,300	1,350	250	1,100
	20,000	7,500	6,300	1,700	4,500
Less Cost centre expenses:					
Finance department			500	100	
Marketing department			400	450	
Personnel & training dept.			300	50	
			1,200	600	1,800
Profit before fixed charges					2,700
Less Fixed charges:					
Accountancy fees				100	
Insurances				160	
Interest				340	
Sundry fixed charges				100	700
Net profit					2,000

The reader will note that the construction of the above profit and loss account is very similar to the form of income statement suggested by the US Uniform System of Accounts for the Lodging Industry dealt with in Chapter 20. Also it should be noted that the profit and loss accounts of the individual hotels would be drawn up as suggested in that chapter (see p. 316).

PROBLEMS

1. Explain what you understand by 'responsibility accounting'.
2. Write short, explanatory notes on:

   (a) cost centre
   (b) profit centre
   (c) investment centre.

3. Distinguish between natural profit centres and artificial profit centres.
4. Draw up an organization chart of any type of business with which you are familiar, and:

   (a) suggest how it might be divided into responsibility centres
   (b) draft a pro forma profit and loss account, showing clearly the areas of executive responsibility.

5. You have just been appointed general manager of a hotel group. You find that different unit managers are remunerated differently by your company. The main methods of remuneration are:

   (a) a straight salary of so much per annum
   (b) a basic fixed salary, plus a percentage commission based on the net profit of the unit (the net profit is, for this purpose, arrived at by deducting a proportion of head-office expenses)
   (c) a basic salary, plus a commission based on the average room occupancy of the unit concerned.

   You are anxious to introduce a uniform method of remunerating your unit managers. State, giving reasons, which of the three methods appears the most satisfactory.

6. Prepare an organization chart for a large tour operator, and suggest how the total operation may be divided into appropriate responsibility centres.

Budgetary control 12

DEFINITIONS

The Institute of Cost and Management Accountants offered the following definitions (*Terminology of Management and Financial Accountancy*, London: Institute of Cost and Management Accountants, 1974, p. 45):

> *Budgets* are 'financial and quantitative statements, prepared and approved prior to a defined period of time, of the policy to be pursued during that period for the purpose of attaining a given objective'.
>
> *Budgetary control* is defined as 'the establishment of budgets relating to the responsibility of executives to the requirements of a policy, and the continuous comparison of actual with budgeted results, either to secure by individual action the objective of that policy or to provide a basis for its revision'.

Let us now look at these two definitions more closely. From the first definition it is clear that the preparation of budgets presupposes the existence of a policy. This, in practical terms, means that before any budgets are prepared it is essential to decide on the aims and objectives of the business and determine how such aims and objectives are to be achieved. In terms of hotel operations, it is necessary to fix a profit target and then prepare a number of budgets covering all income, expenditure, assets and liabilities to ensure that the profit target is reached. Because of the dependence of the hotel profitability on the volume of sales, budgets relating to the revenue-producing departments of the business will feature prominently in the totality of budgetary control. Consequently, operating budgets for room, food and beverage sales and other revenue-producing departments will be in the forefront of all the budgeting undertaken in the hotel. Similar considerations apply to restaurant operations. Here, too, budgets relating to the revenue side of the business will need considerably more careful thought than those relating to operating costs, capital expenditure, etc.

The concept of budgetary control cannot be divorced from that of executive responsibility. Budgets cannot control income or expenditure. They can, and usually do, influence the way in which an executive or manager controls his company, unit or department of a business. It is essential, therefore, that budgets should be prepared after full consultations with those who are to assume responsibility for them. To quote from Charles T. Horngren (*Cost Accounting: A Managerial Emphasis*, 3rd edn, Englewood Cliffs, NJ: Prentice-Hall, 1972, p. 125):

Budgeting is too often looked upon from a purely mechanistic viewpoint. The human factors in budgeting are more important than accounting techniques. The success of a budgetary system depends on its acceptance by the company members who are affected by the budgets.

The second essential point about budgetary control is this. It is not enough to prepare budgets and assign responsibility for them. It is essential to compare, at frequent intervals, actual with budgeted results to ensure that deviations from planned results are kept down to a minimum and that the necessary corrective action is taken as soon as possible after the occurrence of any deviation.

OBJECTIVES AND ADVANTAGES

As stated in the previous section, the most important function of budgetary control is to help the business achieve its objectives in accordance with the stated policy. A system of budgetary control, however, achieves more than this.

When budgets are being formulated the opportunity should be taken to combine the ideas and suggestions of all those responsible for the budgets. The chairman of the budget committee must, therefore, ensure that there is free expression of the views of committee members and full participation by all concerned. Unless this happens, departmental managers will feel that the budgets are being imposed on them.

Most hospitality establishments are highly departmentalized. Yet it is essential that the whole business works as one coherent unit. Co-ordination of the work of all the revenue-producing and other departments is therefore essential. Here, again, the chairman of the budget committee has the specific duty to ensure that the highest degree of interdepartmental co-ordination is achieved. Both interdepartmental co-ordination and greater understanding of the problems faced by various departments are important by-products of the work of the budget committee.

One of the most important tasks of the system of budgetary control is to select appropriate yardsticks for measuring performance. Such yardsticks, or targets, will take different forms depending on the nature of each department. In the revenue-producing departments the targets set for managers will be expressed in terms such as turnover, hotel and restaurant occupancy, average room rate, average spending power, departmental profit, gross profit, etc. In non-revenue-producing departments emphasis will be placed on cost ceilings (expressed in absolute or percentage terms) in relation to total departmental expenditure.

Finally, budgetary control enables the business to make the fullest use of its resources. The sales budget will, amongst others, predetermine the level of activity over the next budget year and thus show what spare capacity will exist over that period. It will then be necessary to decide how it is possible to convert such spare capacity into additional revenue. Appropriate pricing devices and sales promotion techniques may then be used to achieve this objective.

THE OVERALL FRAMEWORK

As may be seen from Figure 12.1, the starting point for the process of budgeting is the determination of the profit target. This having been done, the system of budgetary control is the best practical way of ensuring that the profit target is achieved. Let us now look at the various components of Figure 12.1 in more detail.

Operating and capital budgets

Operating budgets are concerned with the income and expenditure of the business. Budgets are prepared for the various revenue-producing departments of the business, showing the budgeted departmental profit in each case. The total of departmental profits, plus any departmental profits from the minor operated departments, less budgeted undistributed expenses (administration, sales promotion, heat, light, repairs, etc.) will give the budgeted net profit. Thus all the operating budgets are consolidated into a budgeted profit and loss account.

Capital budgets are concerned with the assets and liabilities of a business and are incorporated into the budgeted balance sheet. Both the budgeted profit and loss account and the budgeted balance sheet are known as *master budgets*.

Budget committee

The budget committee usually consists of the senior executives of the business. Invariably the chairman of the budget committee is the chief executive (managing director, general manager, etc.) and the management accountant acts as secretary to the committee. Its main task is to administer the system of budgetary control and specifically:

(a) to prepare draft budgets for submission to the board of directors
(b) to keep under constant review the standard procedures of budgetary control
(c) to monitor the operation of the system and particularly the submission of periodic reports.

In order to ensure the smooth running of the system the budget committee will, with the aid of appropriate specialists prepare a *budget manual*. This usually takes the form of a loose-leaf binder, and sets out in detail the necessary standard procedures, the classification of accounts, a statement of review periods (i.e. frequency with which actual results are compared with budgeted results), dates for submission of budget reports, etc.

An important task of the budget committee is to ensure that budgets are prepared in accordance with the organizational structure of the business. Where an executive has no authority to incur a particular item of expenditure, he or she should not be held responsible for that expenditure. In other words, authority and responsibility should, in this case, be co-extensive. Let us look at two examples.

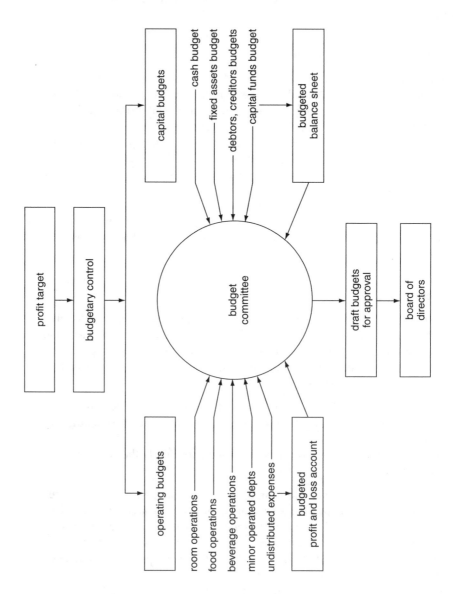

Figure 12.1 The framework of budgetary control

In the case of a restaurant company there is no point in making unit managers responsible for a proportion of head office expenses. A unit manager has no influence on rates of pay offered to head office staff. He or she has no say in the choice of location of the head office and hence no influence on its occupancy costs, etc. Now, from the point of view of the company as a whole, it is clearly essential that the profits of the individual units should be adequate to cover the cost of the head office and leave a satisfactory group net profit. That, however, is a matter for the company as a whole and the responsibility of the board of directors.

Similarly, it makes no sense to include a proportion of occupancy costs, management salaries, advertising, etc. in the Rooms Department budget. The rooms division manager, or whoever has responsibility for this department, has no authority to incur such expenditure and should have no responsibility for it.

To sum up, the budget committee must ensure that lines of authority and responsibility are clearly defined and reflected in the actual budgets that are prepared. To this end it is useful to prepare an organization chart, a simple example of which is given in Figure 12.2.

THE TIME SCALE OF BUDGETARY CONTROL

When we predict the number of customers and their choice of menu items for the next week, we use the technique of volume forecasting. When we predict future developments over the next five years and plan for that period, we use the technique of long-range planning. When we plan for the next year we use the technique of budgeting. This is illustrated in Figure 12.3.

Thus in relation to each segment of the time scale we must choose an appropriate technique for prediction, planning and control purposes. There is always a degree of uncertainty about the future; and the more distant the future the greater the degree of uncertainty. Our predictions in volume forecasting are very detailed. Our budgeted figures are still fairly detailed but less so. Where long-range plans are prepared the figures shown will invariably be considerably less detailed than those included in annual budgets.

Preparation of budgets

The starting point in the process of budgeting is the preparation of the sales budget. The sales budget is the most critical budget because the volume of sales has an important bearing on all variable and semi-variable costs, as indeed on the cash inflows and outflows of the business. It is clear, therefore, that there is no point in attempting to prepare any budgets unless and until the sales budget has been prepared.

Before the preparation of the sales budget it is essential to examine all the key factors (also known as limiting factors). These are factors which operate to limit the volume of output/sales. It will be found, of course, that in market-oriented businesses the most important key factors operate on the revenue, rather than cost, side of the business. Thus, whilst in cost-oriented businesses

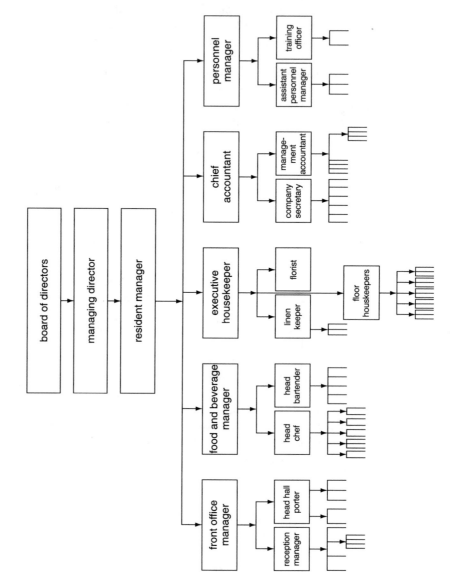

Figure 12.2 Organization chart

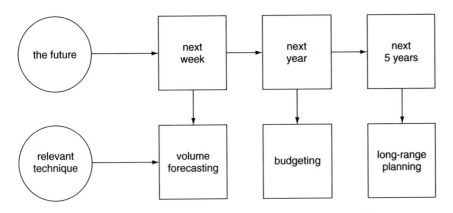

Figure 12.3 The time scale of budgetary control

key factors such as shortages of materials, non-availability of skilled labour and general labour shortages are often the most critical, in market-oriented businesses such key factors are of secondary importance.

PRINCIPAL KEY FACTORS

Accommodation available

This is one of the most critical key factors operating in hotels. When all the rooms are sold, it is impossible to increase the volume of room sales except through an increase in room rates. When the sales budget is being prepared it is essential to examine patterns of occupancy to establish what level of room sales may realistically be expected during the forthcoming budget year. Where there is a high degree of room sales instability, evidenced by pronounced swings in occupancy rates, it is desirable to examine the possibility of shifting demand from peak to off-peak periods.

Seating capacity

This is probably the most powerful key factor operating in restaurants and hotel restaurants. The effects of this key factor may, to some extent, be offset by increasing the number of waiting staff and by appropriate in-company training programmes. Another possibility (and this has been tried successfully in many establishments) is to offer the waiting staff a bonus based on the number of covers served. The exact solution will, in the end, depend on the circumstances of each establishment. In the majority of expensive restaurants most clients will arrive between 7.30 and 8.30 p.m., and will not leave before 10.00 or 10.30 p.m., by which time it is too late to expect many new customers. In such circumstances it would not make much sense to even attempt to increase restaurant occupancy. It is, of course, entirely different in low-ASP establishments where the customer's main objective is to secure a palatable meal—and no more. Speedier service will, in such establishments, be reflected in improved restaurant occupancy and the volume of sales.

Various pricing devices have been extensively employed by high-ASP establishments to combat this key factor. Many restaurants that offer a dinner dance charge about 20 per cent more towards the end of the week than at the beginning of it to shift demand to the less busy periods of the working week. Others impose a minimum charge during the busy part of the week in order to discourage low spenders and, generally, shift demand to slacker periods.

Quality of management

This is an important key factor. Its operation is not, however, evident over shorter periods. Over longer periods, of course, the quality of management will have a direct and powerful influence on the volume of sales.

Shortage of labour

This particular key factor is potentially powerful, but there is no evidence that it exerts much influence on the volume of sales in hospitality. In some locations labour shortages may, in fact, be a severe limiting factor. It seems that such locations are rather exceptional.

Consumer demand

Consumer demand is often found to be a potent key factor. Its operation may be due to several reasons.

The price level of the establishment may be too high, and this may result in a low ASP or NoC or both. Where the price level is thought to be the reason for insufficient consumer demand, it is essential to subject all the tariffs and menus to thorough scrutiny, and examine room sales, menu items offered to customers, as well as all profit margins.

Insufficient consumer demand may also be due to competition. In order to remedy this it is imperative to examine the external environment of the business and answer questions such as the following: Who are our main competitors? What are their strengths? What is our customers' profile? What is it that draws the customer to one establishment rather than another?

Where insufficient consumer demand obtains over long periods, it is essential to undertake a thorough re-appraisal of the whole marketing policy in relation to the existing location. Quite frequently new restaurants are opened in unsuitable locations simply because the proprietors did not undertake a market feasibility study. It should be pointed out that the greater the degree of market orientation of an establishment the greater the need for a proper market feasibility study.

Other key factors

In addition to the key factors dealt with above, several others may operate to restrict the volume of sales. Insufficient capital may make it impossible for a company to acquire further units and thus increase its turnover. For the same reason an establishment may find it difficult to maintain its facilities at an appropriate level of comfort, etc., through insufficient expenditure on repairs, replacements and other items which add to the decor and atmosphere of the establishment. Management may, as a result of its own policy, exclude certain types of customer, e.g. coach tours. In self-service operations cash collection and the time taken by customers in the selection of food items are both important limiting factors.

From what has been said it will be clear that there are a variety of key factors. It is for each establishment to identify the key factors limiting its sales and take steps to remove their negative effect on the volume of sales.

Key factors in tourism

Most of the key factors that operate in hotels and restaurants are also present in the wider field of tourism. When preparing the budget for the forthcoming year, the tour operator has to take into account a number of key factors. The availability of hotel accommodation in the various tourist destinations and the seating capacity available from airlines are probably the most critical of these. Consumer demand is generally stable and changes little from one year to another. There are times, however, when owing to political developments and other factors demand is affected most severely; and this frequently calls for a thorough revision of budgets already prepared.

As far as retail agents are concerned, their fortunes tend to reflect those of tour operators. Any major swings in demand will affect tour operators and travel agents equally.

OPERATING BUDGETS

The method used in the preparation of hotel and catering budgets is now fairly well established. The first step is to predetermine the volume of sales. In order to do this it is essential to examine the following: (a) past sales; (b) current trends; and (c) relevant economic and political aspects.

The analysis of past sales is always the starting point in the preparation of any sales budget. It is necessary to establish the overall trend in the volume of sales as well as the trends in the principal elements of the sales mix. It is useful to calculate the percentage change in room, food and beverage sales as well as changes in the turnover of minor operated departments over the last two or three years. It will not be enough to consider only the absolute sales values. The volume of sales depends on the number of units sold and the price per unit. It follows, therefore, that it is equally important to establish trends in room occupancy, room rates, the number of covers sold and the average spending power.

In addition to past sales, it is essential to look at the reality of the current situation, and decide what trends exist which are likely to influence the volume of sales over the next budget year. Points which are relevant in this context are: trends in hotel and restaurant occupancy; composition of guests by country of origin; trends in the sales mix of the establishment, etc.

The state of the national economy and political developments are sometimes more critical than the internal environment of the business. Government economic and fiscal policies have a powerful effect on the level of disposable incomes of the population. Similarly government decisions have an important effect on the state and prosperity of particular industries and regions. Hospitality establishments which cater for foreign tourists have to look beyond their frontiers, and consider developments overseas and their effect on the inflow of foreign tourists.

When the budgeted volume of sales has been predetermined, it is necessary to decide what turnover will be achieved by each revenue-producing department. From the budgeted room, food and beverage sales as well as sales of minor revenue-producing departments will be deducted budgeted (controllable) departmental expenses. Thus the budgeted departmental profit for each revenue-producing department is arrived at. Where there is an appreciable volume of banqueting sales, a separate budget will be prepared for the department.

The second step is to deal with the multiplicity of (essentially fixed) expenses such as administration and general expenses; advertising and sales promotion; heat, light and power; repairs and maintenance; depreciation, rates and similar expenses. All these are frequently referred to as 'undistributed operating expenses', because in most situations no attempt is made to distribute or apportion them to the revenue-producing departments.

From the point of view of budgetary control two methods of approach are possible here. In smaller units all such expenses may be predetermined for the next budget year without attempting to allocate/apportion them to departments. In larger units it is possible to analyse such expenses as between those which are controllable and those which are not, and allocate the controllable items to the respective non-revenue-producing departments such as accounts; control; personnel and training and maintenance. The uncontrollable expenses would then appear separately and be the responsibility of top, rather than departmental, management. Which of these two solutions is chosen depends on the size and the special circumstances of each hotel. As far as the basic method is concerned there is no difference between hotels and restaurants.

The operating budgets dealt with above may be of two kinds: fixed budgets and flexible budgets. A fixed budget is one which is not influenced by the level of activity. Thus most of the budgets for the undistributed operating expenses (e.g. administrative and general expenses, advertising and sales promotion, repairs and maintenance, etc.) will be fixed budgets because changes in hotel and restaurant occupancy will not have a direct influence on them. With regard to flexible budgets the position is quite different. Expenditure on food, beverages, the cost of sales in the minor operated departments, part-time and casual labour, etc. will be directly influenced by the volume of sales. Such budgets will, therefore, be dependent on and directly influenced by the level of activity. All establishments will, therefore, have some fixed and some flexible budgets, depending on the response of their operating costs to changes in the volume of sales.

FLEXIBLE BUDGETS

The need for flexible budgets arises from the condition of sales instability, which was commented on in Chapter 1. Where the volume of sales is reasonably stable from one week to another, operating budgets may safely assume a particular volume of business. Where, on the other hand, the volume of business is erratic and unpredictable it is not helpful to assume a number of covers or room occupancy that may be materially different from what is actually achieved.

A seaside restaurant catering for day trippers will be subject to substantial fluctuations in the number of covers. When the weather is fine, the number of covers served may be several times greater than that in times of inclement weather. Similar considerations apply to out-of-town museums, zoos and places of historical interest.

An example of a flexible budget is given below. It is assumed that the sales volume may vary from 1,600 to 2,000 covers per month. In relation to each projected number of covers we predetermine the volume of sales, the cost of sales, gross profit as well as the level of semi-fixed costs. Monthly fixed costs are then shown—though some accountants might feel that these need not be given in any great detail. Where this view prevails, one would show just one figure of total fixed costs.

THREE OAKS RESTAURANT
Flexible Budget for Month 7, 19 . . .

No of covers	1,600	1,700	1,800	1,900	2,000
	£	£	£	£	£
Average spending power	20.00	20.00	20.00	20.00	20.00
Sales	32,000	34,000	36,000	38,000	40,000
Less: Cost of sales	11,200	11,900	12,600	13,300	14,000
Gross profit	20,800	22,100	23,400	24,700	26,000
Semi-fixed costs:					
Part-time labour	3,460	3,530	3,600	3,670	3,745
Gas and electricity	865	880	900	920	940
Operating supplies	670	685	700	715	730
Total	4,995	5,095	5,200	5,305	5,415
Fixed costs:					
Wages and salaries	5,500	5,500	5,500	5,500	5,500
Admin. expenses	2,900	2,900	2,900	2,900	2,900
Marketing	800	800	800	800	800
Repairs and maintenance	1,200	1,200	1,200	1,200	1,200
Depreciation	900	900	900	900	900
Total	11,300	11,300	11,300	11,300	11,300
Total operating costs	16,295	16,395	16,500	16,605	16,715
Net profit	4,505	5,705	6,900	8,095	9,285

Sales budget

Of all the budgets that have to be prepared the sales budget is always the most critical, as any change in the budgeted sales volume will have a direct impact on many other budgets. If we project a 10 per cent increase in sales, then this will obviously affect our cash inflow, food and beverage costs and possibly part-time and casual labour. It is for this reason that the sales budget deserves a great deal of attention. Three examples explaining the preparation of sales budgets are therefore given below.

Sales budget example 1

The Trentham Restaurant is a large licensed establishment which operates a system of budgetary control. Its budget year consists of 13 four-weekly periods at the end of which actual sales are compared with the budgeted figures. The sales of the restaurant during the immediate past three years are given below.

Analysis of past sales

	1995	1996	1997
Restaurant sales	448,750	468,050	477,400
% increase on previous year	6.8	4.3	2.0
Bar sales	225,500	237,000	253,350
% increase on previous year	3.9	5.1	6.9
Sundry sales	76,250	80,200	84,950
% increase on previous year	4.8	5.2	5.9
Total sales	750,500	785,250	815,700
% increase on previous year	5.2	4.6	3.9

Additionally, the following information is available.

- Restaurant sales: the sales volume here has been rising in absolute terms, but the rate of increase has been falling off. This is due to limited space in the dining room. It is considered, therefore, that no physical increase in restaurant sales should be expected in 1998.
- Bar sales: the increase in the volume of bar sales has been quite satisfactory. In view of the limiting factor affecting dining-room sales, no further increase in the rate of growth should be expected.
- Sundry sales: this is expected to increase at least as well as in 1997.

From the trends and information given above we are now able to set sales targets for 1998:

- Restaurant sales: although little increase in physical volume can be expected here, we can increase some menu prices and, therefore, secure an increase of 4.5 per cent.
- Bar sales: we should expect an increase in sales of 7.0 per cent.
- Sundry sales: in view of the current trend we should expect an increase of 7.0 per cent.

The budgeted sales for 1998 are therefore:

	£		£
Restaurant sales	477,400	+4.5%	498,880
Bar sales	253,350	+7.0%	271,080
Sundry sales	84,950	+7.0%	90,900
Total sales			860,860

The four-weekly sales targets should then be fixed. Where there are seasonal trends the total budgeted sales would have to be split in accordance with the typical distribution of sales over the budget year. Let us assume, however, that the Trentham Restaurant is non-seasonal, and this will simplify our calculations. These are given below.

$$\text{Restaurant sales} \quad \frac{£498,880}{13} = £38,375.38 \quad \text{say} \quad £38,375$$

$$\text{Bar sales} \quad \frac{£271,080}{13} = £20,852.31 \quad \text{say} \quad 20,855$$

$$\text{Sundry sales} \quad \frac{£90,900}{13} = £6,992.31 \quad \text{say} \quad 6,990$$

$$\text{Total sales} \quad \frac{£860,860}{13} = £66,220.00 \quad \text{say} \quad 66,220$$

The preparation of periodic budget reports and the comparison of actual with budgeted figures are discussed in the next chapter entitled 'Variance analysis.'

Sales budget: example 2

In a real situation the budgeting process enjoins an analytical approach. In Example 1 above, we looked at figures of sales without giving any consideration to the determinants of sales, i.e. the number of covers (NoC) and the average spending power (ASP), and both of these are of immense importance in sales budgeting.

When NoC and ASP figures are used the determination of budgeted sales consists of three basic steps. The first step is to ascertain the most recent trends in NoC and ASP. Next we look at the external environment to decide how such trends may be affected by government fiscal policy, developments in domestic and international tourism, the position of local industries, etc. Finally, we should decide what action we ourselves can take with regard to prices charged, menus, opening hours, etc. It is only at this stage that we are able to determine NoC and ASP levels for the forthcoming budget period.

From the simple example given below it will be seen that where appropriate statistical information is available the preparation of the sales budget is facilitated considerably.

OLD BRIDGE RESTAURANT
ASP and NoC statistics for . . .

	Month					
	1	*2*	*3*	*4*	*5*	*etc.*
Food sales (£):						
Restaurant	13.15	13.43	13.61	13.58	13.62	
Coffee shop	8.52	8.31	8.52	8.63	8.71	
Snack bar	4.15	4.24	3.97	4.16	4.05	
Beverage sales (£):						
Restaurant	5.25	5.41	5.46	5.39	5.54	
Coffee shop	2.49	2.44	2.40	2.57	2.43	
No. of covers:						
Restaurant	2,100	2,075	2,005	1,995	2,010	
Coffee shop	3,160	3,175	3,225	3,305	3,275	
Snack bar	1,800	1,950	1,925	1,875	1,965	

Ideally we should be budgeting for a particular sales volume as well as a particular level of NoC and ASP, and showing these in all sales budgets and relevant reports. An example is given below.

MAGNOLIA HOTEL
Sales Budget for year ending . . .

Department	*No.of covers*	*ASP food*	*Food sales*	*ASP beverages*	*Beverage sales*	*Total sales*
		£	£	£	£	£
Restaurant	25,000	14.00	350,000	5.25	131,250	481,250
Coffee shop	37,500	8.50	318,750	2.50	93,750	412,500
Banqueting	6,400	16.00	102,400	7.50	48,000	150,400
Snack bar	21,400	5.50	117,700	1.50	32,100	149,800
Cocktail bar	14,000	—	—	4.50	63,000	63,000
Total	104,300	—	888,850	—	368,100	1,256,950

Where the procedure is as illustrated in the Magnolia Hotel example, we are likely to control the revenue inflow more effectively. Now and again a decrease in the ASP is compensated by a similar increase in the NoC. In a situation like this if we just look at the resulting sales volume, we will not be aware that important changes are taking place in the basic structure of the sales volume.

Sales budget example 3

The process of budgeting for room sales is essentially similar to budgeting for food and beverage sales. Here too it is essential to maintain the appropriate statistics without which any predictions are bound to prove inaccurate. Specifically, monthly statistics are required in respect of the following.

(a) room sales: including the number of rooms sold (singles and doubles) and the resulting single- and double-room sales.
(b) occupancy statistics: room occupancy (rooms sold as a percentage of rooms available) as well as double occupancy (percentage of rooms sold as doubles rather than singles)
(c) average room rate: which we define as room sales divided by the number of rooms sold.

The Black Swan Hotel is a relatively new property, having been built in the mid-1970s. The hotel has 100 rooms, all of which may be sold as singles or doubles. Throughout 1997 the single rate was £40.00 and the double rate £50.00.

The hotel has a system of budgetary control in operation and particulars of rooms sold and percentages of occupancy are given below. You are required to prepare the hotel's Room Sales Budget for the first half of 1998. The following information should be taken into account.

(a) Owing to an improvement in local business activity, 1998 should see an increase in the number of single rooms sold. This is estimated to improve single occupancy by 5.0 per cent.
(b) Because of adverse political developments in Ruritania some loss of foreign tourists will occur during the month of June. It is anticipated that this will reduce the hotel's double occupancy in June by 10.0 per cent.
(c) New arrangements have just been completed with Scandinavian tour operators whereby heavily discounted accommodation (double rooms only) will be sold as follows:

Month	No. of rooms	Discounted rate
March	280	£29.00
April	430	£31.00

(d) In order to allow for inflation the management will increase room charges as follows: single rate to £43.00 and double rate to £55.00.

Solution

Set out below is a summary of occupancy statistics for 1997. These are monthly statistics, though some hotel accountants would prefer to have such information presented on a weekly basis.

Occupancy Statistics
1997

	Jan.	Feb.	March	April	May	June
Rooms available	100	100	100	100	100	100
No. of days	31	28	31	30	31	30
Rm. nights available	3,100	2,800	3,100	3,000	3,100	3,000
Room occupancy %	28.0	30.0	42.0	57.0	64.0	69.0
Double occupancy %	40.0	38.2	40.5	39.4	39.7	39.0
Rms sold—Single	521	519	775	1,036	1,197	1,262
Double	347	321	527	674	787	808
Total	868	840	1,302	1,710	1,984	2,070
Rm sales—Singles £20,840	20,760	31,000	41,440	47,880	50,480	
Doubles £17,350	16,050	26,350	33,700	39,350	40,400	
Total £38,190	36,810	57,350	75,140	87,230	90,880	
Av. room rate £ 44.00	43.82	44.05	43.94	43.97	43.90	

From the above statistics and the information given in (a) to (c) we may prepare the Room Sales Budget for the first half of 1998 as follows:

Month	Singles Sold	S.Room Sales	Doubles Sold	D. Room Sales	% Room Occup.	% Double Occup.	Av. Room Rate	Total Rm Sales
	—	£	—	£	%	%	£	£
January	547	23,521	347	19,085	28.8	38.8	47.66	42,606
February	545	23,435	321	17,655	30.9	37.1	47.45	41,090
March	814	35,002	807	37,105	52.3	49.8	44.48	72,107
April	1,088	46,784	1,104	50,400	73.1	50.4	44.34	97,184
May	1,257	54,051	787	43,285	65.9	38.5	47.62	97,336
June	1,325	56,975	727	39,985	68.4	35.4	47.25	96,960
Total	5,576	239,768	4,093	207,515	53.4	42.3	46.26	447,283

Let us now explain the figures in the above budget by reference to the month of January. We sold 547 rooms as singles, which is the 521 sold in January last year plus 5 per cent. This, multiplied by the new single rate of £43, gives the single-room sales of £23,521. The number of doubles sold is the same as last year; and this, multiplied by the new double rate of £55, gives double-room sales of £19,085. We sold (547 + 347) 894 rooms out of 3,100 available in January; and this gives the room occupancy percentage of 28.8. We sold 347 rooms as doubles out of a total of 894 rooms sold; and our double occupancy percentage is 38.8. Finally our total room sales amount to £42,606 and this divided by the number of rooms sold (894) gives us the average room rate of £47.66. The above budget shows budgeted room sales for the forthcoming half-year of £447,283, consisting of single-room sales of £239,768 and double-room sales of £207,515. During the next half-year we should achieve single-room occupancy of 53.4 per cent and double-room occupancy of 42.3 per cent. Finally, we should strive to achieve an average room rate of £46.26.

CAPITAL BUDGETS

Examples of capital budgets have already been given. The most important capital budgets in the context of hospitality and tourism operations are cash budgets and capital expenditure budgets.

Cash budget

The main objective of the cash budget is to predetermine the cash inflows, cash outflows and the resulting cash balance over a future period.

In order to determine future cash inflows it is necessary to identify the sources of cash inflows. These will normally be: room, food and beverage sales and sales of the minor operated departments. Each of these sources may generate cash and credit sales. Cash sales constitute an immediate cash inflow. Credit sales, however, take time to result in a cash inflow. Thus credit sales in the banqueting department may take an average of almost two months before conversion into cash (i.e. payment by banqueting customers). On the other hand, credit room sales may take an average of only a few days. It is necessary, therefore, in the case of credit sales to take into account the average time lag in relation to each element of the credit sales mix.

Cash outflows may be categorized variously depending on the actual system of budgetary control in operation. We may divide the total cash outflows under headings such as food costs, beverage costs, cost of sales of minor operated departments, wages and salaries and other expenditure. The alternative, which is preferable and more generally used in larger units, is to divide the total cash outflow under headings such as departmental expenses (distinguishing between cost of sales, departmental wages and salaries and other departmental expenses), controllable departmental expenses of non-revenue-producing departments and other expenses.

In most situations it will be found that there are non-routine receipts and payments, e.g. dividends received on company investments, bank interest received, payments for fixed assets, etc. It is essential to make provision for such non-routine items in each cash budget.

Capital expenditure budget

The capital expenditure budget will make provision for expenditure on kitchen plant and equipment, furniture, extensions to premises and similar items. In most cases the capital expenditure budget will extend over one year. Sometimes, however, it may cover a period of time in excess of one year, particularly in the case of extensions and more substantial projects which take a long time to complete.

This particular budget will, to some extent, be affected by the cash budget as, inevitably, any proposed capital expenditure must depend on the availability of cash over the budget period. The cash budget will, therefore, have to be consulted before a decision is made on the timing of each item of capital expenditure. All new acquisitions of plant, furniture, etc. listed in the capital expenditure budget will be incorporated in the budgeted balance sheet.

Other capital budgets

Debtors' and creditors' budgets are important elements of the system of budgetary control in many organizations. Hospitality establishments however, have a high proportion of cash and short-term credit sales and keep relatively low stocks and, for these reasons, budgets for debtors and creditors are not usually prepared. In any case, figures of the outstanding debtors and creditors may be obtained from the cash budget, as illustrated later in this chapter.

Similarly, one does not often prepare a budget for food and beverage stocks. Where a system of budgetary control is in operation a standard stock level for food and beverages is fixed, and this is quite adequate for most purposes, including the construction of the budgeted balance sheet.

The remainder of this chapter will be devoted to practical examples and illustrations.

Example 1

From the information given below, prepare the cash budget of the Ealing Restaurant.

Budgeted Sales and Expenditure
February–September 19 . . .

Month	Food sales	Beverage sales	Food purchases	Beverage purchases	Labour costs	Other expenditure
	£	£	£	£	£	£
Feb.	16,000	5,000	6,500	2,500	6,200	5,200
Mar.	17,000	5,500	6,800	2,800	6,300	5,200
Apr.	18,000	5,700	7,300	2,900	6,300	5,300
May	18,600	6,200	7,500	3,200	6,400	5,400
June	24,000	6,900	9,500	3,500	7,000	5,700
July	27,800	8,400	11,000	4,300	7,300	6,000
Aug.	23,000	7,100	9,400	3,600	7,000	5,700
Sept.	19,600	6,400	7,800	3,200	6,800	5,400

Take the following into account.

(a) All beverages are sold for cash only. Of the food sales, one half is cash and one half is on credit. Cash in respect of the latter is received after a time lag of one month.
(b) The time lag in the payment of suppliers' accounts is two months; in the case of labour costs and other expenditure it is nil.
(c) The annual interest on the restaurant's investments is receivable in June and amounts to £700.
(d) The restaurant's capital expenditure budget provides for the acquisition in May of new carpets and furniture costing £5,000. The resulting cash out-flow is planned for the month following the acquisition of these assets.
(e) In September the restaurant will redeem £10,000 of its debentures.
(f) The bank balance of the restaurant on 1 April 19 . . ., was £2,000.

The cash budget of the restaurant would be prepared as shown in Figure 12.4.

Cash Budget
for six months ending 30 September 19 . . .

Particulars	April	May	June	July	August	Sept.	Notes
	£	£	£	£	£	£	
Opening balance	2,000	4,600	7,700	8,700	19,000	25,800	
Cash inflow:							
Food sales—cash	9,000	9,300	12,000	13,900	11,500	9,800	
Food sales—credit	8,500	9,000	9,300	12,000	13,900	11,500	£9,800 debtors
Beverage sales	5,700	6,200	6,900	8,400	7,100	6,400	
Other receipts			700				
Total	25,200	29,100	36,600	43,000	51,500	53,500	
Cash outflow:							
Food purchases	6,500	6,800	7,300	7,500	9,500	11,000	£17,200 creditors
Beverage purchases	2,500	2,800	2,900	3,200	3,500	4,300	£6,800 creditors
Labour costs	6,300	6,400	7,000	7,300	7,000	6,800	
Other expenditure	5,300	5,400	5,700	6,000	5,700	5,400	
Other payments			5,000			10,000	
Total	20,600	21,400	27,900	24,000	25,700	37,500	
Closing balance	4,600	7,700	8,700	19,000	25,800	16,000	

Figure 12.4 Solution to question in Example 1

Notes on cash budget

It should be noted that, as previously explained, the cash budget is prepared by extracting appropriate data from other budgets. Any time lags in income and expenditure must be taken into account to show the correct timing of cash inflows and outflows. The cash budget shows the cash (bank) balance month by month as well as the closing balance of the end of the budget period.

Example 2: budgeting in a new business

John Day and Richard Knight are equal partners and proprietors of the Full Circle Restaurant. They started trading in December 19 . . ., where each partner paid £150,000 into their bank account. At the end of that month a summary of their initial cash transactions was prepared as shown below.

Cash Summary December 19 . . .

		£
Capital contribution J.D.		150,000
Capital contribution R.K.		150,000
		300,000
Less Premises (lease 20 years)	£150,000	
Furniture (estimated life ten years)	40,000	
Plant (estimated life ten years)	80,000	
China and cutlery	10,000	
Food stocks	5,000	285,000
Balance of cash available		£15,000

Given in Figure 12.5 are the relevant budgeted figures in respect of the first six months of operations.

Food sales. The partners are of the opinion that these will amount to £40,000 in January, £80,000 in February and £120,000 subsequently. 50 per cent of the sales will be cash sales and the other 50 per cent credit sales. The period of credit extended to customers will be one month.

Gross profit, purchases, etc. The budgeted gross profit is 60 per cent. Half the food cost for any one month will be paid for in cash; the other half will be purchased on credit and paid for during the month following purchase. The restaurant has a standard stock level of £5,000.

Wages and salaries. These will be incurred at the rate of £25,000 per month. No time lag is expected here.

Other expenses. Depreciation in respect of the premises, furniture and kitchen plant will be calculated on the straight-line basis. China and cutlery will be revalued annually, and it is expected that annual losses will be in the region of 20 per cent. Other expenses will be incurred at the rate of £20,000 per month. The time lag in the case of the latter will be one month.

You are asked by the partners to prepare a cash budget, a budgeted profit and loss account for the first six months of operations and a budgeted balance sheet as at 30 June 19 . . .

As may be seen from the cash budget, the restaurant will have a relatively small overdraft at the end of February. Subsequently each month will show an appreciable increase in the bank balance. From the 'Notes' column we can see, that at the end of June, debtors will amount to £60,000, creditors £24,000 and expense creditors (i.e. creditors in respect of restaurant expenses owing but unpaid) £20,000.

Cash Budget
for six months ending 30 June 19 . . .

	Jan	Feb.	March	April	May	June	Notes
	£	£	£	£	£	£	
Opening balance	15,000	2,000	(7,000)	8,000	35,000	62,000	
Cash inflow:							
Cash sales	20,000	40,000	60,000	60,000	60,000	60,000	
Credit sales		20,000	40,000	60,000	60,000	60,000	Debtors £60,000
Total	35,000	62,000	93,000	128,000	155,000	182,000	
Cash outflow:							
Cash purchases	8,000	16,000	24,000	24,000	24,000	24,000	
Credit purchases		8,000	16,000	24,000	24,000	24,000	Creditors £24,000
Wages and salaries	25,000	25,000	25,000	25,000	25,000	25,000	
Other expenses		20,000	20,000	20,000	20,000	20,000	Expense creditors £20,000
Total	33,000	69,000	85,000	93,000	93,000	93,000	
Closing balance	2,000	(7,000)	8,000	35,000	62,000	89,000	

Figure 12.5 Solution to question in Example 2

Budgeted Profit & Loss A/c
for six months ending 30 June 19 . . .

	£	£	£
Sales			600,000
Less Cost of sales			240,000
Gross profit			360,000
Less Expenses:			
Wages and salaries		150,000	
Depreciation:			
Premises	3,750		
Furniture	2,000		
Plant	4,000		
China and cutlery	1,000	10,750	
Other expenses		120,000	280,750
Net profit			£79,250

It should be noted that the budgeted profit and loss account is prepared on a completely different basis from the cash budget. In the latter we are interested in actual flows of cash in and out of the business. In the former what matters are flows of income and expenditure. It is for this reason that depreciation is not shown in the cash budget and the total of other expenses is £120,000 in the budgeted profit and loss account but only £100,000 in the cash budget.

Budgeted Balance Sheet—as at 30 June 19 . . .

Fixed assets	Cost	Depreciation	Net
	£	£	£
Premises	150,000	3,750	146,250
Furniture	40,000	2,000	38,000
Plant	80,000	4,000	76,000
China	10,000	1,000	9,000
	280,000	10,750	269,250
Current assets			
Food stocks		5,000	
Debtors		60,000	
Cash		89,000	
		154,000	
Less Current liabilities			
Trade creditors	24,000		
Expense creditors	20,000	44,000	
Net current assets			110,000
			379,250
Financed by:			
Capital a/c J.D.		150,000	
Capital a/c R.K.		150,000	300,000
Net profit			79,250
			379,250

Example 3: effect of sales mix on profitability

The Westminster Restaurant budgeted in respect of the year ended 31 December 19 . . . for sales of £400,000 and an average spending power of £4.00. The budgeted differential profit margins were as follows.

	Sales mix %	Gross profit %
Soups and appetizers	10	65
Meat and fish	40	45
Vegetables	10	60
Sweets	10	60
Teas and coffees	10	65
Alcoholic beverages	20	60
	100%	

Budgeted labour costs and overheads were £160,000. Of these, fixed costs were £100,000 and variable costs £60,000.

At the end of the budget year it was found that actual sales and the average spending power were as budgeted. The actual sales mix and differential profit margins were as given below.

	Sales mix %	Gross profit %
Soups and appetizers	10	65
Meat and fish	50	40
Vegetables	5	60
Sweets	5	60
Teas and coffees	10	65
Alcoholic beverages	20	55
	100%	

Actual labour costs and overheads were as budgeted but, of the total of £160,000, £80,000 was fixed and £80,000 a variable cost.

(a) Prepare a summary of budgeted and actual results.
(b) Comment on the results achieved.

Solution

The overall budgeted and actual gross profits may be calculated as follows:

Budgeted gross profit

Description	Sales mix		Gross profit	
	%	£	%	£
Soups and appetizers	10	40,000	65	26,000
Meat and fish	40	160,000	45	72,000
Vegetables	10	40,000	60	24,000
Sweets	10	40,000	60	24,000
Teas and coffees	10	40,000	65	26,000
Alcoholic beverages	20	80,000	60	48,000
Total	100%	£400,000	55%	£220,000

Thus the overall budgeted gross profit was £220,000, i.e. 55 per cent of the budgeted sales volume.

Actual gross profit

Description	Sales mix		Gross profit	
	%	£	%	£
Soups and appetizers	10	40,000	65	26,000
Meat and fish	50	200,000	40	80,000
Vegetables	5	20,000	60	12,000
Sweets	5	20,000	60	12,000
Teas and coffees	10	40,000	65	26,000
Alcoholic beverages	20	80,000	55	44,000
Total	100%	£400,000	50%	£200,000

As may be seen from the above table, changes which have occurred in the actual sales mix and differential profit margins have resulted in a lower than budgeted gross profit on food and beverage sales.

Summary of budgeted and actual trading results

	Budget	Actual
	£	£
Sales	400,000	400,000
Cost of sales	180,000	200,000
Other variable costs	60,000	80,000
Fixed costs	100,000	80,000
Net profit	60,000	40,000
	£400,000	£400,000

Actual net profit was £20,000 less than budgeted as a result of the changes which took place in the sales mix and differential profit margins. The change in the composition of labour costs and overheads has resulted in a relatively higher fixed cost. The budgeted C/S ratio was 40 per cent and the actual was 30 per cent. The actual margin of safety must thus have been narrower than budgeted.

PROBLEMS

1. Explain what you understand by:

   (a) budget
   (b) budgetary control.

2. Write an essay on the objectives of budgetary control.
3. Distinguish clearly between:

   (a) operating and capital budgets
   (b) fixed and flexible budgets.

4. Write short, explanatory notes on:

   (a) budget committee
   (b) budget manual
   (c) master budgets.

5. Draw an organization chart for a hotel or restaurant with which you are familiar and describe briefly what operating budgets you would expect the establishment to prepare.

6. State what key factors you would expect to operate in each of the following:

   (a) large seaside resort hotel
   (b) low ASP city restaurant
   (c) medium-priced provincial hotel
   (d) a self-service restaurant
   (e) tour operator
   (f) retail travel agent.

7. Jack Robinson is the owner of the Three Camels travel agency. Given below are his sales for the first six months of 1998.

	Package tours	Rail tickets	Other sales	Total sales
	£	£	£	£
January	50,000	20,000	5,000	75,000
February	60,000	25,000	6,000	91,000
March	70,000	30,000	8,000	108,000
April	110,000	45,000	10,000	165,000
May	60,000	20,000	7,000	87,000
June	40,000	15,000	5,000	60,000

Robinson operates a system of budgetary control and you have been asked to assist in the preparation of his sales budget for the first half of 1999. You are informed that:

(a) The sale of package tours for the first three months of 1999 should only show a modest rise of 5 per cent. During the next three months (April–June) there should be an increase in the sale of package tours of 15 per cent.

(b) Railway tickets have shown a healthy trend in recent years, and it is confidently expected that throughout the first half of 1999 there should be an increase in the sale of railway tickets of 10 per cent.

(c) Other sales—mainly insurance policies—are expected to rise by 5 per cent.

Prepare the sales budget for the first half of 1999.

Assume that the pattern of cash inflow in respect of package tours is as follows:

(a) 20 per cent of package tour sales represents an immediate cash inflow
(b) 40 per cent of package tour sales is converted into cash after one month
(c) the remaining 40 per cent of package tour sales materializes as cash after two months.

Railway tickets and other sales are both cash sales.

You are required to calculate Robinson's total cash inflow for:

(i) March 1999
(ii) April 1999
(iii) May 1999.

8. Given below is an extract from the budgeted profit and loss account of Orbis International Hotel.

	April	May	June	July	August
	£	£	£	£	£
ROOM SALES	500,000	540,000	600,000	680,000	750,000
Payroll	75,000	80,000	87,000	97,000	106,000
Departmental expenses	50,000	53,000	58,000	63,000	71,000
Total	125,000	133,000	145,000	160,000	177,000
Departmental profit	375,000	407,000	455,000	520,000	573,000
Food sales	370,000	380,000	400,000	430,000	440,000
Beverage sales	130,000	140,000	180,000	220,000	220,000
FOOD & BEVERAGE SALES	500,000	520,000	580,000	650,000	660,000
Food and beverage gross profit	340,000	350,000	380,000	420,000	460,000
Payroll	220,000	220,000	240,000	270,000	300,000
Departmental expenses	50,000	50,000	60,000	60,000	70,000
Total	270,000	270,000	300,000	330,000	370,000
Departmental profit	70,000	80,000	80,000	90,000	90,000
UNDISTRIBUTED OPERATING EXPENSES					
Administrative and general	80,000	80,000	82,000	82,000	85,000
Advertising and promotion	25,000	25,000	25,000	25,000	25,000
Heat, light and power	40,000	40,000	33,000	28,000	25,000
Repairs and maintenance	50,000	50,000	50,000	50,000	50,000
Depreciation	25,000	25,000	25,000	25,000	25,000
Total	220,000	220,000	215,000	210,000	210,000

You are required to prepare the cash budget of the hotel for the three months ending 31 August 19 . . . The following notes are to be taken into account.

Rooms operations

(a) Of the total room sales 90 per cent is received in cash and 10 per cent materializes as cash after a time lag of one month.
(b) There is no time lag in the case of payroll.
(c) 50 per cent of the departmental expenses entail an immediate cash outflow; the remainder is paid after a time lag of one month.

Food and beverage operations

(a) 50 per cent of food and beverage sales are cash sales. Of the total of credit sales, half materializes as cash after a time lag of one month and the other half after a lag of two months.
(b) 60 per cent of food and beverage costs entail an immediate cash outflow; the remainder is paid one month following purchase.
(c) There is no time lag in the case of payroll.
(d) 30 per cent of the departmental expenses represent an immediate cash outflow; the remainder is subject to a time lag of one month.

Undistributed operating expenses

(a) Of the total of administrative and general expenses, £60,000 represents an immediate cash outflow and the rest is subject to a time lag of one month.
(b) Advertising and promotion are periodic, irregular payments. £70,000 will be paid for press advertising at the beginning of June.
(c) Heat, light and power are all paid quarterly. During the quarter under review a total of £74,000 will be paid out: £40,000 in July and the balance in August.
(d) Of the total of repairs and maintenance £30,000 is an immediate cash outflow. The rest of this expense is paid periodically but not regularly. It is estimated that £45,000 will have to be paid in August.

Other information

(a) The bank balance of the Orbis International Hotel was £300,000 on 1 June 19 . . .
(b) The capital expenditure budget of the hotel provides for the acquisition of the following items:
    restaurant furniture   £400,000: May
    kitchen plant   £200,000: June
    Both items will be paid for two months after purchase.

9. The Grand Hotel has 100 rooms; its average room rate in 1997 was $40.00. Given below is the Profit and Loss A/c of the hotel for the year ended 31 December 1997

Profit & Loss A/c
for year ended 31 December 1997

	Net sales	Cost of sales	Dept. payroll	Dept. expenses	Dept. profit
	$	$	$	$	$
Rooms	1,073,400	—	230,400	111,200	731,800
Food and beverage	1,127,400	372,200	447,600	115,800	191,800
Minor oper. depts	136,600	61,200	49,000	9,200	17,200
Store rentals	29,400	—	—	—	29,400
Other	44,600	—	—	—	44,600
	2,411,400	433,400	727,000	236,200	1,014,800

Less Undistributed operating expenses:		
Administration and general	197,200	
Marketing	71,200	
Heat, light and power	94,800	
Repairs and maintenance	135,600	498,800
Net profit		516,000

The Budget Committee of the hotel are planning the Budgeted Profit and Loss A/c for the next accounting period and, because of strong inflationary tendencies, expect the following changes in 1998.

(a) Food and beverage costs as well as the cost of sales in the Minor Operated Departments will rise by 10 per cent.
(b) Departmental payroll will increase by 15 per cent.
(c) Departmental expenses will rise by 10 per cent.
(d) Administrative, general, advertising and promotion expenses will rise by 10 per cent. Heat, light, power, repairs and maintenance will, however, increase by 20 per cent.

The General Manager of the Grand Hotel is considering what price level adjustments will be necessary to preserve the profitability of the business. He knows from recent experience that annual price increases of the order of 10–15 per cent do not have an adverse effect on hotel occupancy or sales in other departments. He proposes, therefore, in 1998, to increase prices as follows:

(a) room rate—from $40.00 to $45.00
(b) food and beverage prices—by 12 per cent
(c) MOD charges—by 15 per cent.

You are required to:

(a) prepare the budgeted Profit and Loss A/c of the Grand Hotel for the year ended 31 December 1998
(b) comment on the adequacy of the budgeted gross operating profit for 1998
(c) state clearly any assumptions you have had to make.

10. From the information given below prepare a cash budget for the six months commencing 1 April 19 . . .

Month	Food sales £	Beverage sales £	Food purchases £	Beverage purchases £	Labour costs £	Overheads £
February	60,000	18,000	24,000	9,000	23,000	20,000
March	62,000	19,000	25,000	10,000	24,000	21,000
April	68,000	21,000	27,000	11,000	26,000	22,000
May	71,000	25,000	28,000	12,000	27,000	22,000
June	92,000	27,000	29,000	12,000	29,000	23,000
July	101,000	33,000	31,000	15,000	30,000	22,000
August	91,000	28,000	29,000	14,000	27,000	21,000
September	82,000	26,000	28,000	13,000	24,000	21,000

Notes:

(a) Assume that 80 per cent of food sales are for cash and the balance of 20 per cent on a credit basis with a time lag of one month. All beverage sales are on a cash basis.
(b) The interest on the company's investments, £3,000, will be received in July.
(c) The time lag in the payment of suppliers is two months; in the payment of overheads it is one month; in the case of labour costs it is nil.
(d) New kitchen equipment costing £85,000 will be purchased in May and paid for the following month.
(e) The bank balance of the company on 1 April 19 . . . was £15,000.

11. The Green Valley Hotel has 80 rooms and, amongst others, a successful food and beverage department. The Food and Beverage (F&B) Manager has been asked to prepare an operating budget for his department for 1998. The attached schedule shows the operating results of the food and beverage operation for 1995, 1996 and 1997.
     The following notes are relevant and should be taken into account:

NoC and ASP

It is expected that the upward trend in these figures will continue in 1998. Please assume that the results in 1998 will be at least as good as the best during the last three years.

Gross profit

The policy of the hotel is to achieve a gross profit of 67.0 per cent on food and 62.0 per cent on beverage sales.

Departmental payroll

The General Manager insists that departmental payroll for 1998 should not exceed 37.0 per cent.

Departmental expenses

The General Manager is also of the opinion—which is shared by the Food and Beverage Manager—that departmental expenses should be maintained at the level of 15.0 per cent of departmental turnover.

You are required to assume the role of the Food and Beverage Manager of the Green Valley Hotel and prepare the F&B Operating Budget for 1998. State clearly any assumptions you have made.

Should the departmental profit resulting from your projections amount to less than £140,000 suggest ways and means of ensuring that the 1998 departmental profit shows an improvement of at least 5 per cent on the previous year.

Green Valley Hotel
Food and Beverage Operations: 1995–97

	1995	*1996*	*1997*
No. of covers	30,000	31,200	32,760
ASP—food	£16.00	£16.80	£17.48
ASP—beverage	5.60	5.82	6.12
ASP—total	£21.60	£22.62	£23.60
Food sales	£480,000	£524,160	£572,644
Beverage sales	168,000	181,584	200,492
Total sales	£648,000	705,744	773,136
Food cost	£158,400	£167,732	£188,972
Beverage cost	63,840	70,818	74,182
Cost of sales	£222,240	£238,550	£263,154
GP—food	£321,600	£356,428	£383,672
GP—beverage	104,160	110,766	126,310
GP—total	£425,760	£467,194	£509,982
GP—food	67.0%	68.0%	67.0%
GP—beverage	62.0%	61.0%	63.0%
GP—total	65.7%	66.2%	66.0%
Dept. payroll	£246,240	£261,126	£293,792
Dept. payroll	38.0%	37.0%	38.0%
Dept. expenses	£84,240	£98,804	£92,775
Dept. expenses	13.0%	14.0%	12.0%
Dept. profit	£95,280	£107,264	£123,414
Dept. profit	14.7%	15.2%	16.0%

12. Set out below is the Profit and Loss A/c of the Ponte Vecchio Restaurant in respect of the year ended 31 December 1998.

Profit and Loss A/c

	£	%
Sales—food	300,480	72.7
beverage	112,680	27.3
total	413,160	100.0
Cost of sales—food	102,163	34.0
beverage	50,706	45.0
total	152,869	37.0
Gross profit	260,291	63.0
Less Operating expenses:		
Wages and salaries	102,464	24.8
Employee benefits	13,221	3.2
Direct operating expenses	21,071	5.1
Music and entertainment	7,850	1.9
Advertising and promotion	11,982	2.9
Gas and electricity	18,179	4.4
Administrative and general expenses	17,766	4.3
Repairs and maintenance	4,545	1.1
Rent	18,592	4.5
Depreciation	5,784	1.4
Total	221,454	53.6
Net profit	38,837	9.4

You are required to prepare the restaurant's budget for 1999, taking the following notes into account:

Food and beverage sales

The number of covers has shown a modest increase in recent years and this trend is expected to continue in 1999. The average spending power (ASP) of the restaurant tends to reflect general inflationary trends. The following figures are available.

	1996	*1997*	*1998*
No of covers	22,734	23,802	25,040
ASP—food	£10.70	£11.32	£12.00
beverage	4.00	4.24	4.50

Gross profit margins

The policy of the restaurant is to operate at gross profit margins as follows:

(a) Food: 65%
(b) Beverage: 55%

Wages and salaries

There will be no change in the number of employees, but wage rates and salaries will increase in accordance with current wage rates adjustments which average 7 per cent. Employee benefits should not increase by more than 5 per cent.

Direct operating expenses

An increase of 8 per cent is expected.

Music and entertainment

A new team of musicians and artists will be employed and this will entail an increase of 12 per cent on the expenses incurred in 1998.

Advertising and promotion

It is considered that this should not exceed 2.4 per cent of the sales revenue in 1999.

Gas and electricity

From information available it is clear that this expenditure will not increase by more than 3 per cent.

Administrative and general expenses

The proprietors are determined that this expenditure should be maintained at 4 per cent of the 1999 sales revenue.

Repairs and maintenance

Past experience suggests that this will not cost more than £4,700 during the year to 31 December 1999.

Rent

This will show an increase of 6 per cent.

Depreciation

This will remain as in 1998, i.e. at the level of £5,784.

The proprietors insist that the restaurant must achieve a net profit of at least £50,000 during the year ended 31 December 1999.

13 Variance analysis

INTRODUCTION

Where there is a system of budgetary control in operation, it is essential to ensure that all deviations from budgeted results (variances) are analysed and reasons for their occurrence established. Let us assume that at the end of a budget period the following information is available.

	Budget £	Actual £
Sales	100,000	110,000
Food and beverage costs	40,000	47,000
Labour costs	30,000	33,000
Overhead costs	20,000	21,000
Net profit	10,000	9,000
	£100,000	£110,000

The amount of meaningful information given in the above statement is minimal. We can see that actual sales were 10 per cent above budgeted sales, but we do not know whether this increase is due to a larger number of covers or higher average spending power or both. Similarly we can see that all costs showed some increase in relation to the budget. How much of the increase is due to the higher volume of sales, increased prices paid to suppliers, or inefficiency is not known. Finally, we see that the actual net profit is less than budgeted net profit. As we have not identified the reasons for the variances in sales and operating costs, we are not able to explain why the decrease in the net profit has occurred.

SOME BASIC PRINCIPLES

We have, as yet, no generally accepted method of variance analysis in the hospitality industry. The principles of variance analysis are, however, well established. The aim of the present chapter is, therefore, to show how the basic principles of variance analysis may be applied to hospitality operations.

A sales variance model

Let us assume that a restaurant budgeted for 500 meals and an ASP of £20.00. The budgeted sales were therefore £10,000. At the end of the budgeted period it was found that 600 meals were sold and the ASP was £25.00. Actual sales were, therefore, £15,000 and the overall variance on the sales volume £5,000.

For the purposes of variance analysis the overall variance must be analysed as between ASP variance and NoC variance. The method to be applied is illustrated in Figure 13.1

Six hundred meals were actually sold and resulted in an additional ASP of £5.00 per meal. The ASP variance is, therefore, £3,000. The restaurant sold 100 more meals than it budgeted; and this multiplied by the budgeted ASP of £20.00 gives an NoC variance of £2,000. We may, therefore, analyse the overall variance on sales as follows:

Budgeted sales	£10,000
Add ASP variance	3,000
NoC variance	2,000
Actual sales	£15,000

It is now quite clear that of the total variance of £5,000, £3,000 was due to higher spending by customers and £2,000 to more meals having been sold. The shaded area in the top right-hand corner of Figure 13.1 sometimes creates problems of interpretation. It may be argued that this particular portion of the overall variance is due both to higher spending by customers and to the larger numbers of meals; and there is, of course, substance in this argument. There are two solutions possible. One may show this as a separate ASP/NoC mix variance and ignore the dual nature of the variance, or regard it as part of the ASP variance. The latter is the more common procedure. It is suggested,

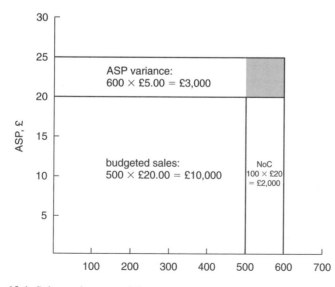

Figure 13.1 Sales variance model

therefore, that the ASP variance should be calculated on the total actual number of covers.

Cost variance models

Let us assume that at the end of the budget period the following data are available.

	Budget	Actual
Number of covers	200	250
Food cost per cover	£5.00	£6.00
Total food cost	£1,000	£1,500

Thus the overall variance is £500. Figure 13.2 shows how the relevant variances may be calculated. We can see that the overall difference between budgeted and actual food cost is due to two factors: (a) a larger than budgeted number of covers; (b) increase in the food cost per cover—presumably due to excessive/inefficient usage of materials (food cost). The NoC variance is (50 × £5.00) = £250, and the food cost usage variance is (250 × £1.00), also £250.

We may reconcile the budgeted and actual food costs as follows:

Budgeted food cost	£1,000
Add NoC variance	250
Usage variance	250
Actual food cost	£1,500

The shaded area in the top right-hand corner of the diagram is in the same category as the ASP/NoC mix variance on sales. Once again, it may be shown

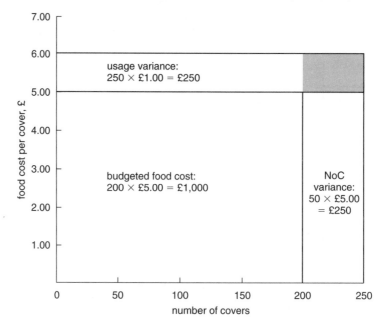

Figure 13.2 Food cost variance model (1)

separately but, for practical purposes, it is best to regard it as part of the food cost usage variance.

Quite frequently in addition to the two variances described above there is also a price variance. The food cost price variance arises when the prices paid to suppliers are in excess of those budgeted. Let us revert to the last example and assume that of the actual food cost per cover 50p was due to higher than budgeted prices paid to suppliers. If that is so we have three variances responsible for the overall difference between budgeted and actual food cost. These are shown in Figure 13.3.

The budgeted and actual food costs may now be reconciled as follows:

Budgeted food cost	£1,000
Add NoC variance	250
Usage variance	125
Price variance	125
Actual food cost	£1,500

After this preliminary consideration of variances, let us explore variance analysis in more detail.

Revenue-based variances

As already explained, in the case of food and beverage sales there are two variances, i.e. the ASP and the NoC variance. At the end of each trading

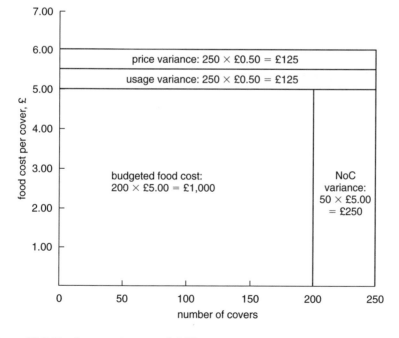

Figure 13.3 Food cost variance model (2)

period it is essential to explain any overall deviations from budgeted results in terms of these two variances.

Example 1: Food and beverages sales

The Trio Restaurant Company operates three small restaurants: A, B and C. At the end of month 5 the following figures were available.

	Budget			Actual		
	NoC	ASP	Sales	NoC	ASP	Sales
		£	£		£	£
Restaurant A	1,000	4.40	4,400	1,100	4.20	4,620
Restaurant B	800	8.20	6,560	760	8.40	6,384
Restaurant C	600	7.00	4,200	660	7.20	4,752

You are required to calculate appropriate variances and reconcile the budgeted and actual sales for the above period, and to set out your figures in the form of a simple tabulated report, addressed to the Sales Manager of the company.

The variances would be calculated as follows:

Restaurant A

Budgeted sales	£4,400
Add NoCV (100 × £4.40)	440
	4,840
Less ASPV (1,100 × £0.20)	220
Actual sales	£4,620

Restaurant B

Budgeted sales	£6,560
Add ASPV (760 × £0.20)	152
	6,712
Less NoCV (40 × £8.20)	328
Actual sales	£6,384

Restaurant C

Budgeted sales	£4,200
Add NoCV (60 × £7.00)	420
ASPV (660 × £0.20)	132
Actual sales	£4,752

The reconciliation of total budgeted and actual sales could take the following form.

Budgeted sales:	Restaurant A	£4,400	£
	Restaurant B	6,560	
	Restaurant C	4,200	15,160
Add Restaurant A—NoCV		440	
Restaurant B—ASPV		152	
Restaurant C—NoCV		420	
Restaurant C—ASPV		132	1,144
			16,304
Less Restaurant A—ASPV		220	
Restaurant B—NoCV		328	548
Actual sales:	Restaurant A	4,620	
	Restaurant B	6,384	
	Restaurant C	4,752	£15,756

There are various ways in which one can tabulate variances. The following is simple and straightforward.

TRIO RESTAURANT COMPANY
Monthly Sales Report

From: Management Accountant   Month: 5
To: Sales Manager   Date: 30 Sept. 19 . .

		Variances		
Unit	*Budgeted sales*	*NoC*	*ASP*	*Actual sales*
	£	£	£	£
Restaurant A	4,400	440	(220)	4,620
Restaurant B	6,560	152	(328)	6,384
Restaurant C	4,200	420	132	4,752
Total	15,160	1,012	(416)	15,756

Example 2: Room sales

The A-N-B Hotel Company operates two hotels, A and B. Given below is information relating to these two units in respect of month 3.

	Budget	*Actual*
Room nights A	2,000	2,200
Room nights B	1,000	900
Average room rate A	£20.00	£21.00
Average room rate B	£12.00	£12.20
Room sales A	£40,000	£46,200
Room sales B	£12,000	£10,980

You are required to calculate appropriate variances and the budgeted and actual room sales of each hotel.

Hotel A:

Budgeted room sales	£40,000
Add room rate variance (£1.00 × 2,200)	2,200
occupancy variance (£20.00 × 200)	4,000
Actual room sales	£46,200

Hotel B:

Budgeted room sales	£12,000
Add room rate variance (£0.20 × 900)	180
	12,180
Less occupancy variance (£12.00 × 100)	1,200
Actual room sales	£10,980

Cost-based variances

In the case of food cost, variance analysis is just the final stage of a long process. The first step, in the whole process of control and variance accounting, is to undertake appropriate yield tests, designed to establish the suitability of ingredients and potential yields in relation to the type of customer catered for. Secondly, standard purchase specifications are prepared. These describe in some detail the size, quality and other properties of the foodstuffs to be purchased from the suppliers. Finally, it is essential to prepare standard recipes for all menu items, showing the ingredients, method of preparation and, usually, the standard cost per portion. A full description of these techniques will be found in Chapter 14.

Example 1: Food cost

The following information is available at the end of a budget period.

	Budget	Actual
Number of covers	1,500	1,600
Food cost per cover	£2.40	£2.60
Total food cost	£3,600	£4,160

You are informed that of the £0.20 increase in the food cost per cover £0.10 is due to higher prices of foodstuffs. Calculate the relevant variances and reconcile the total budgeted and actual food cost.

Budgeted food cost	£3,600
Add NoCV (£2.40 × 100)	240
Usage V (£0.10 × 1600)	160
Price V (£0.10 × 1600)	160
Actual food cost	£4,160

Example 2: labour costs

The cost of labour is in most situations a semi-fixed cost; and the relative proportions of the fixed and variable elements vary from one establishment to another. As a result, different variances are calculated in respect of labour costs by different establishments. Thus where the number of staff is almost constant over longer periods changes in the number of covers will not be reflected in the number of staff employed. In such circumstances there is, naturally, no point in calculating NoC variances. The position is quite different in banqueting operations and outdoor catering where a high degree of adjustment of labour costs to the number of covers is possible. Thus, it is for each establishment to decide what variances will be calculated.

The standard weekly labour cost of an establishment is as follows:

Permanent staff	£1,500
Part-time labour	100
Casual labour	150
Total	£1,750

At the end of week 2 it was found that the actual labour cost was £1,920. You are informed that:

(a) the second chef was given a rise of £25.00 per week
(b) an additional kitchen porter was employed at £125.00 per week
(c) part-time employees have secured a rise in rates of pay of 20 per cent.

Reconcile the budgeted and actual weekly labour cost.

Budgeted labour cost		£1,750
Add Rate of pay variance:		
Permanent staff	£25.00	
Part-time staff	20.00	45
Establishment variance		125
Actual labour cost		£1,920

Example 3: overheads

Most of the expenditure under this heading tends to be of a fixed nature, and does not, therefore, respond much to changes in the level of activity. Few hotels and restaurants calculate variances for this group of expenses. It is desirable, however, to distinguish between fixed overheads and those which are variable. If the appropriate records are available there is no reason why variance analysis should not be applied to the variable element of total overheads. Where, for instance, considerable use is made of disposables (plates, cups, serviettes, tablecloths) the cost of such disposables per cover may be quite appreciable.

The ODG Catering Company has been asked to provide catering facilities at a race meeting. The company has budgeted, amongst other things, for a variable overhead cost per cover of £0.40. The budgeted number of covers was 2,000. On completion of the function it was found that the actual number of covers was 1,900 and total variable overhead cost £836. Explain the overall variance between the budgeted and actual variable overhead cost.

Budgeted overhead cost	£800
Less NoCV (£0.40 × 100)	40
	760
Add Usage V (£0.04 × 1900)	76
Actual overhead cost	£836

Variance analysis: practical applications

The techniques of variance accounting already described in this chapter offer a lot of scope for practical applications in many types of hospitality operation. The preparation of cash budgets, profit & loss a/cs and balance sheets, on the lines suggested here, should present no special difficulties in practice. Similarly, the suggested method of calculating labour cost variances is realistic and lends itself to many applications in the hospitality industry. Finally, our suggested method for calculating variances on sales is both simple and particularly easy to apply: in most hotels and restaurants, we know, on a daily basis, the total of food and beverage sales and the number of covers. The computation of daily/weekly ASP figures is, therefore, a simple matter. There is, in consequence, no reason at all why ASP and NoC variances should not be calculated as a matter of daily and weekly routine. As already explained in Chapter 10, small changes in the sales volume have a powerful impact on net profit. If we are to put the concept of 'revenue accounting' into practice, then the monitoring of sales variances should be given high priority—not only because of the powerful effect of sales variances in net profit, but also because the task is simple and undemanding.

Food cost variances: simplified method

The calculation of variances in respect of food cost is in a different category. Any difference between standard and actual food cost may be due to a number of different causes which, in practice, are difficult to isolate. Thus an increase in food costs due to higher prices paid to suppliers (materials price variance) is difficult to calculate as it necessitates the determination of standard purchase prices and the close monitoring of actual prices paid for, typically, hundreds of individual food items used in most hotel/restaurant kitchens. Similarly, the 'food cost usage variance' may be due to a variety of causes. It need not only refer to larger than standard portion sizes offered to guests, but may also be the result of petty pilfering, waste in the kitchen, etc. In consequence, an increase in food costs due to a 'usage variance' may actually be accompanied by smaller than standard portions being offered to guests!

It is because of these difficulties that many American 'food service operators' and a few catering companies in this country use a system of control which is simple and effective but does not pretend to achieve the impossible: only one overall food cost variance is calculated and no attempt is made to analyse it as between that part of it which is due to usage, volume or prices paid to suppliers. The only prerequisite here is the use of standard recipes to determine the standard food cost per portion of each menu item.

Example

Set out below are particulars of standard portion costs, selling prices and the number of portions sold over a period of one week.

Menu item	Standard food cost/portion £	Selling price £	Portions sold
A	1.00	2.00	15
B	0.50	1.20	15
C	0.75	2.00	13
D	3.00	8.00	25
E	4.00	10.00	30
F	5.00	12.00	42
G	1.00	2.50	18

Other relevant information is given below:

	£
Opening stock	266.75
Closing stock	238.50
Cost of employee meals	30.00
Food purchases	490.70

You are required to calculate:

(a) total food sales
(b) total standard food cost—both cash and %
(c) total standard gross profit—both cash and %
(d) total actual food cost—both cash and %
(e) total actual gross profit—both cash and %
(f) total food cost variance—both cash and %.

Solution

Our first step is to calculate total standard food cost and total food sales. The relevant figures are shown in the table below.

Menu item	Standard food cost/portion	Selling price	Portions sold	Standard food cost—total	Food sales
	£	£		£	£
A	1.00	2.00	15	15.00	30.00
B	0.50	1.20	15	7.50	18.00
C	0.75	2.00	13	9.75	26.00
D	3.00	8.00	25	75.00	200.00
E	4.00	10.00	30	120.00	300.00
F	5.00	12.00	42	210.00	504.00
G	1.00	2.50	18	18.00	45.00
	—	—	—	455.25	1,123.00

(a) Total food sales = £1,123.00

(b) Total standard food cost = £455.25

as a percentage of sales $\dfrac{£455.25}{£1,123.00} \times 100 = 40.5\%$

(c) Total standard gross profit = £667.75

as a percentage of sales $\dfrac{£667.75}{£1,123.00} \times 100 = 59.5\%$

(d) Total actual food cost:

Opening stock	£266.75
Add purchases	490.70
	757.45
Less closing stock	238.50
Cost of food consumed	518.95
Less cost of employee meals	30.00
Actual food cost	£488.95

as a percentage of sales $= \dfrac{£488.95}{£1,123.00} \times 100 = 43.5\%$

(e) Total actual gross profit:

Food sales	£1,123.00
Less actual food cost	488.95
Actual gross profit	£634.05

as a percentage of sales $\dfrac{£634.05}{£1,123.00} \times 100 = 56.5\%$

(f) Total food cost variance:

Actual food cost	£488.95	
Less standard food cost	455.25	
Food cost variance	£33.70	

as a percentage of sales $\dfrac{£33.70}{£1,123.00} \times 100 = 3.0\%$

From the above example the advantages of this method will be readily apparent. First, we have sufficient information relating to both standard and actual percentages of food cost and standard and actual percentages of gross profit. Also the method enables us to control our cash gross profit. The information made available by this method is thus both comprehensive and relevant.

The second main advantage is that we have the overall, total food cost variance—in the above example 3.0 per cent or £33.70—which is quite sufficient for control purposes. No attempt is made to attribute parts of this variance to causes which are frequently impossible to quantify.

BUDGET REPORTS

Where a comprehensive system of budgetary control is maintained, it is essential not only to calculate appropriate variances at the end of each review period but also to ensure that suitable reports are prepared. The control and degree of detail as well as the method of presentation will tend to vary from one type of hospitality establishment to another. Also the information needs of senior managers will tend to vary from one individual to another. It is, therefore, impossible to suggest hard and fast rules on how budget reports are to be prepared. Two fairly typical examples of reports are given below.

In the case of the Arcadia Hotel we show budgeted and actual sales as well as the variances—both quantitative and percentile. Whilst our report deals with sales only, this form of presentation may be applied to any budget. The main advantages of this method of presentation are its simplicity and clarity.

Arcadia Hotel
Sales Report
Monthly Budget Report for May 19 . .

	Sales		Variances	
	Budget	*Actual*	*Amount*	
	£	*£*	*£*	*%*
Rooms:				
Type x	90,000	93,000	3,000	3.3
Type y	70,000	68,000	(2,000)	(2.9)
Total	160,000	161,000	1,000	0.6
Food:				
Grill room	65,000	67,000	2,000	3.1

Coffee shop	40,000	39,000	(1,000)	(2.5)
Banquets	25,000	26,000	1,000	4.0
Total	130,000	132,000	2,000	1.5
Beverages:				
Grill room	26,000	27,000	1,000	3.8
Coffee shop	10,000	9,600	(400)	(4.0)
Banquets	11,000	11,600	600	5.5
Cocktail bar	13,000	14,000	1,000	7.7
Total	60,000	62,200	2,200	3.7
Other sales:				
Telephone	3,000	3,100	100	3.3
Guest laundering	1,700	1,800	100	0.6
Kiosk	4,800	5,100	300	6.3
Golf course	1,500	1,200	(300)	(20.0)
Total	11,000	11,200	200	1.8
Total sales	361,000	366,400	5,400	1.5

In the case of the Blue Lagoon Restaurant we show budgeted and actual figures as well as the relevant percentages. Although quantitative variances are not shown many restaurant operators would probably be satisfied with just the percentages as, traditionally, percentages have played an important role in the control process.

Blue Lagoon Restaurant
Budget Report
for quarter ended 30 September 19 . .

	Budget		Actual	
	£	%	£	%
Food sales	230,000	71.9	224,000	70.9
Beverage sales	90,000	28.1	92,000	29.1
Total	320,000	100.0	316,000	100.0
Food cost	80,500	35.0	81,760	36.5
Beverage cost	36,000	40.0	37,720	41.0
Cost of sales	116,500	36.4	119,480	37.8
Gross profit	203,500	63.6	196,520	62.2
Payroll	86,400	27.0	86,900	27.5
Employee benefits	8,000	2.5	8,220	2.6
Administration expenses	16,320	5.1	14,850	4.7

Marketing	7,040	2.2	7,580	2.4
Music and entertainment	14,400	4.5	12,960	4.1
Direct operating expenses	13,120	4.1	12,640	4.1
Gas and electricity	11,200	3.5	10,740	3.4
Repairs and maintenance	5,760	1.8	4,110	1.3
Depreciation	8,960	2.8	8,960	2.8
Total expenses	171,200	53.5	166,960	52.8
Net profit	32,300	10.1	29,560	9.4

Readers will notice that in both examples we give monthly figures only and do not show cumulative, year-to-date figures. There is no reason why additional columns should not be incorporated into such reports. Too much information, however, may prove counter-productive and make reports less intelligible.

PROBLEMS

1. What are the objectives and advantages of variance analysis?
2. Explain the relationship between budgetary control and variance analysis.
3. A Sales Budget has been formulated using standard costing techniques for five restaurants. At the end of the first week the Sales Manager requires you to prepare a statement showing all the relevant information, including an analysis of appropriate variances. The necessary information is given below.

	Budget		Actual	
Restaurant	ASP	NoC	ASP	NoC
A	£20.00	500	£21.00	460
B	15.00	400	15.00	380
C	10.00	300	9.00	350
D	12.00	400	13.00	420
E	16.00	200	14.00	240

4. From the information given below calculate appropriate variances on sales.

			£
(a) Standard sales	40,000 meals @	£5.00 =	20,000.00
Actual sales	43,000 meals @	£5.50 =	23,650.00
(b) Standard sales	2,500 meals @	£7.50 =	18,750.00
Actual sales	2,400 meals @	£8.00 =	19,200.00
(c) Standard sales	6,000 meals @	£10.50 =	63,000.00
Actual sales	5,908 meals @	£9.50 =	56,126.00

5. Given below are the budgeted and actual figures of the London Oxford Hotel in respect of month 4.

| | Budget | | Actual | |
	ASP	NoC	ASP	NoC
	£		£	
Breakfast	3.80	3,000	3.60	2,900
Lunch	6.80	1,800	6.70	1,850
Dinner	9.40	2,400	9.50	2,500
Nightclub	8.40	1,600	8.70	1,700

You are required to calculate appropriate variances and reconcile the total budgeted and actual sales of the hotel for month 4.

6. Set out below are particulars of standard portion costs, menu prices and portions sold over a period of one week.

Menu item	Standard food cost/portion	Selling price	Portion sold
	£	£	
A	2.20	5.00	20
B	1.00	3.80	30
C	1.50	4.00	40
D	5.00	15.80	30
E	6.40	18.80	40
F	8.20	23.80	20
G	2.20	6.80	40
H	0.80	2.50	30

Other relevant information is given below:

	£
Opening stock	644.80
Closing stock	690.40
Purchases	940.10
Staff meals	70.20

You are required to calculate:

(a) total food sales
(b) total standard food cost—both cash and %
(c) total standard gross profit—both cash and %
(d) total actual food cost—both cash and %
(e) total gross profit—both cash and %
(f) total food cost variance—both cash and %.

7. Gastronomy Ltd provides, amongst other things, a banqueting service, and given below is the company's budget in respect of November 19 . .

Food sales—	2,000 covers @ £13.20		£26,400
Beverage sales—	2,000 covers @ £3.00		6,000
			32,400

Less Food cost—	2,000 covers @ £4.80 = £9,600			
Beverage cost—	2,000 covers @ £1.20 = 2,400	12,000		
Casual labour—	1,800 hours @ £3.00 = 5,400			
Permanent labour—	300 hours @ £4.80 = 1,440	6,840		
Variable overheads—2,000 covers @ £1.20 = 2,400				
Fixed overheads =	3,000	5,400	24,240	
Standard net profit			£8,160	

The actual figures in respect of November 19.. were:

Food sales—	2,100 covers @ £12.60		£26,460
Beverage sales—	2,100 covers @ £3.60		7,560
			34,020

Less Food cost—	2,100 covers @ £4.50 = £9,450		
Beverage cost—	2,100 covers @ £1.50 = 3,150	12,600	
Casual labour—	1,900 hours @ £3.00 = 5,700		
Permanent labour—	270 hours @ £5.40 = 1,458	7,158	
Variable overheads—2,100 covers @ £1.32 = 2,772			
Fixed overheads =	3,000	5,772	25,530
Actual net profit			£8,490

You are required to ascertain what variances have occurred during the above period and present an appropriate statement reconciling the standard and actual net profit.

Note: Having regard to the nature of the operation it is considered that it would be inappropriate to calculate volume variances in respect of labour costs unless the actual number of covers differed by at least 10 per cent from the standard number of covers.

14 Food and beverage control

INTRODUCTION

No textbook of hospitality management accounting can be complete without a chapter on food and beverage control. In non-residential establishments such as restaurants, cafés and fast-food outlets, food and beverage sales account for at least 95 per cent of the turnover. In hotels, food and beverage sales frequently amount to approximately 45 per cent of total revenue. This calls for an effective system of food and beverage control to ensure sound management controls on the one hand and satisfactory profitability on the other.

The food and beverage department has two principal aims. The first—and probably the more important one—is to provide a standard of food and beverage service consistent with the expectations of the guests. If guests' expectations are not met, then clearly this will prejudice the hotel's ability to sell rooms; and, as may be seen in Chapter 17, 'Analysis of departmental profitability', room sales are the most profitable element of the total sales mix. The second aim is to maintain the food and beverage operation within the limits set by the food and beverage departmental budget and thus contribute to the overall profitability of the establishment.

The above principal aims will not be achieved unless enough attention is paid to the following:

(a) As the food and beverage department incurs high fixed costs (mainly payroll and related expenses), it is essential to ensure a satisfactory volume of sales.
(b) The sales volume is determined by two elements: the number of covers and the average spending power. It is important, therefore, to achieve both a satisfactory number of customers and an adequate level of ASP.
(c) Once we have achieved a satisfactory volume of sales, we should ensure that this is converted into the right volume of cash gross profit. Comprehensive controls must, therefore, be introduced to maintain the cost of sales at the right level in relation to departmental turnover.
(d) Finally, we must control not only the cost of sales but also other departmental costs and particularly the cost of payroll and related expenses.

The methodology of food and beverage control is now well understood and follows from the natural course of events in food and beverage operations. Whatever the nature of the hospitality establishment there are always five basic problems. First, food and beverages have to be purchased. Secondly, on delivery, all the incoming goods have to be checked. We then have to store the goods and subsequently issue them to various requisitioning departments. Next, food has to be prepared (whilst most beverages are sold in the same condition as they were purchased, some, such as cocktails, do require processing or preparation). Finally, meals and beverages have to be sold.

At each of these five stages we need appropriate control devices and procedures to ensure that the control system is both comprehensive and effective. In addition to such control devices and procedures we need a number of standards—such as standard purchase specifications, standard recipes and standard food/beverage costs. Such standards lay down norms which should be observed during operations and contribute significantly to the effectiveness of the control system. All the typical food and beverage standards are discussed later in this chapter. Let us now look at the cycle of food and beverage control in detail.

BUYING

The purchasing of food is a skilled and difficult task. It is also one which carries with it a lot of responsibility, if only because of the large amounts of money spent under this heading.

Whilst the purchase of what is commonly described as non-perishables is not unduly difficult, perishable items of food are typically heterogeneous and tend to vary in price from one supplier to another as well as seasonally. In large units—particularly hotels—there is often a full-time purchasing officer, who is responsible for all purchases: food, beverages and non-consumables. In smaller units the non-perishable foods are usually purchased by an assistant manager. The perishables, which include meat, poultry, fish, fruit and vegetables, are invariably purchased by the head chef.

Methods of buying

Whoever is responsible for buying, several methods of buying are almost always available. The methods actually used depend on the size of the unit, its location and the type of menu.

Many large hospitality companies purchase a high proportion of their foodstuffs—particularly the non-perishables—by contract. This method of buying has the advantage of stability of purchase prices and, usually, availability of essential supplies. Another advantage of contract buying is the saving of time: whenever a purchase is made it is not necessary to negotiate the purchase price with the supplier.

Medium-sized and large hospitality units situated close to wholesale markets (such as Smithfield and Billingsgate in London) buy a fair proportion of their perishables direct from such sources. This method of buying guarantees fresh produce and a relatively low price, but it is rather time-consuming and involves the additional cost of transporting the food to the establishment.

Many smaller and medium-sized establishments now take advantage of the recent growth in the 'cash and carry' business. The advantages of this method of buying are relatively low prices, a good choice of foodstuffs (though mainly non-perishables) and flexibility with regard to quantities required. The caterer must, of course, provide his own transport and pay cash. On balance, this appears to be a very convenient method of buying from the point of view of the smaller establishment.

Large establishments which spend considerable sums of money on foodstuffs often use the 'weekly quotation method'. Each week several suppliers will be asked to quote for particular quantities of foods (usually non-perishables). The prices quoted are noted on a 'master quotation sheet'. Other things being equal, the order goes to the supplier who has quoted the lowest price.

Yield testing

Before any buying is done it is essential to undertake appropriate yield tests. There are different kinds of yield testing and the term includes what should properly be described as 'product testing'. The tests may be carried out to establish actual yields (e.g. the percentage of edible meat, after bone loss, fat, etc.) Tests are sometimes undertaken to identify the gastronomic properties of foods: these are, strictly speaking, product tests, but in practice they are regarded as part and parcel of yield testing. Thus a catering company may obtain several different kinds of soup mixes. These will be processed as directed by the manufacturers/suppliers. A panel will then rate each soup mix with regard to taste, flavour, texture, etc. Finally, tests are often undertaken to establish the most economical method of processing. For example, identical joints of meat may be cooked at different temperatures—some in the conventional manner and others foil wrapped—to decide which method gives the best results, i.e. lowest cooking loss. An example of a yield test is given in Figure 14.1

Needless to say, yield testing is an indispensable preliminary for buying as well as the choice of most appropriate cooking methods. In the case of food control we have to undertake yield tests and subsequently produce the

COOKING YIELD TEST CARD

Objective: To measure potential savings by using aluminium foil when roasting meats

Commodity		Oven temperature	Initial weight	Cooked weight	Cooking loss %	Potential savings %
Chicken	Conventional	200 °C	1.42 kg	0.98 kg	31.0	
	Foil-wrapped	200 °C	1.40 kg	1.17 kg	16.4	14.6
Turkey	Conventional	200 °C	7.05 kg	4.67 kg	33.7	
	Foil-wrapped	200 °C	6.92 kg	5.49 kg	20.7	13.0
Topside of beef	Conventional	200 °C	2.72 kg	2.18 kg	19.9	
	Foil-wrapped	200 °C	2.72 kg	2.38 kg	12.5	7.4
Leg of lamb	Conventional	200 °C	2.40 kg	1.64 kg	31.7	
	Foil-wrapped	200 °C	2.49 kg	1.93 kg	22.5	9.2

Figure 14.1 Yield test card

necessary purchase specifications. Neither of these is necessary in the buying of beverages. We are dealing here with standardized products whose properties do not change except over very long periods.

Purchase specifications

When the necessary yield tests have been carried out it is next essential to prepare a 'purchase specification'. A purchase specification is a concise description of an item of food. Different purchase specifications will obviously deal with different attributes of food items. Thus in the case of meat the principal elements will be: country of origin, age, grade, weight, fat and bone content. In the case of poultry the purchase specifications would deal with aspects such as: whether fresh or frozen, rough plucked, eviscerated, weight of bird, percentage of giblets, degree of trimming required, etc. An example of a purchase specification is given in Figure 14.2.

The effect of a well-developed purchase specification is to create a standard product. As soon as the purchase specifications have been prepared they are sent to the suppliers to inform them exactly what is required. Some large hospitality companies include photographs of the food items in purchase specifications to ensure that no misunderstanding with suppliers can take place.

The buying of beverages is to some extent influenced by the system of volume forecasting. Most beverages are not subject to a high degree of perishability. Beers and minerals have a relatively short life and these have to be purchased in accordance with demand predictions from one week to another. In the case of wines and spirits most establishments buy once a month, and the stress is on the replenishment of stocks. The exact quantities purchased are also influenced by factors such as storage space available, discounts offered by the suppliers and government fiscal policy. The clerical procedures here are basically the same as in the case of food purchases.

PURCHASE SPECIFICATION

Best end neck of lamb   *P.S: 109*

Definition
   The portion of meat obtained from the crown best end (i.e. the 6–12 ribs inclusive) split cleanly down the centre of the vertebrae.
Grade of meat
   All best ends to be cut from YM grade New Zealand lamb carcasses.
Weight
   All prepared best ends to weigh between 0.55 and 0.65 kg.
Degree of preparation
   (a) All cut surfaces to be cleaned of bone dust.
   (b) The breast meat to be trimmed off parallel to the chine bone giving a rib bone length of approximately 14 cm.
Delivery notes
   (a) Best ends to be delivered frozen.
   (b) Best ends must be wrapped individually in greaseproof paper.

Figure 14.2 Purchase specification

Administrative and clerical procedures

One of the most important points here is to decide who has authority to originate a purchase order. Practice varies from one establishment to another. It seems that in the majority of establishments the non-perishables are purchased once a month, following stocktaking. The quantities to be purchased would be determined by the head storekeeper and approved by the manager or his deputy. In smaller establishments the head chef, having planned his menus, will decide what perishables are required and take full responsibility for this part of purchasing. Where there is a system of volume forecasting in operation, the perishables required each week are determined by reference to the volume forecast.

Wherever possible written purchase orders should be used. Many hospitality organizations use triplicate purchase orders: the top copy is sent to the supplier, the second copy is sent to the goods received clerk to inform him what goods to expect and the third copy remains in the office for control purposes.

RECEIVING

Of all the stages of the food and beverage control cycle the 'receiving' stage is certainly the easiest. Unfortunately, it is often the most neglected stage, too. Several points are particularly important here.

First, it is essential to make sure that all incoming goods are checked. The quality of the non-perishables tends to remain constant over longer periods. When checking non-perishables the stress will, therefore, be on quantities received. In the case of the perishables both the quality and the quantity must be checked thoroughly. The goods received clerk is not usually competent to judge the quality of meat, fish, etc. received. Consequently, it is essential that the head chef or his deputy checks all the incoming perishables personally.

Secondly, it is necessary to ensure that the goods actually received correspond with the particulars shown in the supplier's delivery note and, of course, the relevant copy of the establishment's purchase order. Particulars of all foodstuffs received are entered in a (usually loose-leaf) goods received book. At the end of each day the goods received clerk will attach to the goods received sheet all delivery notes and the relevant copies of the purchase orders and pass all these to the Control Office.

When receiving foodstuffs both the quantity and the quality must be checked. With regard to incoming beverages emphasis will, of course, be placed on the quantities actually received. Certain items (table wines, minerals, etc.) will have to be subjected to a quality inspection. On the whole, however, quality inspections feature more prominently in the case of food.

STORING AND ISSUING

From the point of view of this stage of the control cycle it is essential to distinguish between perishable and non-perishable foods. On receipt, the perishables are usually transferred direct to the kitchen, and are not normally subject to requisitioning by means of written requisition notes. The utilization of the perishables is under the direct supervision of the head chef. The turnover of such foods is very fast. It is impracticable and, to some extent, unnecessary to keep extensive stock records for the perishables.

With regard to the non-perishables the position is quite different. On receipt they are transferred to the store, and are issued in smaller quantities once or twice a day. To ensure the safekeeping of such foodstuffs, stock records are usually maintained by the vast majority of medium-sized and large establishments.

Perishables

In order to control the weekly consumption of the perishables many establishments keep an analysed Weekly Perishables Book. The opening stock of perishables is entered at the beginning of the week. As the perishables are received from one day to another, the chef's clerk will enter the values of such foods under headings such as: meat, poultry, fish, bacon and sausages, milk and cream, fruit, vegetables, etc. At the end of each week the book will be totalled, the closing stock of perishables deducted and the consumption of perishables thus obtained. An example of a Weekly Perishables Book is given in Figure 14.3

In some establishments it is considered essential to maintain records of the

WEEKLY PERISHABLES BOOK

Week: 26

Date		Meat	Poultry	Fish	Dairy	Fruit	Veg.	Total
June 22	Opening Stock	640.20	310.50	431.50	179.80	110.90	155.10	1,828.00
" 22	Lean Meat Co.	371.70						371.70
" 23	Gormley Farm					162.50	88.74	251.24
" 24	Irish Milk Ltd.				192.20			192.20
" 24	Atlantic Fish Co.			369.80				369.80
	etc.							
" 28	Total	2,470.70	1,211.50	1,612.40	710.70	409.30	603.40	7,018.00
" 28	Closing Stock	580.40	288.30	377.50	157.70	90.50	131.60	1,626.00
" 28	Consumption	1,890.30	923.20	1,234.90	553.00	318.80	471.80	5,392.00

Figure 14.3 Weekly perishables book

more expensive items of perishables such as lobsters, entrecote steaks, Dover sole, etc. To this end a larder control sheet is kept and actual portions/units left at the end of each week are reconciled with the balances shown in the above record. It should be added that this particular record is especially useful in a speciality restaurant. An example is given in Figure 14.4.

Non-perishables

Where detailed records of non-perishables are kept they normally take the form of stock cards or bin cards. Stock cards are usually kept on the loose-leaf principle. Bin cards, which are essentially very similar, are attached to the respective bins, racks, etc. These are, of course, the traditional records. As time goes on more and more hospitality establishments install computerized control systems; and a number of satisfactory computer programs are currently available.

One of the basic documents used in stores control by hotels and restaurants is the requisition note. Where there are several requisitioning departments, coloured requisition notes are often used to easily identify the departments concerned. An example of a requisition note is given in Figure 14.5.

The record which collects data relating to all issues of non-perishables is the weekly issues book. This is completed once a week, and the weekly totals are posted to the appropriate stock cards or bin cards. An example of the weekly issues book is given in Figure 14.6.

The sequencing of items in the weekly issues book may be alphabetical or alphabetical under group headings such as canned fruit, breakfast cereals, etc.

As already indicated bin cards are very similar to stock cards, except that they are not kept in a binder or cabinet but attached to the various bins,

LARDER CONTROL SHEET

Week: 26

Description	Unit	In Out	Mon	Tue	Wed	Thur	Fri	Sat	Sun	Total	Bal.
Lobster	each	In		24				24		48	
		Out			13	2	7	10	5	37	11
Sole	kg.	In	20			10				30	
		Out	5		4			7	13	29	1
Pheasant	each	In		20			10			30	
		Out			10	5	3		7	25	5
etc.											

Figure 14.4 Larder control sheet

STORES REQUISITION 1			
date *16 June 19*	dept. *Still Room*		no. *0.27*
description of items	quantity	unit price	value
Sugar	*5 kg*		
Tea	*2 kg*		
Coffee – Kenya	*1 kg*		
Cadbury's Bournville Cocoa	*1 kg*		
signed *B. Lacey*			

Figure 14.5 Stores requisition. *Note:* the requisition note would not normally be priced when presented to the stores, as requisitioning departments are not normally familiar with the price of each unit. They are often priced subsequently by the food controller's office to ascertain the periodical total of non-perishables consumed.

WEEKLY ISSUES BOOK

week ending *16 Sept. 19..*

Description	Unit	Unit Cost	Sun.	Mon.	Tue.	Wed.	Thur.	Fri.	Sat.	Total	£	p
Asparagus Soup	51	2.00	- - -	2 - -	- - -	- - -	3 - -	- - -	- - -	5	10	00
Blackcurrant Jam	3kg	3.00	- - -	- - -	1 - -	- - -	- - -	- - -	1 - -	2	6	00
Cocoa	4kg	7.20	- - -	- - -	- - -	1 - -	- - -	- - -	- - -	1	7	20
Danish Crown	2kg	1.80	1 - -	- - -	- - -	- - -	- - -	1 1 -	- - -	3	5	40
Eggs – Large	each	0.10	- - 10	- - -	15 20 -	- - -	20 - -	20 15 -	- - -	100	10	00
Farmhouse Soup	can	0.20	- - -	10 - -	- - -	20 - -	- - -	- - -	10 - -	40	8	00

Figure 14.6 Weekly issues book

drawers, etc. In some establishments bin cards are not written up weekly but daily—every time an issue is made or new delivery received.

The storing and issuing of beverages needs a lot of care and attention, if only because of the high volume of beverage stocks. Access to the cellar should be restricted to, frequently, just the cellarman and the hotel manager. The exact cellar records kept vary from one establishment to another. In large units—particularly hotels—cellar records consist of bin cards and the cellar ledger.

A bin card is kept for each item, showing receipts, issues and the running balance. All bin card numbers should correspond with wine list numbers, as it is usual for wine waiters to ask for wines by number rather than by name. A specimen bin card is shown in Figure 14.7

The cellar ledger usually takes the form of a series of double-sided accounts. An account is kept for each item, and movements of beverage stocks are recorded in terms of quantities and values—at cost. Periodically, the cellar ledger is balanced and the individual balances are compared with the actual quantities in stock as ascertained on stocktaking.

In larger hotels there are usually several departments which requisition beverages: dispense bar, cocktail bar, floor service, banqueting, etc. It is essential to maintain appropriate analytical records of issues of beverages to all such departments. The issues may be recorded at selling price, at cost or both. In the majority of medium-sized establishments the issues of beverages are recorded at selling price. An example of a cellar issues book is shown in Figure 14.8.

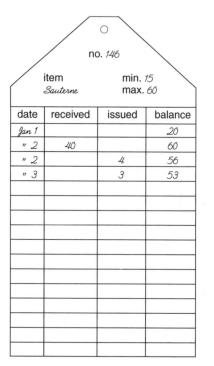

date	received	issued	balance
Jan 1			20
" 2	40		60
" 2		4	56
" 3		3	53

no. 146

item Sauterne   min. 15 max. 60

Figure 14.7 Bin card

CELLAR ISSUES BOOK							
date	req. no.	particulars	bar		dispense		banqueting
Jan 1	003	6 bot. Chanti					66 00
" 1	003	2 bot. Dry Martini					38 00
" 2	004	3 bot. Gordon's Gin			84 00		
		etc.					

Figure 14.8 Cellar issues book

STOCKTAKING

Stocktaking is usually undertaken once a week. To facilitate speed in this routine task it is imperative to have well-designed stock sheets. One of the most important points in this connection is the sequencing of items. In some establishments the items are listed alphabetically under group headings such as breakfast cereals, canned meat, canned fruit, etc. In others all the items are shown alphabetically, irrespective of any grouping. What really matters is that the records should be adequately streamlined. If the foods in the store are kept so that each group of items is separate then we should have the same arrangement in the weekly issues book, keep the stock cards in that sequence and the same sequence in the stock sheets. A simple example of a stock sheet is given in Figure 14.9.

The stocktaking of beverages is an important, though time-consuming, task. In the majority of hospitality establishments it is undertaken at least once a month; this enables the control department to calculate the exact gross profit on beverage sales. The opportunity should be taken to make a note of slow-moving items, as idle beverage stocks can prove very costly to keep.

Pricing of issues

The stock of any one item of food may consist of several lots purchased over a period of time at different prices. Whenever an issue is made to a requisitioning department there is often the problem of which price should be charged. Several solutions are possible.

The usual procedure in most establishments is to charge out the perishables at the actual price paid to the supplier. This is a simple and commonsense solution, since most of the perishables are consumed within a day or two of delivery. Non-perishables are usually held over a period of weeks during which appreciable price fluctuations may take place. The methods of pricing of issues described below apply to all foodstuffs but, in practice, tend to be used mainly in relation to non-perishables.

STOCK SHEET

date *31 March 19..*

Item	qty.	unit price	£ p	Item	qty.	unit price	£ p
Breakfast Cereals							
All Bran	42	0.95	39.90				
Cornflakes	16	0.80	12.80				
Ready Brek	31	1.15	35.65				
Scott's Porage Oats	19	0.70	13.30				
Shredded Wheat	25	1.10	27.50				

Figure 14.9 Stock sheet

(1) Actual price

Food may be charged out at the actual price in two ways. Under the FIFO (first in, first out) method, food is issued from the lot earliest delivered and charged accordingly. Let us assume that there are 100 items of *x*. Of these 20 units were purchased some time ago at 20p per unit and the balance of 80 units was acquired later at 25p per unit. Two requisitions are received: the first for 15 units and the second for 25 units. The charge for the first issue would be

$$15 \times 20p = £3.00$$

The charge for the second issue would be

$$5 \times 20p = £1.00$$
$$20 \times 25p = \underline{\quad 5.00}$$
$$\underline{\underline{£6.00}}$$

Thus, during periods of inflation, whoever comes first gets the benefit of the lower price. Ultimately, whatever has been paid to suppliers is charged out to the requisitioning departments.

Under the LIFO (last in, first out) method the procedure is different. Issues of stock are still made so as to ensure satisfactory rotation of food and prevent perishing, but food is charged out at the latest prices. This ensures that the current price is charged in respect of the requisitions. Let us assume that there are 100 items of *y*: 60 purchased some time ago at 40p per unit, and 40 units acquired recently at 50p per unit. Two requisitions are received: the first for 30 units and the second for 40 units. The charge for the first issue would be 30 × 50p, i.e. £15.00. The charge for the second lot would be:

$$10 \times 50p = £\ 5.00$$
$$30 \times 40p = \ \ 12.00$$

Total £17.00

Both the FIFO and LIFO methods necessitate the keeping of detailed records and are rather infrequently used. They are nevertheless found in some larger units.

(2) Average price

This may be applied in two different ways: one may use a simple average or a weighted average. Let us assume that there are 100 units of *z* in stock: 60 units purchased at 20p and 40 units at 24p. If we used a simple average we would issue the stock at 22p per unit. The weighted average is more accurate because it takes into account the quantities purchased at different prices. With the weighted average method the charge per unit would be:

$$60 \text{ units at } 20p = £12.00$$
$$40 \text{ units at } 24p = \ \ 9.60$$

Therefore

$$\frac{(£12.00 + £9.60) = £21.60}{100} = 21.6p \text{ per unit}$$

The simple average method is rather less accurate and results in marginal over- and under-charging. There are, however, numerous items of food issued each day and the small discrepancies tend to cancel out. The weighted average method is accurate, but it involves time-consuming calculations. It is, therefore, less popular and less frequently used.

(3) Inflated price

This particular method of pricing food issues is not often used. It is, however, now and again applied in situations where it is desired to recover the cost of handling and storage charges. For instance, a small restaurant chain may establish a central purchasing department, and buy in large quantities for subsequent issue to the units operated by the company. To recover the cost of running the purchasing department, all food may be issued at cost plus, say, 10 per cent. A similar procedure could be applied in a large hotel or restaurant with a central meat preparation department.

PREPARING

Total food cost at the end of each trading period depends on two factors: the number of covers and the food cost per cover. It follows, therefore, that if we wish to control the cost of food we must use appropriate techniques to predict the number of covers that will be served. We must also be able to control, in advance of preparation, the cost of each food item. To predict the number of covers we use the technique of volume forecasting. To control the food cost of each menu item we use the technique of pre-costing.

Volume forecasting

The two principal aims of volume forecasting are:

(a) to predict the number of covers that will be served during the next trading period—usually one week
(b) to predict what choices will be made by the customers in relation to the menu items.

In other words, what we must do is this. We must estimate during the course of the current week how many customers will come to lunch and dinner on Monday, Tuesday, etc., throughout the next week. If we decide that 100 customers will come for lunch on Monday, we must then predict what these customers will choose from the menu: how many will have the first course and of those how many will have melon, how many soup, pâté, etc. The same predictions must be made for the main course including vegetables, the sweets, etc. What it amounts to is that we have to predict which menu items will be sold and how many of each.

Once the volume forecast has been made, the predicted quantities of menu items are converted into raw materials equivalents. Immediately, purchase orders are written out and sent to the suppliers to inform them what perishables they are to deliver each day of the following week. Normally, the non-perishables are replenished monthly, independently of the system of volume forecasting. A simple example of a volume forecast is shown in Figure 14.10.

A large hotel would normally have several outlets for its food: the dining room, floor service, banqueting department, etc. Many large hotels prepare a master volume forecast which predicts the number of covers for each outlet. A detailed volume forecast (similar to that shown in Figure 14.10 would then be prepared for each selling outlet. An example of a master volume forecast is given in Figure 14.11

Aids to volume forecasting

The most important aid to volume forecasting is the *sales history*. A sales history is, simply, a record of the number of portions sold of each menu item over a trading period. The period covered by a sales history is usually one, two or four weeks. Figure 14.12 illustrates a fairly typical sales history.

The advantages offered by sales histories are substantial. By studying a sales history we can see the principal trends and such relationships as: the

WINDSOR RESTAURANT
Volume Forecast: *Luncheons—Week 16*

Menu	Mon	Tue	Wed	Thu	Fri	Sat
Fruit juice	7	9	11	13	15	17
Honeydew melon	8	10	11	12	16	19
Lentil soup	5	6	8	10	12	16
Smoked salmon	6	6	7	10	12	15
Dover sole	7	8	10	12	18	24
Roast chicken	8	10	11	14	20	26
Mixed grill	10	10	12	15	20	27
Irish stew	5	7	7	9	12	13
Creamed potatoes	10	12	17	20	28	35
Fried potatoes	14	15	21	29	40	45
Cauliflower	20	23	29	37	50	60
Runner beans	15	17	22	25	36	40
Apple flan	10	11	14	18	24	31
Creme caramel	6	8	11	14	18	25
Peach melba	9	10	11	13	14	15
Total covers	30	35	40	50	70	90

Figure 14.10 Volume forecast for restaurant

percentage of the total number of customers who take the first course, the sweet, tea and coffee; the popularity of the various menu items; the pattern of business over the working week, etc.

Volume forecasting can never be 100 per cent correct. It is preferable, however, to predict subject to an error of 10–15 per cent than not attempt any predictions and, at the end of the day, find that a third of the food remains unsold.

Another important aid to volume forecasting is *cyclic menus*. A cyclic menu is one which normally covers a period of 10–28 days. With a ten-day cycle we have ten menus. We start with the menu for day 1 and, having served

EALING HOTEL
Master Volume Forecast—Week 22

		Sun	Mon	Tue	Wed	Thu	Fri	Sat
Room occupancy—%		40	65					
Restaurant:	Breakfast	90	135					
	Luncheon	220	340					
	Dinner	160	235					
Floor service:	Breakfast	430	645 etc.					
	Luncheon	20	33					
	Dinner	60	85					
Banqueting:	Luncheon	20	15					
	Dinner		30					
Total covers		1000	1518					

Figure 14.11 Master volume forecast for hotel

SALES HISTORY
Fortnight Commencing 1 May 19..

Menu item	Sun	Mon	Tue	Wed	Thu	Fri	Sat	Sun	Mon	Tue	Wed	Thu	Fri	Sat
Sea Food Cocktail	20	15	20	25	24	30	28	21	16	25	30	35	34	45
Chilled Melon	5	10	15	20	16	20	22	4	11	20	25	25	30	40
Quiche Lorraine	10	15	15	20	25	20	30	10	16	15	20	25	26	25
Consommé Croûte-en-pot	15	20	20	25	30	40	35	15	21	20	20	26	35	30
Filet of Brill Marguery	8	12	10	20	5	20	15	10	12	15	20	20	25	25
Scampi Provencale	10	4	15	20	19	20	25	8	18	20	20	25	35	45
Sweetbreads Maréchale	12	12	15	14	15	18	25	14	15	15	22	25	25	25
Sirloin Steak Belle Hélène	14	16	20	15	21	32	35	12	15	20	26	30	25	25
Charcoal Grilled Cutlets	6	6	10	21	25	20	15	6	5	10	7	11	15	20
New Potatoes	10	20	25	35	35	41	42	12	20	30	40	54	65	75
Parisienne Potatoes	12	10	15	18	20	29	31	10	18	20	25	26	30	40
Croquette Potatoes	25	25	25	35	38	39	42	25	27	28	30	30	30	25
Broccoli Spears	15	16	20	30	32	38	42	15	20	30	40	44	55	65
Braised Celery	15	14	18	25	28	32	28	17	20	28	30	36	40	50
Stuffed Tomatoes	17	19	21	35	34	36	41	15	25	22	25	30	30	25
Assorted Dairy Ice Creams	20	25	30	35	34	43	44	15	20	30	35	40	45	55
Sweets from the Trolley	15	20	2	28	32	37	46	20	25	35	45	55	60	70
English Cheeses	13	14	18	25	28	29	24	13	13	15	15	16	20	15
Coffee	48	57	68	87	95	106	112	50	65	78	95	111	125	138
Total Number of Covers	50	60	70	90	95	110	115	50	65	80	95	111	125	140

Figure 14.12 Sales history

the tenth menu, revert to menu 1, and so on. The main advantage of this arrangement is that there is a fixed pattern over time which facilitates the identification in trends and thus makes volume forecasting less difficult.

Pre-costing

Pre-costing is a technique whereby the food cost of each menu item is predetermined prior to food preparation. The most important instrument of pre-costing is the *standard recipe*.

A standard recipe must be distinguished from a basic or international recipe. The latter gives general guidance on the preparation of a menu item. It is not a recipe designed for any particular type of customer, and is in practice interpreted differently by different chefs. A standard recipe is one which has been prepared for use in a particular establishment. It follows, therefore, that it must necessarily take into account the type of customer, his or her spending power, etc. A standard recipe will show in detail the ingredients, the method of preparation and the standard cost per portion. The latter should be based on periodic standard purchase prices, as explained earlier in this chapter.

Apart from their pre-costing function, standard recipes offer several other advantages: they facilitate buying and the preparation of food; they enable the establishment to offer a standard product and thus ensure a high degree of permanency in the gastronomic standards of the establishment. An example of a standard recipe is given in Figure 14.13.

The fourth stage of the control cycle—'preparing'—is most critical in the case of food. Over production results in waste which has an adverse effect on gross profit. Where insufficient food is prepared, customers have to be satisfied with a second choice which tends to prejudice customer loyalty. With regard to beverages, there is hardly any 'preparing' or processing done. We purchase quantities of beverages in larger units and sell these—normally in the same form—in smaller units. The similarity with retailing is rather obvious. Now and again the barman will mix a cocktail, but this will be taken care of by an appropriate recipe and constitutes a small proportion of total beverage sales. Pre-costing in the case of beverages, though easier than in the case of food, is essential. Volume forecasting is not, as we are not dealing with perishable items.

SELLING

We now come to the last stage of the control cycle. Let us start with pricing.

As indicated in earlier chapters, before an establishment is opened it is essential to formulate its price policy. From the point of view of operational food cost control this means that the management will have already decided on the basic price level for its food operations; management will also have decided on the overall gross profit on food sales as well as the differential profit margins for the various elements of the food sales mix.

In day-to-day food operations we do not, therefore, have to concern ourselves with basic pricing decisions. We do, however, have to ensure that, at the end of each trading period, actual profit margins are as close as possible to those predetermined by management. At this stage of the food cost control cycle pricing is a routine matter. We know what gross profit is to be achieved on any one menu item. By reference to the appropriate standard recipe we may ascertain the standard food cost per portion—the rest is simple arithmetic.

Restaurant checking systems

Most hotels and restaurants operate some kind of checking system. There is a variety of systems in operation, but they all tend to fall into three categories

STANDARD RECIPE no. *136*

Name of item: *Bitoks à la Russe*

Quantity	Unit Cost	Cost of Ingredients	Ingredients	Method of Preparation
1.500kg	£2.60	£3.90	Beef—thick flank	1. Mince beef and pork finely.
0.500kg	2.20	1.10	Pork—shoulder	2. Chop onions finely and sauté in beef dripping, allow to cool.
0.500kg	0.80	0.40	Onions	3. Soak crumbs in milk for 10 mins, then add to beef, pork and onions in a large bowl.
0.060kg	0.64	0.04	Beef dripping	4. Add whole eggs, salt, pepper, nutmeg and parsley, mix to a smooth paste.
0.700kg	0.72	0.50	White breadcrumbs	5. Weigh out into portions.
¾ l	0.36	0.27	Milk	6. Dust with flour, shape like tournedos
0.060kg	2.50	0.16	Chopped parsley	7. Sauté on both sides in clarified butter.
4	0.08	0.32	Eggs—standard	8. Place in serving dish and coat with sauce smitaine.
0.060kg	0.30	0.02	Salt	
0.030kg	3.00	0.10	White pepper	
0.007kg	4.00	0.04	Nutmeg	
0.250kg	0.30	0.08	Plain flour	
0.500kg	1.60	0.80	Cooking butter	

Total Cost	£7.73	Portion size:	Other information:
No. of Portions	30	raw weight 0.115kg	cooking temperature: stove top
Portion Cost	£0.26	cooked weight –	cooking time: 10 mins.

Figure 14.13 Standard recipe

depending on the number of checks (i.e. food and beverage requisitions) produced by the waiter.

With the 'single checking system' only one copy of the check is produced, and this is sent either to the kitchen or the dispense bar. In the case of the 'duplicate checking system' there are two copies of the check; one copy is sent to the cashier who uses such checks to write up customers' bills: the other copy serves as a food or beverage requisition. The 'triplicate checking system' is used predominantly in high-ASP establishments. The three copies of the check are used as follows: one goes to the cashier; one is sent to the kitchen or dispense bar; the third copy is kept by the station head waiter to remind him of what menu items have been ordered by the guests.

Cash and credit sales

At the end of each service the cashier will have to prepare a summary of cash and credit sales, and both these elements have to be checked thoroughly. With regard to cash sales, the total of such sales will have to agree with the total of cash taken—after, of course, taking into account the cashier's floats. In the case of credit sales it will be necessary to ensure that copies of all bills are sent to the accounts department and debited to the personal accounts of the customers concerned.

TOTAL OR SELECTIVE CHECKING?

Many establishments—particularly larger hotels—maintain large control departments. In some cases a high proportion of the total work done in the control department consists of the verification of charges made to customers. After each service copies of the checks received by the kitchen, dispense bar and the cashier as well as all copies of customers' bills arrive in the control office. All checks are then compared with the items detailed on customers' bills to ensure that there are no over-charges or under-charges.

This total checking approach was widely practised until quite recently. Rising labour costs, however, tend to make this practice prohibitive and currently many establishments are changing over to selective checking. It makes little sense to employ a control clerk at £200 per week who, after one week's work, will have discovered under- and over-charges to the value of £10, and frequently after the departure of the customers concerned.

Most large and medium-sized establishments have now installed a fully computerized control system that includes revenue control. Most systems in operation offer a number of advantages, amongst which speed and accuracy feature prominently. Also, a computerized revenue control system facilitates the preparation of periodic reports and operating statistics.

Computerized systems of revenue control have done away with the need for large control departments; and have produced a situation that is far less labour-intensive. Where, therefore, there is a comprehensive computerized system of revenue control the problem of selective checking no longer exists. We control all the revenue and do so effectively and speedily.

FOOD AND BEVERAGE TRANSFERS

At the end of each trading period it is essential to ascertain the separate results achieved by the food and beverage operations. Food sales and beverage sales are invariably recorded separately; also, food stocks are kept separately from beverage stocks. It is the cost of food and beverages consumed that requires our attention. During the course of each trading period we have a number of what are known as 'food and beverage transfers'. A few examples are given below.

(a) Food consumed by the employee. The cost of employee meals should not be included in the cost of food sales but treated as a cost of labour (and usually debited to the Employee Benefits A/c).

(b) Any wine transferred to the kitchen requires a similar adjustment: the cost of such wine should be deducted from beverage cost and added to food cost.

(c) Frequently, smaller amounts of food are transferred to the bar, e.g. nuts, crisps, oranges, lemons, etc. The cost of such food should be credited to (deducted from) food cost and debited to (added to) beverage cost.

(d) Food and beverages are occasionally used for entertaining business associates, travel agents, etc. Where hospitality of this nature is offered, the net value of such food and beverage (i.e. the sales value minus the gross profit loading) should be deducted from food cost and beverage cost and added to an appropriate account (e.g. Marketing A/c, Public Relations A/c). Where food and beverages are used for a staff party, the cost of such food and beverages should be deducted from food cost and beverage cost and added to the cost of 'employee benefits.'

It is only after making the appropriate adjustments in respect of food and beverage transfers that we are able to arrive at the net cost of food and beverages consumed. Where such adjustments are ignored, the resulting figures of gross profit on food and beverages cannot be accurate.

Example

The following figures were extracted from the books of the Magnolia Restaurant at 31 December 1998.

	Food £	*Beverages* £
Sales	820,000	285,000
Purchases	305,000	105,000

You are required to make appropriate adjustments in respect of the food and beverage transfers shown below and calculate the gross profit on food and beverage operations.

(a) The cost of employee meals was £13,100.
(b) Wines used for cooking amounted to £7,800.
(c) Food transferred to the cocktail bar amounted to £1,900.

(d) Hospitality offered by the restaurant to business associates cost, at selling price: food £1,000 and beverages £625. Assume that the gross profit loading was 60 per cent.

You are informed that opening stocks were: food £10,500 and beverages £14,200. Closing stocks were: food £11,200 and beverages £18,400.

The net cost of food sales was:

		£
Opening stock		10,500
Add purchases		305,000
		315,500
Less closing stock		11,200
Cost of food consumed		304,300
Add wines for cooking		7,800
		312,100
Less employee meals	£13,100	
food for cocktail bar	1,900	
food for hospitality (40% of £1,000)	400	15,400
Net cost of food sales		296,700

The net cost of beverage sales was:

		£
Opening stock		14,200
Add purchases		105,000
		119,200
Less closing stock		18,400
Cost of beverages consumed		100,800
Add food consumed		1,900
		102,700
Less wines for cooking	£7,800	
wines for hospitality (40% of £625)	250	8,050
Net cost of beverage sales		94,650

We are now able to calculate the gross profits:

	Food sales		Beverage sales	
	£	%	£	%
Sales	820,000	100.0	285,000	100.0
Less net cost of sales	296,700	36.2	94,650	33.2
Gross Profit	523,300	63.8	190,350	66.8

BEVERAGE CONTROL

We have so far in this chapter concentrated very largely on food control. Techniques such as yield testing, volume forecasting and standard recipes are relevant to food rather than beverage control. Yet, clearly, beverage sales are not only an important part of the sales mix of hospitality establishments but also more profitable than food sales. A brief description of beverage control is, therefore, now offered.

As far as gross profit control is concerned, there are two distinctly different approaches possible. In some establishments it will be decided on the basis of past experience what percentage of beverage gross profit should be achieved. This percentage is then used as a target, and is sometimes described as 'standard gross profit'. Subsequently, from one week/month to another, the periodic actual gross profit will be compared to the standard gross profit. Any variances between the standard and actual gross profits will then be investigated. An example is shown in Figure 14.14.

From Figure 14.14 we can see that the restaurant expects the beverage operation to produce a gross profit of 60.0 per cent. During the month under review the actual gross profit was 58.5 per cent, and there was a negative variance of 1.5 per cent.

A more analytical and therefore effective approach to gross profit control is to rely on the concept of *potential sales value*. An example will make this clear. If we buy a bottle of Scotch at £12.00 and sell it as thirty individual tots at £1.20 each, the sales value potential is (30 × £ 1.20) £36.00 (and the beverage gross profit £24.00).

With this approach, every time beverages are requisitioned from the cellar, their value is debited to the bar concerned at selling price. Every time, therefore, a bottle of Scotch is transferred to a bar and subsequently sold, we

CHERRY BLOSSOM RESTAURANT
Report on Beverage Operations, May 19..

	This month		Last month	
	£	%	£	%
Opening stocks	4,830		5,250	
Add Purchases	13,440		13,020	
	18,270		18,270	
Less Closing stocks	6,930		6,300	
Cost of beverage sales	11,340	41.5	11,970	42.2
Sales	27,300		28,350	
Less Actual beverage cost	11,340	41.5	11,970	42.2
Actual gross profit	15,960	58.5	16,380	57.8
Standard gross profit	16,380	60.0	17,010	60.0
Variance	(420)	(1.5)	(630)	(2.2)

Figure 14.14 Beverage trading account

should see an increase in the level of cash, £36.00. With this method of control we know exactly how much cash should have been taken and how much gross profit earned. It should be noted that with computerized procedures this method of control presents no problem as all the necessary data are always available.

Example

A cocktail bar sells a limited range of drinks. The table in Figure 14.15 shows the relevant portion costs, selling prices and the number of drinks sold. From this information we arrive at the potential beverage cost, the sales value potential as well as the potential gross profit. The totals in columns 5, 6 and 7 are standards against which we should compare actual results. We can see that the cocktail bar should have taken cash amounting to £15,430; it should have incurred a beverage cost of £3,779.85 and earned a gross profit of £11,650.15.

Let us assume that the actual results for the control period in question were:

	£	%
Sales (takings)	15,290.00	100.0
Less Beverage cost	3,810.00	24.9
Gross profit	11,480.00	75.1

It is clear that the cash actually taken was £140 less than potential takings. The cost of sales was £30.15 more than potential beverage cost and, finally, actual gross profit was £170.15 less than potential gross profit.

OPERATIONAL ANALYSIS

In addition to the routine controls already described in this chapter, it is desirable to undertake, either routinely or occasionally, further analyses of various aspects of the food and beverage operation. Whether such analyses are regarded as routine or *ad hoc* depends on the circumstances and requirements of each business.

Much emphasis was placed in Chapter 10 on the interpretation of the PM profile which, it will be remembered, indicated the relative impact of each key factor on the net profit of a business. The PM profile is always a good and reliable guide to the kind of operational analyses that should be undertaken.

Thus in the case of a restaurant it may be found that the sales volume profit multiplier has a relatively high value. This would point to the need for effective and comprehensive controls of the number of covers and average spending power—both of which are determinants of the sales volume. Establishments which experience substantial fluctuations in their food and beverage sales may find that they need particularly effective controls over their labour costs to ensure satisfactory profitability; and appropriate routine controls would then be introduced with a view to ensuring a sufficient degree of adjustment of labour costs to the ever-changing sales volume. Finally, in cost-oriented operations the cost of sales and direct labour are usually

COCKTAIL BAR
Analysis of beverage operations for June 19..

Description	Portion cost	Selling price	Portions sold	Potential bev. cost	Potential sales value	Potential gross prft
(1)	(2)	(3)	(4)	(5)	(6)	(7)
	£	£	–	£	£	£
Scotch	0.40	1.60	2,150	860.00	3,440.00	2,580.00
Gin and tonic	0.38	1.50	2,070	786.60	3,105.00	2,318.40
Vodka	0.35	1.40	1,050	367.50	1,470.00	1,102.50
Napoleon brandy	0.42	1.70	1,525	640.50	2,592.50	1,952.00
Martini and soda	0.35	1.50	3,125	1,125.25	4,822.50	3,697.25
				3,779.85	15,430.00	11,650.15

Figure 14.15 Use of potential sales value concept

represented by relatively high profit multipliers; and this points to strict, and ideally routine, controls over these two categories of expense.

A full treatment of operational analysis of food and beverage operations would be outside the scope of this chapter; and, therefore, a few selected examples are given to indicate the main types of operational analysis that should be undertaken.

ASP and NoC analysis

The volume of sales has, in all kinds of food and beverage operations, a powerful impact on profitability. As already suggested, therefore, strict control should be exercised over both average spending power and the number of covers. The table in Figure 14.16 illustrates a simple, yet useful, method of calculating and monitoring the relevant weekly and monthly figures. An additional advantage of the analysis is that we are able to predict for each day of the week the number of covers and in this way adjust the number of waiting staff accordingly.

Waiters' sales mix and ASP performance

There is a great deal of difference between the periodic calculation of sales mix or ASP figures and the actual of the sales mix or ASP of an operation. Implicit in the concept of control is not only the strict monitoring of the relevant figures but also the taking of swift positive measures to correct any undesirable trend. A number of hotels and restaurants have recently started controlling the sales mix and ASP achieved by individual waiters, as it is the effect of each waiter's sales effort that determines the total overall results for the business as a whole.

OPERATIONAL ANALYSIS: ASP and NoC
Month 4 ended 5th November 19..

	Monday		Tuesday		Wednesday		Thursday		Friday		Saturday	
	£	NoC	£	NoC	£	NoC	£	NoC	£	NoC	£	NoC
Week 1	801	103	960	121	1,320	165	1,310	169	1,770	201	675	82
Week 2	855	107	1,020	125	1,251	174	1,265	161	1,902	219	594	77
Week 3	891	110	950	115	1,305	159	1,292	165	1,907	223	709	91
Week 4	820	99	1,035	127	1,271	160	1,245	163	1,820	215	640	82
Monthly totals	3,367	419	3,965	488	5,147	658	5,112	658	7,399	858	2,618	332
Weekly averages	842	105	991	122	1,287	165	1,278	165	1,850	215	655	83
Average spending power	£8.02		£8.12		£7.80		£7.75		£8.60		£7.89	

Figure 14.16 ASP and NoC analysis

WAITERS' SALES ANALYSIS
Week ended: 31 January 19..

Name		Starters	Main course	Sweets, teas, coffee	Beverages	Total sales	NoC	ASP
Brown, Jack	£	225	825	150	300	1,500	125	12.00
	%	15.0	55.0	10.0	20.0	100.0	—	—
Davies, Ron	£	288	784	192	336	1,600	131	12.21
	%	18.0	49.0	12.0	21.0	100.0	—	—
Finney, Phillip	£	168	868	126	238	1,400	119	11.76
	%	12.0	62.0	9.0	17.0	100.0	—	—
Jennings, Paul	£	252	686	168	294	1,400	114	12.28
	%	18.0	49.0	12.0	21.0	100.0	—	—
Lipsey, Fred	£	204	648	132	216	1,200	103	11.65
	%	17.0	54.0	11.0	18.0	100.0	—	—
Total sales	£	1,137	3,811	768	1,384	7,100	592	11.99
	%	16.0	53.7	10.8	19.5	100.0	—	—

Figure 14.17 Waiters' sales analysis

Figure 14.17 shows a convenient and effective method of controlling not only the number of covers and the ASP, but also the sales mix of each member of the waiting staff.

Weekly sales analysis

All hotels and restaurants should, in accordance with the concept of revenue accounting, complete a detailed weekly sales analysis. This may take various forms and the suggested layout in Figure 14.18 may be adapted to suit a variety of different operational requirements. It is stressed again that the figures produced should be studied and acted upon. In this example Friday and Saturday are, clearly, the busiest days. Although we have a high number of covers per waiter, we also have relatively low ASP figures. This may suggest that the five waiters available are unable to provide the kind of service which is conducive to a satisfactory sales effort. One should, in such circumstances, investigate the desirability of employing more waiting staff. Quite frequently it is found that the additional cost of labour is easily offset by the resulting benefits of improved service to guests, and higher levels of ASP.

Different waiters achieve different levels of ASP. Thus Jennings sells (£12.28−£11.65)= 63p per cover more than Lipsey; and in view of the very different ASP figures it is clear that there must be under-achievement in terms of the total sales volume of the business.

Waiters who make the effort to sell the starters, sweets, teas and coffees tend generally to achieve a high level of individual ASP.

As starters, sweets, teas, and coffee are ordinarily sold at above-average gross profit margins what matters is not only the total volume of food and beverage sales, but also the sales mix actually achieved. Finney and Jennings both sold food and beverages of £1,400, but because the latter secured a more favourable sales mix he must have made a greater contribution to total gross profit.

WEEKLY SALES ANALYSIS
Week ended: 3 MAY 19..

	Mon	Tue*	Wed	Thu	Fri	Sat	Total
No. of covers	61	71	82	101	145	160	620
	£	£	£	£	£	£	£
Food sales	620	740	825	1,050	1,470	1,620	6,325
Beverage sales	300	320	350	440	630	690	2,730
Total sales	920	1,060	1,175	1,490	2,100	2,310	9,055
ASP—food	10.16	10.42	10.06	10.40	10.14	10.12	10.20
ASP—beverage	4.92	4.51	4.27	4.35	4.34	4.31	4.40
ASP—total	15.08	14.93	14.33	14.75	14.48	14.34	14.60
No. of waiters	4	4	4	5	5	5	—
Sales per waiter	£230	£265	£294	£298	£420	£462	—
Covers per waiter	15.3	17.8	20.5	20.2	29.0	32.0	—

Figure 14.18 Weekly sales analysis

PROBLEMS

1. Write a short essay on the objectives of food and beverage control.
2. (a) Identify the principal stages of the food and beverage control cycle.

(b) Comment on the relative importance of each stage in
  (i) a high-ASP restaurant
  (ii) an industrial canteen.

3. Write short, explanatory notes on

(a) methods of buying
(b) product testing
(c) yield testing.

4. Explain in detail how you would undertake a yield test for canned fruit salad.
5. Write a purchase specification for

(a) lamb cutlets
(b) broilers.

State clearly what assumptions you have made.
  6. Design a complete set of stock records for a large, medium-ASP restaurant.
  7. Explain what you understand by

(a) LIFO
(b) FIFO.

  8. Design a system of volume forecasting for a 200-bedroomed hotel.
  9. Prepare a standard recipe for any item of your choice. Describe in detail the type of customer for whom it is intended.
10. Distinguish clearly between basic and standard recipes.
11. Set out below are particulars of food and beverage sales and covers served by five waiters in respect of Week 5.

Waiter	Starters	Main course	Sweets	Teas & coffees	Beverages	No. of covers
	£	£	£	£	£	
Adam	215	795	90	70	270	128
Brian	165	830	60	65	270	122
Charles	245	815	115	90	295	131
Dennis	180	810	105	75	250	124
Edward	145	845	75	65	210	126

You are required to prepare a Waiters' Sales Analysis which will show clearly:

(a) the total volume of food and beverage sales for each waiter and the establishment
(b) individual waiters' and total sales mix
(c) individual waiters' and total ASP.

Also comment on the relative performance of the individual waiters.
12. Compare and contrast the problems faced in food cost control and beverage cost control.

13. From the data given below prepare the Bar Trading A/c for the months of May and June 19...

	May £	June £
Beverage sales	22,500	26,800
Opening stock	26,700	20,100
Closing stock	20,100	18,300
Purchases	4,100	9,600
Beverages for cooking	240	260
Staff disco	130	140
Entertaining	260	280
Head office	240	160
Cooks' beer	140	180
Spoilage	20	10

14. The following figures were extracted from the records of the Pacific Restaurant at 31 December 1999:

	Food £	Beverages £
Sales	395,000	130,400
Purchases	142,700	47,900

You are required to make appropriate adjustments in respect of the food and beverage transfers listed below. Also calculate the gross profit on food and on beverage operations.

(a) The cost of employee meals was £6,900.
(b) Wines used for cooking amounted to £3,400.
(c) Food transferred to the cocktail bar amounted to £850.
(d) Hospitality offered to tour operators and travel agents cost, at selling price, food £2,000 and beverages £1,250. You are informed that the food and beverage gross profit loading is to be taken at 60 per cent.

Opening stocks were: food £5,400, beverages £6,900. Closing stocks were valued as follows: food £5,200, beverages £8,700.

Accounting and operating ratios 15

When planning a new hospitality establishment, or subsequently measuring its performance, certain essential relationships between various quantities are to be expected. Thus we expect a certain relationship between capital employed and net profit; between net sales and net profit; between rooms available and rooms occupied, etc. All such relationships may be expressed by means of ratios. Where a hotel has 200 employees and 100 rooms the ratio of employees to rooms is 2:1. Where food sales are £1,000 and the resulting gross profit is £600, there is a gross profit ratio of 10:6 or 60 per cent.

KINDS OF RATIOS

In each hospitality establishment it is possible to calculate dozens of different ratios, and some of these will inevitably be more meaningful than others. Also different ratios measure different kinds of relationships. It is useful, therefore, to classify ratios according to various criteria.

An *accounting ratio* is one which is calculated in respect of a longer period, say six or twelve months, and is derived from the balance sheet or profit and loss account. Examples of accounting ratios are return on capital employed, net profit ratio, current ratio, etc.

An *operating ratio* is calculated in respect of a short period, typically a day, week or month and is based on information obtained from various reports, documents and operating statements. Examples of operating ratios are ratios of occupancy, gross profit, sales mix, average spending power, etc.

It should be realized that some ratios may be both accounting and operating ratios. Thus gross profit and net profit ratios may be either accounting or operating ratios depending on how frequently they are calculated and whether they were derived from the profit and loss account or some weekly operating statistics.

Operating ratios, because they are calculated in respect of short periods, enable management to take swift remedial action. When, for instance, it is found at the end of a week that the hotel's bar profit is unsatisfactory, management may take immediate action designed to prevent further losses of bar profit in subsequent weeks.

A *balance sheet ratio* is an accounting ratio derived from the balance sheet. Examples of balance sheet ratios are return on capital employed, current ratio and acid test ratio.

A *profit and loss ratio* is an accounting ratio derived from the profit and loss account. Examples of such ratios are net profit ratio, gross profit ratio and ratios of departmental and operating expenses to net sales.

Finally, ratios may be divided into *cost-based* and *revenue-based* ratios. The former deal with costs in relation to net sales; the latter are concerned with the revenue side of the business. Examples of cost-based ratios are food cost in relation to food sales, beverage cost in relation to beverage sales, departmental payroll in relation to departmental sales, etc. Examples of revenue-based ratios are net profit ratio, gross profit ratio, average spending power, average room rate, sales mix, etc.

In addition to the ratios referred to already many hospitality establishments produce statistics relating to matters such as sales per room available, sales per seat available, sales per employee, etc. Strictly speaking such figures are neither accounting nor operating ratios and should be referred to as *operating statistics*.

CHOICE OF RATIOS

It will be readily appreciated that the choice of appropriate ratios for planning and control purposes must be influenced by the orientation of the business. As already explained, market-oriented businesses are very dependent on consumer demand and their profitability is greatly influenced by the price level and the volume of sales. Hence in all market-oriented businesses a great deal of prominence should be given to revenue-based ratios.

Taking the hospitality industry as a whole, it will be realized that the ratios used by different sectors of the industry will vary considerably. In hotels and restaurants a great deal of importance will be attached to ratios such as the rate of occupancy, average spending power, average room rate and sales mix. In establishments which tend to be more cost-oriented (e.g. industrial and staff canteens) cost-based ratios will be regarded as at least as critical as revenue-based ratios.

ACCOUNTING RATIOS

Return on capital employed

This particular ratio measures the relationship between net profit and capital employed. As explained in Chapter 9, this is the most important single measure of profitability. The formula to be applied is

$$\frac{\text{Net profit (£20,000)}}{\text{Capital employed (£100,000)}} \times 100 = 20\%$$

The figure of net profit may be either before or after tax. The figure of capital employed is usually defined as total assets less current liabilities.

Capital gearing ratio

The term 'gearing' refers to the relationship between ordinary share capital and fixed interest capital such as preference shares and debentures. A company which has a high proportion of fixed interest capital in relation to ordinary share capital (equity capital) is said to be 'highly geared'. Where that is so, small changes in net profit will have a substantial effect on the profits available to ordinary shareholders. When a new business is being planned, it is essential to ensure that the proportions of fixed interest and equity capital are right, as too high a proportion of preference shares and other fixed interest capital may result in undue fluctuations in the profits available to ordinary shareholders. The formula to be used is

$$\frac{\text{Equity capital (£300,000)}}{\text{Fixed interest capital (£100,000)}} = 3:1$$

A capital gearing ratio of $3:1$ would usually be regarded as satisfactory. On the other hand, a ratio of $1:3$ would tend to indicate an unduly high proportion of fixed interest capital, likely to result in pronounced fluctuations in ordinary dividends.

Net profit ratio

This measures the relationship between net profit and net sales. The formula is

$$\frac{\text{Net profit (£25,000)}}{\text{Net sales (£100,000)}} \times 100 = 25\%$$

It is not easy to suggest what net profit ratio should be aimed at in any one business. Most hotels and restaurants tend to aim at 20–25 per cent. The exact ratio must ultimately depend on the special circumstances of each business as indeed its asset turnover—as explained in Chapter 9.

Gross profit ratio

This measures the relationship between gross profit and net sales. The formula is

$$\frac{\text{Gross profit (£60,000)}}{\text{Net sales (£100,000)}} \times 100 = 60\%$$

Gross profit is defined as net sales less the cost of food sold, after making an appropriate allowance for the cost of staff meals, which should be regarded as part of the cost of labour. Gross profit on beverage sales is often referred to as 'bar profit', and is calculated in the same manner.

Gross profit margins vary considerably in hotels and restaurants. In the case of food sales gross profit normally varies between 50 per cent and 70 per cent. In general, the higher the ASP the higher the gross profit margin. Banqueting food sales attract a somewhat higher percentage of gross profit than à la carte sales. The latter usually produce a rather higher percentage of gross profit than table d'hôte sales.

The gross profit on beverage sales is a similar percentage to that on food sales. The overall percentage of bar profit depends largely on the level of prices charged as well as on the sales mix. The higher the proportion of beers, minerals and soft drinks to total beverage sales, the lower the overall percentage of bar profit. On the other hand, where spirits and fortified wines constitute a high proportion of beverage sales, the overall gross profit will tend to be quite high.

With regard to the minor operated departments, gross profit margins will invariably be lower than those on food and beverage sales. What actual percentage should be expected depends essentially on what is being sold: the gross profit on flowers, gifts, theatre tickets, etc. will not normally be uniform. Hence each establishment must decide for itself what results should be expected.

Current ratio

The current ratio measures the relationship between current assets and current liabilities. Thus where current assets amount to £3,000 and current liabilities are £2,000, the current ratio is 3 : 2. Working capital is the difference between current assets and current liabilities and, in the above example, amounts to £1,000. The current ratio may also be expressed by using the following formula:

$$\frac{\text{Current assets (£3,000)}}{\text{Current liabilities (£2,000)}} = 1.5$$

In very general terms, hospitality companies need less working capital than firms and companies in the manufacturing industries, though clearly an excess of current assets over current liabilities is required. A more detailed treatment of working capital will be found in Chapter 18.

Acid test ratio

This measures the relationship between liquid assets and current liabilities. Liquid assets are cash and current assets which are easily convertible into cash. Traditionally, stocks are not included in liquid assets, but one could argue that, in the case of food and beverage stocks, conversion into cash is considerably easier than the conversion of raw materials in the manufacturing industries. The formula for the calculation of the acid test ratio is

$$\frac{\text{Liquid assets (£2,400)}}{\text{Current liabilities (£2,000)}} = 1.2$$

Current liabilities are a claim on the resources of the business. Liquid assets are the resources available to meet such claims. Quite clearly, therefore, whatever the nature of the business the acid test ratio should be at least 1 : 1. Where it is less than 1 : 1 the business is not in a position to meet its immediate commitments.

Rate of stock turnover

The rate of stock turnover measures the speed with which stocks move through the business. A high rate of stock turnover indicates low stocks in relation to the volume of sales; and, conversely, a low rate of stock turnover indicates that high stocks are being kept in relation to the volume of sales. The formula which is easiest to apply is

$$\frac{\text{Cost of sales (\pounds 40,000)}}{\text{Average stock at cost (\pounds 1,000)}} = 40 \text{ (times)}$$

In the case of food operations the rate of stock turnover will usually vary between 30 and 50, which means that the typical stock of food held by the establishment is usually re-sold or replenished between 30 and 50 times a year. The exact rate of stock turnover will depend on factors such as the type of menu, methods of purchasing, storage space available, etc.

With regard to beverage sales, the position is rather different. Many hotels and restaurants (particularly high-ASP establishments) consider it imperative to maintain a good cellar. Wines and spirits are not perishable commodities and, during inflationary periods, it is often a good investment to keep wines and spirits in the cellar rather than hold cash balances, even on deposit. In many popular, low-ASP establishments, the rate of stock turnover for beverages is in the region of 12, which means that the average stock is replenished monthly. In high-ASP establishments the rate of stock turnover is considerably lower, frequently in the region of 4–6.

Average collection period

This measures the speed with which debts are collected from customers. Let us assume that a non-seasonal restaurant has annual credit sales of £26,000 and that debtors at the end of the year amount to £1,500. The average collection period may be calculated as follows:

| Annual credit sales | £26,000 |
| Therefore, credit sales per week | £500 |

Hence:

$$\frac{\text{Debtors (\pounds 1,500)}}{\text{Credit sales per week (\pounds 500)}} = 3 \text{ weeks}$$

It is not easy to suggest what the average collection period should be in any particular type of business, as much depends on the special circumstances of each case. In some hotels the average length of stay is only 2–3 days; in others it may well be over one week. The longer the average length of stay the larger the figure of debtors at any time and the longer the average collection period. Much also depends on the sales mix of the establishment. A high proportion of banqueting business is done on credit. The higher the proportion of banqueting sales the higher, clearly, the average collection period. Similar considerations apply in the case of food and beverage sales to non-residents who have arranged credit facilities with the establishment.

Whatever the special circumstances of a business, it is essential to formulate a credit policy to ensure that debts are collected speedily. The slower the process of debt collection the greater the likelihood of bad debts.

Average payment period

This is a similar concept to the average collection period. The average payment period measures the period of credit received from the suppliers. It is calculated by dividing the figure of creditors by the average credit purchases per week, e.g.

$$\frac{\text{Creditors (£1,400)}}{\text{Credit purchases per week (£200)}} = 7 \text{ weeks}$$

A long average payment period is not necessarily a blessing. When suppliers' accounts are not paid within the discount period cash discounts may be lost; and the loss thus incurred may be greater than the benefit resulting from a longer average payment period.

OPERATING RATIOS

Hotel occupancy

Traditionally hotel occupancy has been measured in two ways. *Room occupancy* measures the relationship between rooms available and rooms occupied. Where a hotel has 200 rooms and of these 130 are occupied, the rate of room occupancy is

$$\frac{\text{Rooms occupied (130)}}{\text{Rooms available (200)}} \times 100 = 65\%$$

Guest occupancy, on the other hand, measures the relationship between guest capacity and the number of guests. The formula is

$$\frac{\text{No. of guests (180)}}{\text{Guest capacity (300)}} \times 100 = 60\%$$

Guest occupancy is generally regarded as the more accurate measure of hotel occupancy, as double rooms are sometimes sold as singles and this is not reflected in the percentage of room occupancy.

Guest occupancy, though more accurate than room occupancy, is open to criticism too. A double room will not normally fetch the price of two single rooms. Hence the same percentage of guest occupancy can result in different amounts of room sales, depending on whether beds are sold mainly in double or single rooms. Another disadvantage of these two measures of hotel occupancy is that it ignores the price level of the hotel. When room rates are stable over a period of time a given percentage of occupancy has a particular meaning in terms of room sales. During periods of price competition (sometimes associated with excessive room capacity), hotels frequently offer substantial discounts on room sales, not only to tour operators but also to individual clients. In such circumstances a given percentage of occupancy is rather meaningless unless one also knows the average room rate.

In addition to the two traditional measures of hotel occupancy, three other measures/indicators have recently been used, particularly by the larger hotel companies.

Yield

This expresses actual room sales as a percentage of potential room sales. This indicator is especially useful in situations where substantial discounts are offered by hotels to tour operators, industrial and commercial clients—companies as well as individuals. For this purpose 'potential yield' means the volume of rooms sales that would be achieved if all rooms were sold at published tariffs. Where, therefore, a hotel may potentially take £8,000 per day, and its actual rooms sales are £6,000, the percentage yield is:

$$\frac{\text{Actual room sales (£6,000)}}{\text{Potential room sales (£8,000)}} \times 100 = 75\% \text{ (yield)}$$

Example

A hotel has 100 rooms priced as follows:

		£
(a) 60 singles, priced at £40	=	2,400
(b) 40 doubles, priced at £50	=	2,000
Room sales potential, per day	=	£4,400

On 17 May 19 . . actual room sales are as follows:

		£
Singles:		
20 sold at £20 each	£400	
20 sold at £30 each	600	
10 sold at £40 each	400	1,400
Doubles:		
20 sold at £25 each	£500	
10 sold at £45 each	450	
5 sold at £50 each	250	1,200
Actual room sales	=	£2,600

The hotel had a high percentage of room occupancy:

$$\frac{\text{Rooms occupied (85)}}{\text{Rooms available (100)}} \times 100 = 85.0\%$$

yet, because of heavy discounting, its percentage yield was only

$$\frac{\text{Actual room sales (£2,600)}}{\text{Potential room sales (£4,400)}} \times 100 = 59.1\%$$

Where the practice of discounting is quite prevalent, it is essential to report to management both indicators (room occupancy and percentage yield to ensure a realistic and balanced view of the performance of the rooms department.

Room density index (RDI)

This measures the relationship between the number of guests and occupied rooms. When we have 120 guests in 100 rooms, the RDI is

$$\frac{\text{No. of guests (120)}}{\text{Occupied rooms (100)}} = 1.2$$

The room density index is normally used as an alternative to the percentage of double occupancy, which is described below.

Percentage double occupancy

The percentage of double occupancy shows the proportion of rooms sold as doubles rather than singles. If we sell 200 rooms, and of these 50 as doubles, our percentage of double occupancy is 25 per cent. It should be noted that we are not concerned with available but occupied rooms only. An easy formula for calculating double occupancy is given below.

No. of guests	120
Less Occupied rooms	80
Double occupied rooms	40

In this particular case we sold 80 rooms and of these 40 as doubles: our double occupancy percentage is, therefore, 50 per cent.

Statistics of double occupancy are maintained for two main reasons. First, we need to know projected double occupancy levels in determining room rates. Secondly, double occupancy has an obvious effect on profitability, as a room sold as a double will normally fetch a higher price than when it is sold as a single. Most British and European city hotels tend to achieve a double occupancy of 20–40 per cent. Resort hotels, on the other hand, tend to secure very high levels of double occupancy, frequently in excess of 75 per cent.

Hotel occupancy statistics—example

From the following figures given below calculate:

(a) % room occupancy
(b) % guest occupancy
(c) room density index
(d) % double occupancy.

	Day 1	*Day 2*	*Day 3*
A: Available rooms	100	100	100
B: Guest capacity	150	150	150
C: Occupied rooms	80	60	80
D: No. of guests	120	72	104

Solution

		Day 1	Day 2	Day 3
A: $\dfrac{\text{Rooms occupied}}{\text{Rooms available}} \times 100$	=	80.0%	60.0%	80.0%
B: $\dfrac{\text{No. of guests}}{\text{Guest capacity}} \times 100$	=	80.0%	48.0%	69.3%
C: $\dfrac{\text{No. of guests}}{\text{Occupied rooms}} \times 100$	=	1.50	1.20	1.30
D: $\dfrac{\text{No. of guests} - \text{occupied rooms}}{\text{Occupied rooms}} \times 100$	=	50.0%	20.0%	30.0%

As will have been observed, both the room density index and the percentage of double occupancy measure the same thing: the relationship between the number of guests and occupied rooms. It is not surprising, therefore, that this is reflected in the relevant figures in our solution. When the room density index is 1.50 we immediately know that double occupancy is 50 per cent. The same applies to Day 2 and Day 3 when the figures are 1.20 and 20 per cent and 1.30 and 30 per cent respectively.

Restaurant occupancy

This is a similar concept to that of hotel occupancy. It measures the relationship between seating capacity and the number of covers served. The formula is

$$\frac{\text{No. of covers served (300)}}{\text{Seating capacity (100)}} \times 100 = 300\%$$

Quite obviously, the higher the percentage of restaurant occupancy the fuller the use that is being made of the facilities of the restaurant. One must remember, however, that different types of restaurant operation tend to produce different restaurant occupancies. In 'fast-food' operations it is often possible to reach occupancies in excess of 400 per cent. In very high-ASP restaurants occupancies in excess of 200 per cent are rather uncommon. Restaurant occupancy may be calculated on a daily basis and/or separately for lunch and dinner.

Average room rate

This measures the relationship between room sales and the total number of rooms occupied. The formula for the calculation of the average room rate is

$$\frac{\text{Room sales (£2,000)}}{\text{Rooms occupied (100)}} = £20$$

Average rate per guest

This measures the relationship between room sales and the total number of guests. The formula to apply is

$$\frac{\text{Room sales (£2,000)}}{\text{Total number of guests (120)}} = £16.67$$

During longer periods of economic stability, both the average room rate and the average rate per guest will tend to remain relatively stable. As mentioned earlier in this chapter, there are circumstances now and again when room rates are cut by hoteliers quite substantially to avoid excessive spare capacity. Where that situation obtains, it is essential to calculate the average room rate and the average rate per guest at frequent intervals, as percentages of room or bed occupancy tend, in such circumstances, to be less meaningful.

Average spending power

This measures the relationship between food and beverage sales and the number of covers. Thus where food and beverage sales are £800 and the number of covers 100, the average spending power is

$$\frac{\text{Food and beverage sales (£800)}}{\text{Number of covers (100)}} = £8.00$$

ASP calculations are undertaken differently by different establishments. In some cases there is a single daily figure of ASP calculated. In other cases the ASP is worked out separately for lunch and dinner. Finally, some large restaurants calculate separate ASP figures for lunch and dinner and analyse these as between food and beverage sales. Following our earlier discussion of the profit sensitivity of hotels and catering establishments, it need hardly be stressed that statistics relating to the ASP (as indeed the average room rate or rate per guest) are of vital importance.

Sales mix

The term 'sales mix' refers to the percentage composition of total sales. A large hotel may have a sales mix such as the following:

	%
Room sales	45.0
Food sales	30.0
Beverage sales	15.0
MOD sales	10.0
Total	100.0

As each element of the sales mix produces a different C/S ratio, it is essential to control the sales mix at frequent intervals. Thus room sales invariably show a higher C/S ratio than food and beverage sales, and the latter a higher C/S ratio than sales in the minor operated departments. As a result, when total sales are constant but there is a change in the sales mix, there may be important changes in the total net profit of the establishment. As an example, an increase in the sales of cigarettes and cigars of £1,000 may result in an increase in total net profit of £200. The same increase in room sales may well increase net profit by £900. Hence, what matters is not only total sales but also the sales mix.

In addition to calculating the sales mix as shown above, it is desirable to calculate the sales mix for food and beverages, and show the composition of food sales and beverage sales under headings such as soups and appetizers, meat and fish, vegetables, sweets, teas and coffees, beers and minerals, table wines, fortified wines, spirits, etc. Again, each element of the food and beverage sales mix will attract a rather different rate of gross profit and thus produce a different C/S ratio. Frequent and regular sales mix calculations are, therefore, imperative.

Gross profit

This is both an accounting and an operating ratio, depending on its frequency of calculation. This ratio has already been dealt with earlier in this chapter.

After-wage profit

This is sometimes referred to as the 'net margin'. It may be defined as net sales less cost of sales and labour costs. The formula for the calculation of the after-wage profit is:

$$\frac{\text{After-wage profit (£3,500)}}{\text{Net sales (£10,000)}} \times 100 = 35\%$$

This particular operating ratio is particularly useful in situations where a high proportion of labour costs is of a variable nature, and where it is important to control labour costs as much as food and beverage costs. In most seasonal establishments the cost of labour will vary quite considerably over the calendar year and, in such circumstances, it is essential to ensure a correct adjustment of labour costs to the volume of sales. Hence the usefulness of this particular operating ratio.

Departmental profit

Departmental profit (in some countries described as 'departmental income') may be defined as departmental sales less all departmental (controllable) expenses. Typically, therefore, there are three deductions from departmental sales before one arrives at departmental profit: (a) cost of sales; (b) labour costs; (c) other departmental expenses. It will be realized that in the case of the rooms department there is, for obvious reasons, no deduction for cost of sales. The figure of departmental profit is usually expressed as a percentage of departmental sales, e.g.:

$$\frac{\text{Departmental profit (£1,900)}}{\text{Food and beverage sales (£10,000)}} \times 100 = 19\%$$

This particular ratio is very useful in the majority of hotels, as indeed in large restaurants which operate a system of departmental accounting. The ratio is useful not only from the point of view of departmental accounting but is also valuable for purposes of budgetary control and decision making.

Net profit

This has already been dealt with under the heading of 'Accounting ratios' earlier in this chapter.

OTHER RATIOS AND STATISTICS

In addition to the accounting and operating ratios described above, there are other ratios and statistics used in hospitality operations. Some of these are described below.

Many hotel companies calculate each year the total revenue inflow per room available. The figure of *sales per room available* may then be used for comparative and control purposes. In the case of restaurants the corresponding measure is that of *sales per seat available*, which again is a useful figure. Some hotels and restaurants calculate each year the figure of *sales per employee* which would have similar uses to the statistics on sales per room available and sales per seat available.

All such additional statistics are useful not only from the point of view of current operational efficiency but also as basic data indispensable for the planning of new units.

Cost-based ratios

The operating ratios dealt with so far are all revenue-based ratios. Even in market-oriented establishments it is essential to calculate certain cost-based ratios. Although the profitability of the market-oriented establishment is determined largely by factors operating on the revenue side of the business, the best results will not be achieved unless due attention is paid to operating costs.

In all revenue producing departments it is necessary to control the *cost of sales*: food cost, beverage cost and the commodity costs of the minor operated departments. In each case the cost of sales is expressed by a percentage of the relevant departmental sales, as illustrated below.

$$\frac{\text{Food cost (£1,680)}}{\text{Food sales (£4,000)}} \times 100 = 42\%$$

Needless to say, where gross profits are calculated and controlled periodically (which is almost universal practice in the hotel and catering industry) the percentages of departmental cost of sales are produced as a matter of course.

Similar considerations apply to departmental wages and controllable expenses. In many hotels and restaurants these are calculated weekly, or at other frequent intervals, and expressed as percentages of departmental sales.

Finally, we have a group of expenses described as undistributed operating expenses. These are:

(a) administrative and general
(b) marketing
(c) guest entertainment
(d) property operation, maintenance and energy costs.

These too are calculated at frequent intervals and expressed as percentages of total sales or, sometimes, room sales.

OPERATING RATIOS IN TOURISM

Tour operators are in some respects in a similar situation to hotels. They have traditionally faced a great deal of competition, with the result that their profit margins have always tended to be modest. In a situation like this it is important to concentrate on the management of the revenue inflow rather than on cost control.

All tour operators pay particular attention to their current revenue inflow vis-à-vis the position last year. They know from experience what percentage of total revenue should have been achieved by the end of March, April, etc. A concurrent problem is that of spare capacity. Where it is anticipated that a departure is not likely to be fully booked, the tour operator will offer sufficient discounts to encourage potential holiday-makers to book and travel, frequently during the last few days before departure. Statistical predictions of take-up for various departures are of critical importance. Information on sales mix as between various destinations and hotels is also important; the relevant statistics are monitored very closely indeed.

In addition to the information prepared by head-office staff a great deal of valuable statistical information will be received—on a regular basis—from the tour company's representatives. All tour operators receive reports on customer complaints; these are analysed as between various hotels as well as in respect of the nature of the complaint (room, food, facilities, etc.).

Some retail travel agents are small in size, employing typically not more than a few persons. This small size of business operation militates against the introduction of elaborate management information systems. Nevertheless most travel agents prepare some statistical information for control purposes. Examples of such information are: monthly sales figures, commission earned on the sale of package tours, independent tours, railway tickets and insurance policies. Where several booking clerks are employed their productivity is sometimes measured in terms of time taken per transaction or the number of transactions per day.

Other travel agents belong to large organizations (e.g. Thomas Cook) and these have elaborate management information systems and supply a fully comprehensive range of operating statistics to their headquarters. The statistics would cover the whole spectrum of business activity, including sales, sales mix, cash and credit sales, and number of packages sold as well as sales of insurance policies, railway tickets and foreign currency.

PROBLEMS

1. Distinguish clearly between accounting and operating ratios. Give three examples of each.
2. What justification is there for the distinction between cost-based and revenue-based operating ratios? Answer the question by reference to the concepts of 'cost accounting' and 'revenue accounting'.
3. State which factors determine the choice of operating ratios in any one type of business.
4. Define each of the following:

   (a) return on capital employed
   (b) net profit ratio
   (c) capital gearing ratio
   (d) gross profit ratio
   (e) current ratio
   (f) acid test ratio
   (g) rate of stock turnover
   (h) average collection period
   (i) average payment period.

5. What are the respective advantages and disadvantages of the concepts of 'room occupancy' and 'guest occupancy'?
6. Explain what you understand by:

   (a) average room rate
   (b) average rate per guest
   (c) average spending power.

7. Explain what you understand by:

   (a) percentage yield
   (b) double occupancy
   (c) room density index.

8. From the following information calculate:

   (a) percentage room occupancy
   (b) percentage guest occupancy
   (c) room density index
   (d) percentage double occupancy.

	Hotel A	Hotel B	Hotel C
Available rooms	100	150	200
Guest capacity	200	200	300
Occupied rooms	75	125	175
No. of guests	100	150	225

9. A hotel company operates three units. The information given below is in respect of 14 September 19 . . .

	Hotel Milano	Hotel Torino	Hotel Roma
No. of rooms available	100	200	150
Guest capacity	150	300	200
No. of rooms occupied	80	120	120
No. of guests	100	180	156
Room sales	£3,600	£4,200	£6,000

You are required to calculate for each hotel:

(a) average room rate
(b) average rate per guest
(c) guest occupancy
(d) room occupancy
(e) double occupancy.

10. Given below are particulars relating to the trading results of the Broadway Restaurant.

	April	May	June
Number of covers	8,000	8,400	9,200
	£	£	£
Food sales	128,000	130,200	138,000
Beverage sales	36,000	39,900	48,300
Total sales	164,000	170,100	186,300
Food gross profit	80,640	78,120	80,040
Beverage gross profit	20,520	23,940	29,460
Total gross profit	101,160	102,060	109,500
Labour costs	42,640	42,530	42,850
Overhead costs	34,440	34,020	35,390
Total	77,080	76,550	78,240
Net profit	24,080	25,510	31,260

You are required to:

(a) calculate appropriate operating ratios
(b) state which factors have influenced the profitability of the restaurant.

16 Financial statement analysis

INTRODUCTION

The main purpose of the chapter which follows is to suggest a practical method of analysing and interpreting financial statements, with particular emphasis on the profit and loss account. The emphasis on the profit and loss account stems from practical considerations. All practising managers and senior executives see a profit and loss account once a month and, indeed, have responsibility for it; and only a small percentage of such managers and senior executives will see a balance sheet or a cash flow statement more than once a year. Most certainly the majority of hospitality managers who are employed by groups or chains, rather than individual establishments, never have the opportunity to see a full set of financial statements of the organization which employs them.

When we interpret a set of figures it is important to have some point of reference or standard against which to assess current results. When we are told that a hotel last month achieved room sales of £150,000 then this in itself means little. It is only when we relate last month's volume of room sales to room sales achieved during the corresponding period of the previous year, or if we relate it to the volume of budgeted room sales for that month, that the figure of £150,000 begins to acquire some meaning.

In the three examples which follow we suggest a method of analysis and interpretation which is based on current practice and is generally accepted as comprehensive. It is stressed, however, that the figures and ratios used—although typical of British and European hotel and restaurant operations—are not necessarily indicative of results that should be expected in any one given situation.

Example 1: Hotel profit and loss a/c

The balances shown below were extracted from the Grand International Hotel at 31 December 1998.

	£
Net sales:	
Rooms	2,350,000
Food	1,725,600
Beverages	764,800
MOD	54,600

Cost of sales:

Food	672,300
Beverages	267,200
MOD	37,900

Departmental payroll:

Rooms	493,300
Food	603,400
Beverages	175,100
MOD	12,200

Departmental expenses:

Rooms	194,900
Food	125,500
Beverages	31,100
MOD	1,400
Administration and general expenses	531,700
Advertising and sales promotion	139,600
Heat, light and power	151,200
Repairs and maintenance	235,600
Insurance, local taxes	127,700
Depreciation	315,400

You are required to:

(a) prepare the hotel's profit and loss account
(b) calculate appropriate ratios
(c) comment on the hotel's financial performance.

GRAND INTERNATIONAL HOTEL
Profit and loss a/c for year ended 31 December 1998

Department	Net sales	Cost of sales	Dept. payroll	Dept. expenses	Dept. profit
	£	£	£	£	£
Rooms	2,350,000	—	493,300	194,900	1,661,800
Food	1,725,600	672,300	603,400	125,500	324,400
Beverages	764,800	267,200	175,100	31,100	291,400
MOD	54,600	37,900	12,200	1,400	3,100
	4,895,000	977,400	1,284,000	352,900	2,280,700

Less Undistributed operating expenses:		
Administration & general expenses	531,700	
Advertising & sales promotion	139,600	
Heat, light & power	151,200	
Repairs & maintenance	235,600	
Insurance & local taxes	127,700	
Depreciation	315,400	1,501,200
Net profit		£779,500

We now calculate the appropriate ratios, percentages and comment as follows.

Sales mix

Rooms	48.0%
Food	35.3%
Beverages	15.6%
MOD	1.1%
	100.0%

The hotel seems to have a strong food and beverage operation as food and beverage sales represent 50.9 per cent of total revenue. Other sales, 1.1 per cent, are minimal, and it is clear that a greater effort could be made to improve sales in the minor operated departments.

Gross profit

Food	61.0%
Beverages	65.1%
MOD	30.6%

Most good-class hotels operate at a food gross profit of about 65 per cent; and so the 61.0 per cent seems rather modest. On the other hand few hotels manage to achieve a beverage gross profit of more than 60 per cent, in view of which the 65.1 per cent seems quite high. We do not know what the minor operated departments are and, therefore, it is difficult to comment on this particular result.

Departmental payroll

Rooms	21.0%
Food	35.0%
Beverages	22.9%
MOD	22.3%

The percentage of payroll in the rooms department looks very acceptable as most larger hotels tend to have a payroll cost of 20–25 per cent in the rooms department. Food operations are generally labour-intensive, and in many UK hotels payroll in the food department is about 45 per cent of food sales. The 35.0 per cent achieved by this hotel seems, therefore, very satisfactory. Beverage sales, on the other hand, require relatively little labour: many hotels have a payroll of approximately 20 per cent in this department, and 22.9 per cent seems reasonable. As we do not know what is included in the other departments it is impossible to comment on the payroll cost of 22.3 per cent.

Departmental controllable expenses

Rooms	8.3%
Food	7.3%
Beverages	4.1%
MOD	2.6%

Departmental controllable expenses in the rooms department are generally below 10.0 per cent of room sales. The 8.3 per cent here seems very reasonable. Food operations show a departmental cost of 7.3 per cent, which is rather low: in most hotels this will tend to be nearer 10.0 per cent. Beverage sales entail few departmental expenses and so the result here, 4.1 per cent, would indicate that somewhat above-average expenses are being incurred in this operation. Again we are not able to comment on the 2.6 per cent in the other departments as the nature of these minor operated departments is not known.

Departmental profits

Rooms	70.7%
Food	18.8%
Beverages	38.1%
MOD	5.7%

Room sales tend to produce, in good-class hotels, a departmental profit of about 70.0 per cent and our result here is probably about satisfactory. The departmental profit on food is good because, as already indicated, the low level of departmental payroll. Also the departmental profit on beverage operations is very acceptable indeed: the reasonable level of payroll and the high percentage of gross profit have given a very satisfactory departmental profit. Again no comment may be offered on departmental profits in the minor operated departments.

Composition of departmental profits

Rooms	72.9%
Food	14.2%
Beverages	12.8%
MOD	6.4%
Total	100.0%

We may see very clearly from our analysis that the rooms department generates almost three-quarters of the total of the departmental profit. This result is quite typical of many large, good-class hotels. Whilst the total contribution of the food and beverage operation (27.0 per cent) is good, the other departments' contribution to the total departmental profit is almost insignificant.

Undistributed operating expenses

Administration and general	10.9%
Advertising and promotion	2.9%
Heat, light and power	3.1%
Repairs and maintenance	4.8%
Local taxes and insurance	2.6%
Depreciation	6.4%
Total	30.7%

Administration and general expenses, advertising and promotion as well as depreciation: all these seem to be quite high in relation to what one would normally expect. Heat, light and power costs appear to be low for this type of operation. No comment is possible on the other expenses here as we know nothing about the age of the property or its location.

Net profit

The hotel achieved a net profit of 15.9 per cent of its total sales volume. This seems to be very satisfactory. We would require a great deal of additional information about the hotel to comment more fully.

Example 2: Restaurant profit and loss a/c

Set out in Figure 16.1 is the profit and loss a/c of a restaurant in respect of the year ended 31 December 19 . . . Calculate appropriate ratios.

Solution:

Sales mix

Food sales	64.3%
Beverage sales	31.4%
Tobacco sales	4.3%
Total sales	100.0%

Gross profit

Food sales	63.3%
Beverage sales	55.9%
Tobacco sales	13.3%

Composition of gross profit

Food sales	69.2%
Beverage sales	29.9%
Tobacco sales	0.9%
Total sales	100.0%

Operating expenses

Payroll and related expenses	20.7%
Administrative and general	5.5%
Gas and electricity	1.2%
Advertising and sales promotion	1.3%
Repairs and maintenance	1.1%
Rent and rates	10.2%
Depreciation	4.1%
Total	44.1%

Net profit

As % of total sales	14.7%

ASP	£
Food sales	8.68
Beverage sales	4.24
Tobacco sales	0.58
Total sales	£13.50

Profit and Loss a/c
For year ended 31 December 19 . .

Department	Sales	Cost of sales	Gross profit
	£	£	£
Food	450,000	165,000	285,000
Beverages	220,000	97,000	123,000
Tobaccos	30,000	26,000	4,000
Total	700,000	288,000	412,000
Less Operating expenses:			
Payroll and related expenses		145,000	
Administrative and general		39,000	
Gas and electricity		8,200	
Advertising and sales promotion		9,100	
Repairs and maintenance		7,400	
Rent and rates		71,200	
Depreciation		29,100	309,000
Net profit			£103,000

NB: You are informed that the restaurant served 51,852 covers during the year under review.

Figure 16.1 Profit and loss a/c of a restaurant

Example 3: Hotel balance sheet

Set out below is the balance sheet of the Metropolitan Hotel Limited as at 31 March 19 . . .

Balance Sheet
as at 31 March 19 . .

	Cost (£000)	Depreciation (£000)	Net (£000)
Fixed assets			
Freehold premises	620	—	620
Furniture and equipment	150	100	50
China, glass, etc.	—	—	13
	770	100	683
Investments			
Shares in A–Z plc			5
Current assets			
Food and beverage stocks		11	
Debtors		12	
Cash		14	
		37	

Less Current liabilities		
Creditors	31	
Advance deposits	1	32
Net current assets		5
Total assets less current liabilities		693
Less Long-terms liabilities		
Tourism Finance plc		400
		293
Financed by:		
Ordinary shares of £1.00 each		220
Profit and loss a/c		73
		293

Comment on the financial position of the hotel.

Solution:

Current ratio

This is 1.16, which means that for every £1.00 the hotel owes in current liabilities it has £1.16 in current assets. At least, on the face of it, this seems reasonable.

Acid test ratio

If we exclude food and beverage stocks from the current assets, the acid test ratio is 0.81. Hence for every £1.00 the hotel owes in current liabilities it has only £0.81 in liquid assets. This is not a happy situation to be in as difficulties may be experienced in paying the creditors.

Return on capital

If, for this purpose, we define capital as the total of assets at the disposal of the hotel, the return on capital is

$$\frac{£73,000}{£725,000} \times 100 = 10.1\%$$

If, we define capital as total assets less current liabilities, the return on capital is

$$\frac{£73,000}{£693,000} \times 100 = 10.5\%$$

Different companies use different definitions of capital; what is important is that we should use the same definition consistently from one year to another.

Other comments

(a) Of the original cost of furniture and equipment (£150,000) £100,000 has already been written off by way of depreciation. One would assume, therefore, that some of these assets are approaching the end of their useful life and will soon have to be replaced.

(b) The hotel has a high proportion of loan capital (£400,000) in relation to its equity capital (£220,000) and is, therefore, highly geared. This implies a high degree of instability in the payment of dividends on the ordinary shares of the company.

PROBLEMS

1. The figures shown below were extracted from the books of the Washington Hotel at 31 December 19 .. You are required to prepare, in good style, the profit and loss account of the hotel and comment on its financial performance.

	£
Net sales:	
Rooms	1,450,100
Food	871,600
Beverages	361,100
Other	27,200
Cost of sales:	
Food	344,500
Beverages	113,800
Other	13,000
Departmental payroll:	
Rooms	271,700
Food	323,600
Beverages	91,300
Other	4,100
Departmental expenses:	
Rooms	119,900
Food	67,900
Beverages	16,800
Other	400
Administration and general expenses	251,000
Advertising and promotion	67,400
Heat, light and power	73,600
Repairs and maintenance	105,200
Local taxes and insurance	130,700
Interest	84,200
Depreciation	169,700

2. Set out below is the profit and loss a/c of a 100-bedroomed hotel for the year ended 31 December 1998.

Profit and Loss a/c for year ended 31 December 19 . .

Department	Sales	Cost of sales	Dept. payroll	Dept. expenses	Dept. profit
	£000	£000	£000	£000	£000
Rooms	1,148	—	250	116	782
Food	850	322	312	64	152
Beverages	328	108	86	14	120
Others	24	10	6	2	6
	2,350	440	654	196	1,060

Less Undistributed operating expenses:		
Administration and general	210	
Marketing	64	
Energy	70	
Repairs and maintenance	105	
Rent, insurance and interest	201	
Depreciation	160	810
Net profit before tax		£250

You are required to calculate appropriate ratios and comment on the financial position of the hotel.

3. Set out below is the profit and loss a/c of a hotel. You are required to comment on the performance of the hotel in respect of the year ended 30 June 19 . . .

LAX INTERNATIONAL HOTEL
Profit and Loss a/c for year ended 30 June 19 . .

Department	Sales	Cost of sales	Dept. payroll	Dept. expenses	Dept. profit
	£000	£000	£000	£000	£000
Rooms	800	—	160	60	580
Food	400	140	170	20	70
Beverages	200	100	50	10	40
M.O.D	100	30	20	10	40
	1,500	270	400	100	730

Less Undistributed operating expenses:		
Administrative and general	160	
Marketing	80	
Guest entertainment	60	
Repairs, maintenance and energy	150	
Financial charges	80	530
Net profit		£200

4. The following balance sheet and profit and loss account have been presented to the proprietor of the Zimbabwe Café.

Balance Sheet
as at 31 December 1998

	Cost £	Depreciation £	Net £
Fixed assets			
Buildings	200,000	—	200,000
Kitchen plant	72,000	32,000	40,000
Furniture	56,000	16,000	40,000
Cutlery, glass, etc.	24,000	4,000	20,000
	352,000	52,000	300,000
Current assets			
Food stocks		12,000	
Beverage stocks		24,000	
Debtors		4,000	
Cash		20,000	
		60,000	
Less Current liabilities			
Creditors	32,000		
Accrued expenses	8,000	40,000	
Net current assets			20,000
Net assets			320,000
Financed by:			
Capital a/c at 1 Jan 1998			272,000
Add Net profit			48,000
			320,000

Profit & Loss A/c
for year ended 31 December 1998

	Sales £	Cost of sales £	Gross profit £
Food sales	400,000	160,000	240,000
Beverage sales	200,000	100,000	100,000
Total	600,000	260,000	340,000

Less Operating expenses:		
Payroll and related expenses	164,000	
Administrative and general	36,000	
Advertising and promotion	12,000	
Energy	12,000	
Repairs and maintenance	16,000	
Depreciation	52,000	292,000
Net profit		48,000

You are informed that stocks at 1 January 1998 were as follows:

Food	£20,000
Beverages	£16,000

The café buys all its food and beverages on credit. Of the total sales volume, £480,000 was cash and £120,000 credit sales.

You are required to calculate appropriate ratios and comment on the operating results of the café as disclosed by the accounts.

Analysis of departmental profitability

17

The purpose of this chapter is, as indicated by its title, to suggest how one should analyse the profitability of the revenue-producing departments of a hotel. This we will do by examining the problems inherent in cost apportionment, as this—where practised—has far-reaching implications. The second part of the chapter will be devoted to the application of some of the concepts and techniques we are already familiar with (contribution, C/S ratio, breakeven analysis, etc.) to departmental profitability.

ALLOCATION AND APPORTIONMENT OF EXPENDITURE

The preparation of a hotel departmental profit and loss account necessitates a close examination of the expenditure of all the revenue-producing departments as well as the associated cost centres. In the case of some of the expenses, we have no problem in deciding where such expenses clearly and naturally belong. We know that payroll in the rooms department should be a charged against room sales, the cost of beverages consumed is obviously a charge against beverage sales, and repairs to kitchen equipment are clearly and indisputably a charge against food sales. In all these cases it is quite apparent where the expense has arisen, and we simply charge it against the revenue of the department which has had the sole and exclusive benefit of such expenditure. All expenses in this category are said to be *allocated*.

Other expenses such as management salaries, rents, rates, depreciation of premises, marketing, financial charges, etc., are in a wholly different category. These are incurred for the benefit of the hotel as a whole and cannot be directly or immediately associated with the operation of any one individual department. All such 'common' or 'indirect' costs can only be split or divided between the departments concerned on some basis such as departmental sales volumes, space occupied, number of employees, departmental payroll, number of covers served, etc., whereby an assumed proportion of each expense is charged against the departments concerned. All such costs are said to be *apportioned*.

As there are a number of alternative methods of apportionment available for dividing most indirect costs, different accountants may choose different methods of apportionment and arrive at different departmental net profit figures. It is worth noting that proponents of cost apportionment tell us *how* to apportion; they seem to have few convincing arguments with regard to *why* we should apportion, or why we should attempt to arrive at a figure of net profit for each revenue-producing department.

It seems that the correct view to take is this. We should regard the total hotel operation as one coherent, integrated package which should, in total, provide a satisfactory profit. It is not right or sensible to insist that all individual elements of this package (rooms, food, beverages, etc.) should produce an equal contribution to total profit, or that they should share equally or proportionately in the absorption of indirect costs. And so whilst we do want to control the results (sales, departmental expenses, profit margins) of the revenue-producing departments, what matters in the final analysis is the size of the total of departmental profits in relation to the total of indirect costs (undistributed operating expenses).

This is illustrated in Figure 17.1, where we see that different departments achieve substantially different levels of departmental profits. The hotel net profit of £200,000 is equal to the excess of the total of departmental profits (£1,200,000) over the total of indirect costs (i.e. undistributed operating expenses of £1,000,000). Whichever methods of apportionment we choose—whether we charge rather more of the indirect costs against room sales, or rather less against the sales of the minor operated departments—our net profit will still be £200,000.

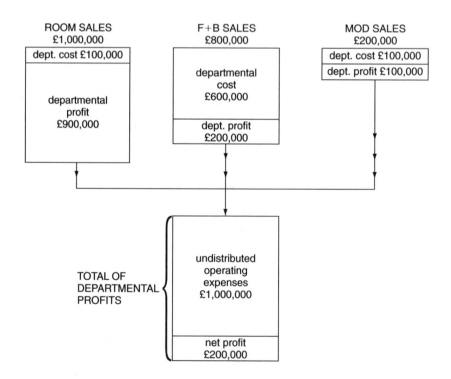

Figure 17.1 Cost apportionment and net profit

Example

Set out below is the profit and loss a/c of the Zanzibar Valley Hotel.

Profit and Loss a/c
for year ended 31 December 19..

Department	Sales	Cost of sales	Dept. payroll	Dept. expenses	Dept. profit
	£000	£000	£000	£000	£000
Rooms	990	—	240	35	715
Food	330	140	155	15	20
Beverages	100	40	20	5	35
Sundries	80	—	—	60	20
	1,500	180	415	115	790

Less Undistributed operating expenses:		
Administration expenses	150	
Insurances and local taxes	100	
Management salaries	90	
Repairs and maintenance	50	
Depreciation	55	
Marketing	25	470
Net profit		£320

You are required to apportion the undistributed operating expenses:

(a) first, on the basis of: rooms—60 per cent; food—25 per cent; beverages—10 per cent; and sundries—5 per cent
(b) next, on the basis of departmental sales volumes.

Comment on the resulting figures of departmental net profits.

Solution

If we apportion the undistributed operating expenses in accordance with instruction (a), the results will be as follows.

Profit and Loss a/c
for year ended 31 December 19..

Department	Sales	Total dept. expenses	Dept. profits	Indirect costs	Dept. net profits
	£000	£000	£000	£000	£000
Rooms	990	275	715	282	433
Food	330	310	20	118	(98)
Beverages	100	65	35	47	(12)
Sundries	80	60	20	23	(3)
	1,500	710	790	470	320

If we apportion the undistributed operating expenses on the basis of instruction (b) our results will be as follows.

Profit and Loss a/c
for year ended 31 December 19..

Department	Sales	Total dept. expenses	Dept. profits	Indirect costs	Dept. net profits
	£000	£000	£000	£000	£000
Rooms	990	275	715	310	405
Food	330	310	20	104	(84)
Beverages	100	65	35	31	4
Sundries	80	60	20	25	(5)
	1,500	710	790	470	320

The first and most important fact which emerges from the above accounts is that different methods of apportionment result in substantially different results in terms of departmental net profits. The reasons for these anomalies are that (a) there is no reliable, rational or logical method of cost apportionment, and (b) we simply do not know how apportionment should be attempted. Those few who are in favour of the apportionment of indirect costs suggest that we should use a method which is 'fair and equitable'. The problem is, however, that the concepts of fairness and equity are, in this context, loose and imprecise and tend to be interpreted differently by different accountants.

It is quite likely that, whatever method of apportionment we use, the food or the combined food and beverage operations will always show an apparent departmental net loss. Be that as it may, the fact is that we cannot sell the rooms unless we also offer food and beverages. Our final conclusion, therefore, is this: when preparing a hotel profit and loss account we should allocate as much as we possibly can, but refrain from apportionment.

ASPECTS OF DEPARTMENTAL PROFITABILITY

In this second section of the present chapter we will illustrate and analyse the main aspects of departmental profitability. Following our conclusions relating to the apportionment of fixed costs, our analysis will only go as far as departmental profits: no attempt will be made to establish how much net profit is commonly earned by the various revenue-producing departments of hotels. The examples which follow are based on the figures from the Grand International Hotel in Chapter 16.

Room operations

From the various examples given in this book it will have been noticed that a hotel rooms department invariably produces a high percentage of departmental profit. In order to carry out the analysis of departmental profitability we have to be able to divide all the departmental expenses as between those which are fully fixed and those which are fully variable. If we assume that departmental payroll and departmental expenses are 80 per cent fixed and 20 per cent variable, we may analyse the room department's operations as follows.

	£
Departmental payroll	493,300
Add Departmental expenses	194,900
Total departmental expenses	688,200
Fixed 80%	550,560
Variable 20%	137,640

We may now show the composition of room sales:

	£	%
Fixed costs	550,560	23.4
Variable costs	137,640	5.9
Departmental profit	1,661,800	70.7
Total	2,350,000	100.0

Also we may calculate the room department's contribution and C/S ratio, as shown below.

	£	%
Sales	2,350,000	100.0
Less variable costs	137,640	5.9
Contribution, C/S ratio	2,212,360	94.1

It is clear from the above figures that room sales are an extremely profitable source of business. In this particular case, after we have reached the

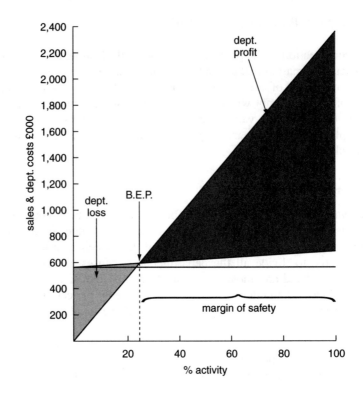

Figure 17.2 Profitability of rooms department

break-even point, every increase in room sales of £1,000 entails a variable cost of £59 and adds £941 to our net profit. The profitability of the rooms department is illustrated in Figure 17.2 where—it will be noticed—we have a very low break-even point and a wide margin of safety.

Food operations

Here again our assumption is that 80 per cent of the departmental payroll and departmental expenses is fixed and the balance of 20 per cent variable. We find the fixed and variable costs as follows.

		£
Departmental payroll		603,400
Add Departmental expenses		125,500
Total		728,900
Fixed 80%		583,120
Variable 20%	145,780	
Add Cost of sales	672,300	818,080

The composition of the food sales of the hotel is:

	£	%
Fixed costs	583,120	33.8
Variable costs	818,080	47.4
Departmental profit	324,400	18.8
Total	1,725,600	100.0

We may now calculate the food department's contribution and C/S ratio.

	£	%
Sales	1,725,600	100.0
Less Variable costs	818,080	47.4
Contribution, C/S ratio	907,520	52.6

Quite clearly the hotel's food department is not nearly as profitable as the rooms department. We have a relatively low percentage of departmental profit and a considerably lower C/S ratio. After reaching the break-even point an increase in food sales of £1,000 entails a variable cost of £474 and the resulting addition to net profit is £526. This is illustrated in Figure 17.3.

Beverage operations

We continue our assumption relating to the division of departmental expenses as between fixed and variable costs, which are as follows.

		£
Departmental payroll		175,100
Add Departmental expenses		31,100
	Total	206,200

	£	£
Fixed 80%		164,960
Variable 20%	41,240	
Add Cost of sales	267,200	308,440

We next show the composition of the beverage sales.

	£	%
Fixed costs	164,960	21.6
Variable costs	308,440	40.3
Departmental profit	291,400	38.1
Total	764,800	100.0

Finally we calculate the beverage department's contribution and C/S ratio.

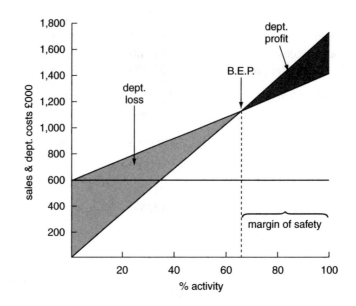

Figure 17.3 Profitability of food department

	£	%
Sales	764,800	100.0
Less Variable cost	308,440	40.3
Contribution, C/S ratio	456,360	59.7

Hotel beverage departments show generally significantly better results than food departments. This is due to the fact that beverage operations are less labour intensive than food operations. Thus whilst the majority of hotel departments operate at a departmental payroll of between 35 per cent to over 45 per cent, the corresponding percentages for hotel beverage operations is 15–25 per cent. As most of the payroll costs are fixed rather than variable, this difference between food operations and beverage operations has several consequences.

(a) Food departments have a relatively higher percentage of fixed costs—frequently of the order of 20 per cent in relation to departmental sales.
(b) Beverage departments tend to produce a considerably higher percentage of departmental profit; here again whilst the departmental profit on food is frequently of the order of 10–15 per cent, many beverage departments achieve a departmental profit of between 30 per cent and 40 per cent.
(c) Thus whilst in many cases food operations manage little more than just to break even, beverage operations tend to show results which are very satisfactory in terms of the departmental profit achieved. This is illustrated in Figure 17.4.

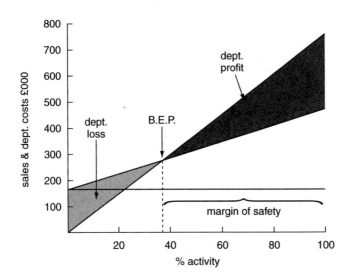

Figure 17.4 Profitability of beverage department

DEPARTMENTAL PERFORMANCE STANDARDS

Many hotel companies, both in the UK and overseas, have in recent years developed company performance standards for the main revenue-producing departments. Standards relating to food and beverage gross profit performance have now been used by British hotels and restaurants for several decades. The recently developed standards, therefore, relate to departmental labour costs.

The two examples which follow are based on standards developed by a UK hotel company after a detailed study of past performance and a thorough assessment of current operational conditions. It is worth pointing out that a company operating a number of hotels would not, indeed should not, have one set of standards, as the nature of business, type of client, age of the property, etc; may all vary considerably from one hotel to another. And so just as we have different standard recipes within a hotel group, from one unit to another, so our performance standards should not be uniform for the whole group, but developed specifically for each individual hotel.

Example 1

F & B PERFORMANCE STANDARDS		
Food service		*Per waiter/waitress*
Breakfast	full service	20 covers
	part self service	24 covers
Lunch/dinner	restaurant	12 covers
	coffee shop	15 covers
Banquets	where basic charge under £18.00	12 covers
	where basic charge £18.00 and over	10 covers

Beverage service

Restaurant	drinks at table	40 covers
Coffee shop	drinks at table	50 covers
Banquets	cash or account orders	40 covers
	bar operation	40 covers

Example 2

PAYROLL AS % OF DEPARTMENTAL SALES

Food sales

Restaurant	45%
Coffee shop	40%
Breakfasts	40%
Banqueting	35%

Beverages

Restaurant	17½%
Coffee shop	15%
Banqueting	15%
Bar operation	15%

The development of departmental performance standards is not necessarily a time-consuming task. The benefits resulting from such standards, however, are very real, both in the context of control of current operations as well as in annual budgeting.

PROBLEMS

1. Set out below is the profit and loss a/c of the London Tourist Hotel.

Profit and Loss a/c

Department	Sales	Cost of sales	Dept. payroll & expenses	Dept. profit
	£000	*£000*	*£000*	*£000*
Rooms	700	—	180	520
Food and beverages	500	175	275	50
Minor operated depts.	200	125	45	30
	1,400	300	500	600

Less Undistributed operating expenses:

Administration and general	125	
Marketing	35	
Energy	50	
Property operation and maintenance	80	
Depreciation and fixed charges	160	450
Net profit		150

Please assume that: (a) undistributed operating expenses are a fully fixed cost; (b) £400,000 of departmental payroll and expenses is the fixed element and the balance (£100,000) is wholly variable.

You are required to:

(a) prepare a break-even chart of the London Tourist Hotel
(b) prepare a break-even chart for the food and beverage department of the hotel, indicating clearly the present volume of departmental profit as well as the departmental profit which would be achieved if food and beverage sales were increased to £600,000
(c) calculate the departmental C/S ratios for (a) rooms department, (b) food and beverage department and (c) minor operated departments
(d) ascertain the effect on total hotel net profit of the increase in food and beverage sales to £600,000.

2. Set out below is the profit and loss a/c of the Stratford Tourist Hotel.

Profit and Loss a/c

Department	Sales	Cost of sales	Dept. payroll	Dept. expenses	Dept. profit
	£000	£000	£000	£000	£000
Rooms	800	—	160	60	580
Food	400	160	180	40	20
Beverages	200	70	50	10	70
Other sales	100	40	20	10	30
	1,500	270	410	120	700

Less Undistributed operating expenses:		
Administration and general	160	
Marketing	40	
Energy	90	
Repairs and maintenance	70	
Depreciation and fixed charges	190	550
Net profit before tax		£150

Please assume that (a) 'Undistributed operating expenses' are a fully fixed cost; (b) 'Departmental payroll' and 'Departmental expenses' may be divided into fully fixed cost of £477,000 and variable element of £53,000.

You are required to:

    (a) prepare departmental break-even charts for (i) rooms department; (ii) food department; (iii) beverage department; (iv) other sales

    (b) calculate each department's contribution and C/S ratio and comment on their respective profitability.

3. Argue the case for and against the apportionment of indirect costs in hotel profit and loss accounts.

The management of working capital 18

INTRODUCTION

It is possible to distinguish two kinds of capital in any one business. First, there is fixed or permanent capital, represented by fixed assets such as land, buildings, kitchen plant, furniture, etc. All such assets are purchased with the intention of being retained in the business. Secondly, there is working capital, whose main function is to support the current financial operations of the business.

Current assets consist of cash and items which will sooner or later be converted into cash. Thus current assets represent a source of liquid resources; current liabilities represent a claim on such liquid resources. Clearly, therefore, there should be some kind of relationship between current assets and current liabilities.

The excess of current assets over current liabilities is described as *working capital*. Where current assets amount to £5,000 and current liabilities are £4,000, we have a working capital of £1,000. As explained in a previous chapter, the relationship between current assets and current liabilities may be expressed by means of the current ratio. In this particular case the current ratio is 5:4 or, by dividing current assets by current liabilities, 1.25.

From the point of view of the liquidity of the business what matters is not only the relationship between current assets and current liabilities, but also the composition of the current assets. Let us look at the balance sheet below.

Extract from
Balance Sheet as at . . .

	£	£	£
Current assets			
Stocks		70,000	
Debtors		20,000	
Cash		10,000	
		100,000	
Less Current liabilities			
Creditors	40,000		
Accrued expenses	30,000	70,000	
Working capital			30,000

The business has a current ratio of 10 : 7 and a working capital of £30,000, which in most hotel companies would be considered satisfactory. Yet if we look at the composition of the current assets, we can see that the position is not entirely satisfactory. Immediate commitments amount to £70,000, and we have a cash balance of £10,000. Debts, which may take several weeks to convert into cash, amount to £20,000. A large proportion of the stocks may take months to materialize as cash.

Hence, in addition to the current ratio it is essential to calculate the acid test ratio, i.e. the relationship between liquid assets and current liabilities. Liquid assets consist of cash and items which are easily convertible into cash. Thus in most situations we regard debtors as liquid and stocks as non-liquid. To come back to our last balance sheet, the acid test ratio is 3 : 7 and it is clear that the liquidity of the business is unsatisfactory, as in most businesses an acid test ratio of at least 1 : 1 is regarded as essential.

HOW MUCH WORKING CAPITAL?

Working capital requirements vary from one industry to another and, indeed, one business to another. It is impossible, therefore, to lay down general rules universally applicable to any one sector of the hospitality industry.

From published information it is clear, however, that hotels and restaurants need less working capital than comparable businesses in other industries. For instance, in the majority of European hotels current assets are only marginally greater than current liabilities. There are two main factors responsible for this. First, a substantial proportion of hotel revenue is obtained from room sales, which are not supported by stocks. Secondly, a high proportion of the revenue of hotels and restaurants is represented by cash sales and sales on short-term credit.

The working capital requirements of a particular business can only be assessed by reference to a number of factors which together determine how much working capital is required. The main factors are listed below.

The period of credit given to customers is important. Generally, the longer this period the less liquid the business and the more working capital required.

Similar considerations apply to the period of credit received from suppliers: the longer the period of credit allowed by them the less working capital required.

Also important is the length of what is described as the 'production cycle', i.e. the period from the purchase of raw materials to the sale of the finished product. A long production cycle is normally associated with high stock levels and hence a relatively large amount of working capital.

Seasonality is a factor which affects a large number of hospitality establishments and influences the level of working capital. Where the pattern of revenue inflow is appreciably different from the pattern of cash expenditure, a relatively larger margin is required between current assets and current liabilities. Thus where most of the revenue is received between April and September and the heaviest expenses are payable between October and March, a relatively larger amount of working capital will normally be required.

Finally, the sales mix of the establishment is also an important factor. Room sales are not supported by stocks; food sales necessitate the keeping of relatively high stocks; beverage sales—particularly in high-ASP establishments—require the strongest support in terms of stock levels. Thus where room sales constitute a high proportion of the sales mix then—other things being equal—a smaller amount of working capital will be required. In the case of restaurants, licensed establishments usually have a higher current ratio than unlicensed establishments.

CONTROL OF WORKING CAPITAL

In order to ensure an adequate level of liquid resources, working capital should be reviewed regularly and frequently. It is useful to tabulate the components of working capital over a period of time and then examine the main trends in total working capital and the various current assets and current liabilities. A specimen statement of working capital is shown in Figure 18.1.

Components of working capital

From what has already been said it will be appreciated that it is not enough to control the total working capital; what matters as well are the individual items comprising it, and unless these are reviewed regularly and frequently, many an embarassing situation may have to be faced.

Cash position

It is probably true to say that most businesses are operating on a reasonably adequate credit balance at the bank. Many seasonal hospitality establishments find, however, that the inflow of cash does not coincide with the way in which

COLWYN BAY HOTEL
Statement of working capital

	31 Dec. 19..		31 Mar. 19..		30 June 19..	
	£	£	£	£	£	£
Current assets						
Cash at bank	19,700		16,400		13,700	
Debtors	4,500		4,800		5,000	
Stocks	18,000	42,200	18,250	39,450	17,800	36,500
Current liabilities						
Creditors	15,400		17,050		19,000	
Accrued expenses	2,500	17,900	3,100	20,150	3,000	22,000
Working capital		£24,300		£19,300		£14,500
Current ratio		2.36		1.96		1.66
Acid test ratio		1.35		1.10		0.85

Figure 18.1 Statement of working capital

expenditure is spread over the calendar year. In such circumstances a need for a substantial cash balance may well arise at a time when the cash resources are depleted. Further, whenever an outlay of cash becomes necessary as a result of replacements, renewals, or purchase of new equipment, etc., the cash position worsens considerably. A watchful eye must then be kept on the bank balance to ensure that there is enough cash left for current operations.

However, whatever the particular circumstances of a business the cash position is certainly a matter deserving special attention. As already explained in Chapter 10, the most effective method of controlling the cash resources is to operate to a cash budget.

Debtors

In hospitality establishments selling on credit the size of the bank balance at any time depends as much on the inflow of cash from debtors (guests, banqueting debtors, expense account debtors) as on cash sales. It is clear, therefore, that a strict check must be kept on all outstanding debts owing from customers. As a result, a frequent—preferably monthly—review of the relevant ledger accounts is essential.

A monthly statement of debtors, as illustrated in Figure 18.2, shows all the debts outstanding and at the same time draws attention to those which are overdue. A regular review of debtors helps to improve the cash position and avoid bad debts.

Stocks

Careful attention should be paid to the stock levels at all times. In businesses having a well-organized system of stores control appropriate stock levels are worked out for all items and, in this way, the value of stocks carried will not rise out of proportion to the amount of business transacted.

Where elaborate stock records are not kept—and this applies in the majority of hospitality businesses—a periodic review of stock levels is essential. A practical way of doing this is, on stock-taking, to go through the stock sheets and examine them in detail, making a note of any items which are in excess or short of normal requirements. All such items would then be taken into account in subsequent ordering.

Quite apart from particular items of stock it is important to ensure that the total of stocks kept does not increase unnecessarily as, obviously, an investment in idle and perishable stocks is a poor investment. A suitable form of a monthly report on stock levels is given in Figure 18.3.

Creditors

Just as a business expects its customers to settle their accounts regularly it must also ensure that it settles its own debts to its suppliers. This is so for two reasons; first to ensure the goodwill and the co-operation of its suppliers; secondly, delay in paying suppliers' accounts inevitably results in loss of cash discounts. A monthly review of such accounts is, therefore, also necessary.

WESTMINSTER RESTAURANT
Monthly statement of debtors
31 May 19 . .

Customer's name and address	Date incurred	Amount	Totals
		£	£
Debts due less than one month			
Total		4,505.00	4,505.00
Debts due more than one month			
A. Brown, Esp., 17 Green Lane, W5	Apr. 4	167.00	
B. Dawson Ltd., Oak Rd., N27	Apr. 16	273.00	
M. King & Sons, 4 Half Acre, EC5	Apr. 22	815.00	
E.M. Steel, Esq., 16 Mole Ave., SW17	Apr. 7	743.00	
M.S. Williams, Esq., 41 Bridge Lane, W5	Apr. 13	1,242.00	3,240.00
Debts due more than two months			
S. Cook Ltd., 12 Milford Rd., W7	Mar. 14	226.00	
W.E. Fenton, Esq., 4 Mill Lane W1	Mar. 7	84.00	
W.S. Lane, Miss, 11 Acton Rd., E17	Mar. 22	167.00	477.00
Debts due more than three months			
M.I. Elder, Esq., 21 Stamford Rd., SW1	Feb. 16	191.00	
T.O. Gorman, Miss, 10 Sutton Rd., W7	Feb. 3	118.00	309.00
Debts outstanding—Total			£8,531.00

Figure 18.2 Monthly statement of debtors

MULTIPLE CATERING COMPANY
Food stock levels
as at 31 January 19..

	Consumption	Average stock at cost	Monthly stock turnover This month	Last month
Restaurant A	£20,000	£5,000	4.0	3.7
Restaurant B	14,000	4,000	3.5	4.4
Restaurant C	6,250	2,500	2.5	4.1
Restaurant D	9,600	2,000	4.8	3.6
Restaurant E	8,000	2,000	4.0	4.1

Figure 18.3 Report on food stock levels

EFFECT OF BUSINESS TRANSACTIONS ON WORKING CAPITAL

Effective control of working capital necessitates a thorough understanding of how business transactions affect the working capital of the business. We may divide all transactions into three categories.

(a) those that operate to increase working capital
(b) those that operate to decrease working capital
(c) those that have no effect on the working capital.

Let us consider some transactions which increase working capital. If a loan is raised, the effect is to increase long-term liabilities (non-current component) and, simultaneously, to increase cash. The result is an increase in current assets and, current liabilities having remained constant, we obtain an increase in working capital. If more shares or debentures are issued the result is the same: an increase in a non-current component (share capital or debentures) and a corresponding increase in current assets (cash), leading to an increase in working capital. The earning of profits has the same effect: to increase the profit and loss account balance (non-current component) and a corresponding increase in current assets.

Transactions which operate to decrease current assets are those which result in the incurring of losses, granting of loans and withdrawal of capital. The purchase of fixed assets for cash will, of course, decrease working capital. If the purchase is financed by a long-term loan there will be no effect on working capital as both aspects of the transaction affect non-current components of the balance sheet.

Any amounts transferred to reserve will not have any effect on working capital as, simply, two non-current components (profit and loss account and general reserve) are involved. The same applies to any amounts written off goodwill or preliminary expenses. Also any transactions which result in a substitution of one current asset for another will have no effect on working capital, e.g. the purchase of food and beverage stocks for cash or the collection of cash from debtors. Finally, transactions which affect simultaneously current assets and current liabilities will have no effect on working capital, e.g. credit purchases and the payment of accrued expenses.

A clear understanding of how transactions affect working capital enables us to explain any changes in the amount of working capital from one balance sheet to another. Indeed, until recently it was usual for most businesses to prepare—at least annually—a funds flow statement (also known as a 'statement of source and applications of working capital'). However, following a recent recommendation from the accounting profession, we now prepare cash flow statements. These explain changes in the cash position from one balance sheet to another.

CASH FLOW STATEMENTS

The format and content of cash flow statements were recommended by the accounting profession in 1991 in the accounting standard known as Financial Reporting Standard No 1 (FRS1). The format of FRS1 was subsequently amended in 1996; the example in Figure 18.4 is based on the latest recommendations. Let us first look at each major heading in detail.

Cash inflow from operating activities

The cash inflow from operating activities may be shown in two different ways. We may use what are known as the 'direct method' and the 'indirect method'. We use the indirect method in Figure 18.4. The difference between

Cash Flow Statement
format and content

	£	£
Cash flow from:		
Operating activities		
Operating profit before tax	x	
Add back depreciation	x	x
	---	---
Add increase in creditors	x	
Less increase in stocks	(x)	
increase in debtors	(x)	(x)
	---	---
Net cash flow from operating activities		x
Returns on investments and servicing of finance		
Interest received	x	
Interest paid	(x)	
	---	---
Net cash inflow from returns on investments and servicing of finance		x
Taxation		
Tax paid	(x)	
	---	---
Net cash outflow from taxation		(x)
Capital expenditure and financial investment		
Purchase of fixed assets	(x)	
Sales of tangible fixed assets	x	
	---	---
Net cash outflow from capital expenditure and financial investment		(x)
Acquistions and disposals		
Sale of Gourmet Restaurants Ltd	x	
	---	---
Net cash inflow from acquisitions and disposals		x
Equity dividends paid		
Payment of ordinary dividends	(x)	
	---	---
Net cash outflow from equity dividends paid		(x)
Management of liquid resources		
Sale of government securities	x	
	---	---
Net cash inflow from sale of govt. securities		x
Financing		
Issue of ordinary share capital	x	
Repurchase of debenture loan	(x)	
	---	---
Net cash inflow from financing		x

Increase (Decrease) in cash		x

Figure 18.4 Cash flow statement

the two methods may be explained as follows. The direct method identifies the actual operating receipts and payments. Cash inflows here will include receipts from residents and from food and beverage outlets, including banqueting receipts. From this total we deduct the cash outflows in respect of food and beverage purchases, payroll and related expenses and other operating costs. Where appropriate there will be deductions in respect of fees for management contracts and/or franchise fees. The direct method is quite easy to apply as it looks at actual cash inflows and cash outflows from operations.

The indirect method determines the net cash inflow (cash inflow less cash outflow) by adjusting the operating profit for non-cash items and changes in working capital. An example is given below.

	£	£
Operating profit	x	
Add back depreciation	x	x
Add increase in creditors	x	x
		x
Less increase in stock	(x)	
increase in debtors	(x)	(x)
Net cash flow from operating activities		x

Depreciation is a non-cash expense; and as it has already been deducted in arriving at operating profit, has to be added back. An increase in creditors implies a saving of cash (as goods etc. have been obtained on credit) and so this adds to the cash generated by operations. An increase in stock represents a corresponding decrease in cash, and is therefore shown as a deduction from the cash inflow. Similarly an increase in debtors implies a decrease in cash generated by operations. It is in this manner that profit is converted into cash.

Returns on investments and servicing of finance

Under this heading we show cash inflows and cash outflows in respect of any interest received or paid, as well as any dividends received by the company. Ordinary dividends paid are shown later in the statement.

Taxation

Here we show the cash outflow resulting from the payment of tax liabilities.

Capital expenditure and financial investment

Under this heading we show cash outflows in respect of any purchases of fixed assets, as well as cash inflows resulting from the disposal of fixed assets.

Acquisition and disposals

This heading is for cash outflows and cash inflows relating to the acquisition or disposal of a trade or business.

Equity dividends paid

Ordinary dividends paid by the business are shown under this heading.

Management of liquid resources

This heading is for dealings in current asset investments held as readily disposable stores of value. Examples of such investments are government securities.

Financing

This relates to transactions such as the issue of shares (resulting in a cash inflow), repayment of loans (cash outflow) etc.

As may be seen in Figure 18.4 the cash flow statement is a logically structured statement showing all cash inflows, cash outflows and the net cash flow. It is of immense value to top management in its task of managing the liquid resources of the business and a valuable adjunct to the balance sheet and profit and loss account.

Example

Set out below is the balance sheet and profit and loss account of Hospitality Ventures Ltd. You are required to prepare a cash flow statement of the company.

Hospitality Ventures Ltd.
Balance Sheets as at 31 Dec.

	1998		1998		1999		1999
	£	£	£	£	£	£
Fixed assets at cost			320,000			400,000
Less Depreciation			120,000			160,000
			200,000			240,000
Current assets						
Stocks		42,180			56,540	
Prepayments		2,000			2,000	
Debtors		15,600			18,420	
Bank		8,400			6,952	
		68,180			83,912	
Less Current liabilities						
Creditors	9,220			9,880		
Accruals	2,000			2,000		
Taxation	3,060			4,100		
Proposed dividends	5,000			7,500		
	19,280			23,480		
Net current assets			48,900			60,432
			248,900			300,432

Less Long-term liabilities

Debenture loan	40,000	60,000
	208,900	240,432

Financed by:

Share capital	130,000	140,000
Profit and loss account	78,900	100,432
	208,900	240,432

Profit & Loss A/c
for year ended 31 Dec. 1999

	£
Operating profit before tax	33,132
Tax on operating profit	4,100
	29,032
Profit and loss account b/f	78,900
	107,932
Proposed dividends	7,500
Net profit c/f	100,432

Solution

Hospitality Ventures Ltd.
Cash Flow Statement for year ended 31 Dec. 1999

	£	£
Cash flow from operating activities		
Operating profit before tax		33,132
Add back depreciation		40,000
		73,132
Add increase in creditors	660	
Less increase in stock	(14,360)	
Less increase in debtors	(2,820)	(16,520)
Net cash flow from operating activities		56,612
Returns on investments and servicing of finance		NIL
Taxation		
Tax paid		(3,060)
		53,552

Capital expenditure and financial investment		
Purchase of fixed assets		(80,000)
		(26,448)
Acquisitions and disposals		NIL
Equity dividends paid		
Ordinary dividend paid		(5,000)
		(31,448)
Management of liquid resources		NIL
Net cash flow before financing		(31,448)
Financing		
Issue of shares	10,000	
New loan	20,000	30,000
Reduction in cash		(1,448)

Explanatory notes

(a) The cash balances may be reconciled as follows:

	£
Opening cash balance	8,400
Less reduction in cash	1,448
Closing cash balance	6,952

(b) In the cash flow statement we show, under the heading 'financing', two cash inflows: issue of shares £10,000 and new loan £20,000. In the comparative balance sheet we see that the share capital increased from £130,000 in 1998 to £140,000 in 1999. Also there is a corresponding increase in the debenture loan from £40,000 to £60,000.

(c) The dividend in the profit and loss account for the current year is only a proposed dividend and will not actually be paid until next year. In the cash flow statement we show the proposed dividend for the previous year, £5,000, which materialized as a cash outflow during 1999.

(d) Similar considerations apply in the case of taxation. Tax in respect of the current year, £4,100, will be paid during the following year. What is payable this year—and shown as a cash outflow—is the tax liability on the 1998 profit, which is £3,060.

PROBLEMS

1. 'The current ratio is an index of the short-run solvency of the business.' Discuss.
2. How important is working capital in hotels and restaurants?
3. Enumerate the principal factors which determine the working capital of a business.
4. From the data below prepare a statement of working capital.

	30 June £	30 September £	31 December £
Debtors	9,000	9,500	10,500
Creditors	31,000	34,000	37,000
Pre-paid expenses	1,000	3,000	1,500
Accrued expenses	6,000	4,000	7,000
Cash at bank	20,000	14,000	11,000
Stock	4,000	5,000	6,000

5. Given below is a list of certain transactions of the Hollings Hotel.

Jan. 1   Issued £100,000 9 per cent debentures.
"   2   Purchased furniture for cash—£16,000.
"   3   Purchased kitchen equipment for £100,000 of which £20,000 was paid in cash as a deposit and the balance was financed by a loan from X Ltd for a period of three years.
"   4   Did a banquet for ABC Club which resulted in a profit of £4,000.
"   5   Purchased beverage stocks for cash—£10,000.
"   6   Purchased food on credit—£3,000.
"   7   Collected debts from customers—£4,000.
"   8   Repaid long-term loan—£10,000.
"   9   Sold old restaurant furniture for cash—£5,000.
"   10   Paid accrued expenses of £2,500.

You are required to explain the effect of each of the above transactions on: (a) the working capital; and (b) the cash position of the hotel.

6. Set out below are comparative balance sheets of the Bibendum Hotel Co. You are required to prepare in good style a cash flow statement of the hotel.

Bibendum Hotel Co.
Balance Sheet

	1998			1999		
	Cost	Depreciation	Net	Cost	Depreciation	Net
	£	£	£	£	£	£
Fixed assets						
Land and buildings	400,000	—	400,000	500,000	—	500,000
Plant and equipment	200,000	50,000	150,000	240,000	60,000	180,000
Furniture	100,000	40,000	60,000	150,000	60,000	90,000
	700,000	90,000	610,000	890,000	120,000	770,000
Current assets						
Stocks		30,000			20,000	
Debtors		10,000			20,000	
Cash		100,000			50,000	
		140,000			90,000	

Less Current liabilities

Creditors	50,000			40,000	
Accruals	20,000	70,000		10,000	50,000
Net current assets			70,000		40,000
			680,000		810,000

Financed by:

Ordinary share capital	580,000	680,000
Profit and loss account	100,000	130,000
	680,000	810,000

7. The information given below was extracted from the records of the Portsmouth Catering Company in respect of the year ended 31 December 1987.

	Food cost	Opening stock	Closing stock	Stock turnover 1986
	£	£	£	Times
Jolly Farmer	200,000	6,000	8,000	31
Black Swan	400,000	12,000	9,000	34
Windsor	320,000	10,000	9,000	42
Decameron	570,000	13,000	12,000	35

  You are required to calculate the rate of stock turnover of each unit for 1987 and present an appropriate report on stock levels to management.

8. In order to control the working capital of a business it is essential to control the principal elements of working capital. Explain how you would control the following in a large hotel: (a) cash; (b) food stocks; (c) beverage stocks; (d) debtors; (e) creditors.

9. Discuss the role of cash budgeting in the context of working capital control.

10. What is the principal aim of the cash flow statement?

11. Explain the difference between operating profit and 'net cash flow from operating activities'.

12. Explain how we use the 'direct method' and the 'indirect method' in arriving at the 'net cash inflow from operating activities.'

13 Mary Dixon is the owner of the Serendipity Leisure Centre, and set out below are the balance sheets of the centre as at 31 December 1998 and 1999. Mary is surprised that, in spite of an impressive increase in the net profit of the centre, the cash balance has decreased by £10,000.

Serendipity Leisure Centre
Balance Sheets

	Cost	1998 Depreciation	Net	Cost	1999 Depreciation	Net
	£	£	£	£	£	£
Fixed assets	200,000	50,000	150,000	260,000	60,000	200,000
Current assets						
Stock		25,000			15,000	
Debtors		125,000			120,000	
Prepayments		5,000			10,000	
Cash		100,000			90,000	
		255,000			235,000	
Less Current liabilities						
Creditors	75,000			25,000		
Accrued expenses	10,000	85,000		5,000	30,000	
Net current assets			170,000			205,000
			320,000			405,000
Financed by:						
Capital account			270,000			320,000
Add Net profits			80,000			125,000
			350,000			445,000
Less Drawings			30,000			40,000
			320,000			405,000

Prepare Mary's cash flow statement and comment on the cash position of the leisure centre.

Assessment of capital projects 19

INTRODUCTION

The present chapter is mainly about two things: profitability and choice. In Chapters 9 and 10 the concepts of profitability, the meaning of return on capital, profit sensitivity analysis and some similar matters were examined. The consideration of profitability was related mainly to situations where resources had already been committed.

Let us now look at the problem of choice. Funds are always scarce in relation to investment opportunities. This applies to national governments, business enterprises and all of us as individuals. If a government spends more money on the construction of new roads, there is less money to spend on social security, education, etc. If a hotel company spends more money on the modernization of existing units, it will have less money for expansion. Finally, if an individual starts spending more money on entertainment, he or she will have less money to spend on books, clothing, travel, etc.

Thus in all these cases the fundamental problem is the same: available funds are always insufficient to satisfy all possible claims: a choice has to be made. The aim of the present chapter is, therefore, to explain the main methods of assessing capital projects in the context of the principal objective of the business enterprise, i.e. profitability. Three main methods will be examined here: pay-back, return on investment and discounted cash flow.

PAY-BACK METHOD

The concept of pay-back is simple. In this particular method we relate the savings of cash expenditure (or additional cash profits) to the cost of the relevant capital expenditure to decide how long it will take a project to pay for itself. The time taken is known as the pay-back period.

Imagine that a person spends 10p a day on matches. One day the individual decides to purchase a lighter for £4.00. Quite clearly—if we ignore the cost of flints and the fuel—the pay-back period is 40 days.

Example

A travel agency maintains a manual system of accounting. The annual cost of the system is as follows.

Salaries	£	£
(a) book-keeper	15,000	
(b) cashier	12,000	
(c) clerk	12,000	39,000
Stationery		1,200
Total		40,200

The proprietor intends to computerize the department. The cost of a suitable computer is £18,000 and it will have an effective life of five years. The annual cost of the new system is estimated as follows.

Salaries:	£	£
(a) book-keeper	15,000	
(b) clerk/cashier	12,000	27,000
Depreciation of computer		3,600
Stationery, maintenance, etc.		4,200
Total		34,800

Now, what are the annual savings of cash expenditure resulting from the new system? Surely, the answer is £40,200 less (£27,000 + £4,200) = £31,200, i.e. £9,000. It should be noted that we have ignored the cost of depreciation as this does not entail a cash outflow. Consequently the pay-back period is:

$$\frac{\text{Cost of computer £18,000}}{\text{Annual cash savings £9,000}} = 2 \text{ years}$$

The cash outlay on the computer will thus be recovered over a period of two years.

The pay-back method has certain advantages and disadvantages. The most important advantage of this method is its simplicity. The concept of the pay-back period is easy to grasp and meaningful. Similarly, the method is easy to apply: all we have to do is divide the cost of the project by the relevant savings of cash expenditure (or additional cash profits). Other things being equal the shorter the pay-back period the more attractive the project. Finally, the pay-back method is useful in the case of risky projects, where the prediction of profitability is difficult. In such situations the recovery of the initial cost of the project may well be an important criterion from the point of view of decision making.

Let us now look at the disadvantages of this method. The most serious criticism is that it has the wrong orientation. Pay-back is concerned with the recovery of the cost of a project and not its profitability. And, the fact remains that we are in business to make a profit, not to recover capital costs. Secondly, the method ignores the time value of money, i.e. it assumes that £1.00 in the future has the same value as £1.00 now. This, clearly, is incorrect; and we shall be returning to this topic later on in this chapter. Finally, the method concentrates on the first few years of a project and ignores what happens after the pay-back period. A project may have a short pay-back period but, subsequently, make little contribution to the profits of the business, and vice versa. The important point is how much a project contributes to the profits of a business throughout its effective life.

Example

A catering company is considering two alternative projects costing £200,000 each. Given below are the estimated cash savings in relation to each project.

Year	A £	B £
1	80,000	30,000
2	70,000	30,000
3	50,000	40,000
4	40,000	40,000
5	30,000	60,000
6	10,000	100,000
	£280,000	£300,000

Project A has a pay-back period of three years; in the case of project B the pay-back period is five years. In spite of this the savings of cash expenditure in the case of project B are greater.

It is because of these limitations of the pay-back method that it is not usually applied on its own. Invariably all the three methods described in this chapter are applied before a decision is made.

RETURN ON INVESTMENT METHOD

In the return on investment method we are interested in the relationship between net profit and the cost of the project. What matters here is the relationship between the additional resources to be invested in a project and the resulting addition to total profits. The formula for this method is:

$$\frac{\text{Average net profit}}{\text{Average cost of project}} \times 100 = \text{return on investment}$$

The concept of the 'average' cost of a project needs some explanation. Where a project consists of depreciable assets—which is so in the majority of cases—the initial cost of such assets is recovered over a period of time by debiting depreciation in the profit and loss account. Where the cost of an asset is £10,000 and its effective life five years, then assuming that the straight-line method of depreciation is used, the position is as shown in Figure 19.1.

Each year the charge to the profit and loss account is £2,000. The amount invested in the asset is £8,000 at the end of the first year, £6,000 at the end of the second year, and so on. Consequently, the average amount invested in the

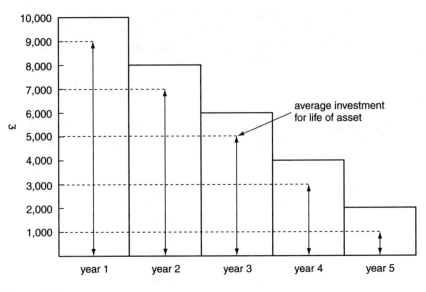

Figure 19.1

asset during the first year is £9,000; during the second year £7,000, and so on. Taking the whole life of the asset the average investment is £5,000.

Readers should, at this stage, note one essential difference between the pay-back method and the return on investment method. In the former we relate savings in cash expenditure to the cost of the project. In the latter we are not concerned with cash but the accounting concept of net profit. We thus ignore depreciation in the pay-back method, but do take it into account in the return on investment method.

Example

A company is considering two alternative projects with an estimated effective life of six years, as shown below.

	A	*B*
Average cost of project	£200,000	£200,000
	£	£
Resulting profits:		
Year 1	100,000	20,000
2	80,000	30,000
3	50,000	40,000
4	40,000	50,000
5	20,000	80,000
6	10,000	90,000
	£300,000	£310,000
Average net profit	£50,000	£51,667
Return on investment	25.0%	25.8%

The advantages of the return on investment method are important. It is quite simple to understand and apply and it has the right orientation: unlike the pay-back method, it is concerned with profitability. Its main disadvantage is that it ignores the time value of money. Thus it would appear from the last example that project B is more attractive than project A. If we took into account the timing of the profits resulting from the two projects we would certainly see that, in fact, project A is the more profitable.

DISCOUNTED CASH FLOW (DCF) METHOD

We mentioned earlier in this chapter the importance of the time element in relation to the value of money. The problem of the time-value may be explained as follows: £1.00 now is worth more than £1.00 in, say, a year's time, because if invested now at, say, 10% it will increase in value to £1.10. Similarly £1.00 now is equivalent (assuming compound interest at 10%) to £1.21 in two years' time.

We may express this compounding process as shown below:

£1.00 will accumulate to:
(a) £1.00 $(1 + r)$ ... in one year's time.
(b) £1.00 $(1 + r)^2$ ... in two years' time.
(c) £1.00 $(1 + r)^3$ ... in three years' time.
Where r denotes the relevant rate of interest.

We may now calculate the present value of £1.00 at some point in time in the future, as follows:

£1.00 receivable in n years' time is now worth: $\dfrac{£1.00}{(1 + r)^n}$

Consequently:

(a) £1.00 receivable in one year's time is worth £1.00/(1.10) = £0.909
(b) £1.00 receivable in two years' time is worth £1.00/(1.10)^2 = £0.826
(c) £1.00 receivable in three years' time is worth £1.00/(1.10)^3 = £0.751

The process of finding the present day value of money receivable (or indeed payable) in the future is known as discounting. In DCF calculations we would not resort to the use of a formula as in the above examples. Instead we would consult DCF tables where the conversion factors are given for different rates of interest and period of time (see Appendix).

Example 1

Peter lends Paul £1000. The latter promises to repay the loan at the rate of £200 a year over five years. Let us assume that Peter can invest any sum at 10 per cent per annum. What is the present-day value of the amounts repaid by Paul?

Year	Amount repaid	Conversion factor	Present value
1	£200	0.909	£181.80
2	£200	0.826	£165.20
3	£200	0.751	£150.20
4	£200	0.683	£136.60
5	£200	0.621	£124.20
	£1,000		£758.00

Solution

Hence, although the total repaid by Paul over five years amounts to £1,000, its present-day value is only £758. Thus by lending the money Peter is, in fact, losing £242.

As may be seen from our illustration the more distant in time a sum of money, the lower its present-day value. Also, as will be noticed by referring to the Appendix, the higher the rate of interest at which future cash flows are discounted, the lower their present-day values. Thus it is the distance in time and the rate of interest which together determine the present-day value of any amount receivable or payable in the future. This is illustrated in Figure 19.2.

Figure 19.2 contains two sets of bars. Those shaded darker represent present-day values of £1,000 discounted at 15 per cent. The other bars represent present-day values of £1,000 discounted at 10 per cent.

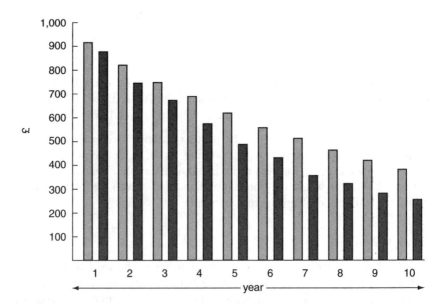

Figure 19.2 Effects of time and interest on present-day values of future cash flows

Example 2

A restaurant is replacing existing furniture. The cash price, payable immediately, is £10,000. Alternatively, the suppliers are prepared to accept the following arrangements:

(a) an immediate payment of £1,000 and £3,500 a year over three years.
(b) an immediate payment of £1,000 and £3,000 a year over four years.

Assume that the appropriate rate of interest is 12 per cent and advise the restaurant on the most advantageous method of payment.

Solution

Alternative (a)

Year	Payment	Conversion factor	Present value
1	£3,500	0.893	£3,125.50
2	£3,500	0.797	£2,789.50
3	£3,500	0.712	£2,492.00
			8,407.00
Add Initial payment			1,000.00
Total			£9,407.00

Alternative (b)

Year	Payment	Conversion factor	Present value
1	£3,000	0.893	£2,679.00
2	£3,000	0.797	£2,391.00
3	£3,000	0.712	£2,136.00
4	£3,000	0.636	£1,908.00
			9,114.00
Add Initial payment			1,000.00
Total			£10,114.00

Hence, of the three possible methods of payment, alternative (a) appears to be the most attractive.

Where future cash flows are identical in amount it is not necessary to convert them to present-day equivalents individually. Table II of the Appendix gives the cumulative factors. Thus, for alternative (a):

£3,500 × 2.402 = £8,407;
and for alternative (b)
£3,000 × 3.037 = £9,111.

The difference of £3 (between £9,114 and £9,111) is marginal and is due to the rounding of conversion factors.

NET PRESENT VALUE METHOD

In this method we assume a particular rate of interest and discount the relevant future cash flows to arrive at their present-day values. The excess of the discounted total over the cost of the project is known as the 'net present value' (NPV) or 'net gain'. Quite clearly, the greater the net present value the more attractive the project.

Example

A leisure centre is considering two projects, each involving a capital cost of £200,000. The life of each project is five years and the resulting cash flows are expected to be as shown below. Assume the appropriate rate of interest to be 10 per cent.

Solution

Year	Conversion factor	Project A		Project B	
		Cash inflow	Present value	Cash inflow	Present value
		£	£	£	£
1	0.909	100,000	90,900	30,000	27,270
2	0.826	80,000	66,080	60,000	49,560
3	0.751	60,000	45,060	70,000	52,570
4	0.683	40,000	27,320	80,000	54,640
5	0.621	20,000	12,420	80,000	49,680
		£300,000	£241,780	£320,000	£233,720
Less cost of project			200,000		200,000
Net present value			£41,780		£33,720

The position is, therefore, as follows. Project A will generate an actual cash inflow of £300,000 and this has a present-day value of £241,780. Its net present value—or net gain—is £41,780. Project B will generate an actual cash inflow of £320,000 but because of the unfavourable cash inflow profile (higher cash inflow figures materialize towards the end of the life of the project) its present-day value is £233,720. Its net present value is therefore £33,720. Other things being equal, Project A is preferable to Project B.

INTERNAL RATE OF RETURN METHOD

In this method we discount future cash flows at various rates of interest until the discounted total equals the cost of the project. The rate of interest which is effective in achieving this is the internal rate of return (IRR). Where there are several projects being contemplated, the one showing the highest internal rate of return is normally chosen.

Example

A hotel company is proposing to undertake a project costing £33,450 and having an effective life of five years. The project will result in savings of cash expenditure as shown below. Calculate the internal rate of return on this project.

The only possible approach is to proceed by trial and error. Let us, therefore, try 10 per cent.

Year	Cash inflow £	DF 10%	Present value £
1	10,000	0.909	9,090
2	11,000	0.826	9,086
3	11,000	0.751	8,261
4	8,000	0.683	5,464
5	5,000	0.621	3,105
	£45,000		£35,006

The discounted total of £35,006 is well in excess of the cost of the project, and clearly we have not used a high enough rate of interest for discounting future cash flows. Let us try 14 per cent.

Year	Cash inflow £	DF 14%	Present value £
1	10,000	0.877	8,770
2	11,000	0.769	8,459
3	11,000	0.675	7,425
4	8,000	0.592	4,736
5	5,000	0.519	2,595
	£45,000		£31,985

Having used 14 per cent for our purpose we have obtained a discounted total well below the cost of the project. Let us, then, try 12 per cent.

Year	Cash inflow £	DF 10%	Present value £
1	10,000	0.893	8,930
2	11,000	0.797	8,767
3	11,000	0.712	7,832
4	8,000	0.636	5,088
5	5,000	0.567	2,835
	£45,000		£33,452

It is clear that the internal rate of return is 12 per cent as this discounts the future cash flows to (practically) the exact cost of the project.

DCF: SOME FURTHER EXPLANATIONS

As already explained in the DCF method, we are not concerned with the accounting concept of profit but, simply, the flows of cash into and out of the business.

When we calculate the net profit of a project we must take into account all revenue expenditure including depreciation. However, depreciation is a non-cash expense: we debit it in the profit and loss account, but there is no corresponding outflow of cash. Depreciation must, therefore, be ignored in DCF calculations.

Taxation is an important factor which must be taken into account. The payment of tax liabilities represents a substantial cash outflow. It must, therefore, be shown as a deduction from any cash profits resulting from a project.

DCF calculations are frequently influenced by government policy. A company may be able to claim a cash grant or subsidy on certain investment projects. When that is so then, clearly, the grant or subsidy must be regarded as an addition to the cash inflow.

Finally, we come to the rate of interest. The choice of the rate of interest for DCF purposes is not a simple matter, and different companies may justifiably use somewhat different rates of interest when assessing their projects. Ultimately the choice should be made on the basis of the cost of capital to the company. Where a project is financed by a bank loan obtained at, say, 14 per cent, the cash flows resulting from the project should be discounted at 14 per cent. Where a project is financed from the internal funds of the company, it is necessary to calculate the average cost of capital to the company from all the actual sources: ordinary shares, preference shares, debentures, etc. The cost of capital will then be influenced by the ordinary and preference dividends paid as well as the debenture interest. The cost of servicing such capital will point to the rate of interest that must be chosen for DCF purposes.

CAPITAL PROJECTS WITH INDETERMINATE PROFITABILITY

Our consideration of the methods of assessment of capital projects has, so far, centred around projects that have measurable consequences on the profitability of the business. There are, however, many projects that have a measurable cost but whose consequences on the earnings of the business are almost impossible to assess.

Education and training projects are, no doubt, in this category. The cost of a proposed training department is fairly easy to calculate. There is often no doubt that the introduction of a training programme is highly desirable and likely to lead to greater efficiency. However, the precise effect of improved efficiency on turnover, operating costs and profitability is not, by any means, certain.

The provision of improved canteen facilities in a factory is certainly likely to have a positive effect on the morale and health of the employees. To what extent this is going to improve the earnings of the business is quite uncertain. Many prestige projects are in this category: expensive cars for company executives, big executive desks, expensive carpets in offices, etc.

In all these cases an assessment of the proposed capital expenditure is difficult. Yet whenever resources are to be committed a decision one way or another must be made. One possible solution is to rely on the collective value-judgement of the decision-makers (e.g. board of directors, budget committee). When there are several such projects possible, the individuals concerned should be asked to indicate their respective preferences as between the various projects and to state their degree of preference (e.g. essential, desirable, possible). It is then possible to quantify the general opinion and express it in terms of a collective and definite decision.

PROBLEMS

1. Explain what you understand by the 'pay-back period'. Enumerate the main advantages and disadvantages of the pay-back method.
2. Describe the return on investment method. How does it differ from the pay-back method?
3. Compare and contrast the NPV method with the IRR method.
4. Jack lends £1,000 to Jill, who promises to repay the loan at the rate of £250 a year over four years. Assume that the relevant rate of interest is 10 per cent.

    (a) What is the present-day value of the amounts repaid by Jill?
    (b) How much is Jack losing by lending the money?
5. A hotel company is contemplating a project costing £283,000 and having an effective life of five years. The resulting cash inflows are projected as follows:

Year	Cash inflow £
1	70,000
2	70,000
3	80,000
4	80,000
5	100,000

(a) Assuming that the appropriate rate of interest is 10 per cent, what is the net present value of the project?

(b) By trial and error find the internal rate of return on this project.

6. A hotel company is planning a reorganization of its banqueting department. The cost of the project is £795,000 and its life ten years. The projected cash inflows are estimated as follows:

Year	Cash inflow £
1	120,000
2	130,000
3	140,000
4	160,000
5	160,000
6	170,000
7	170,000
8	180,000
9	180,000
10	200,000

The directors of the company insist that all new projects must show an internal rate of return of at least 13 per cent. You are required to:

(a) assess the project, using the NPV method, assuming that the appropriate rate of interest is 10 per cent

(b) find the internal rate of return for the project

(c) comment briefly on your results.

7. A company is considering a capital project costing £400,000. The sales forecast, together with the forecast expenditure are shown below.

Year	Sales	Cost of sales	Other v'ble costs	Fxd costs excl. dep'n	Depreciation
	£	£	£	£	£
1	200,000	60,000	20,000	30,000	100,000
2	300,000	90,000	30,000	30,000	100,000
3	400,000	120,000	40,000	30,000	100,000
4	300,000	90,000	30,000	30,000	100,000
	1,200,000	360,000	120,000	120,000	400,000

You are required to:

(a) calculate the pay-back period for the project
(b) calculate the return on this investment
(c) assess the project by means of the DCF method, assuming that the appropriate rate of interest is 10 per cent
(d) prepare a break-even chart for the above project and comment appropriately.

8. It is proposed to mechanize the wash-up department of a large restaurant. The cost of an appropriate dishwashing machine is £190,000, and installation costs are estimated at £10,000. The estimated life of the machine is six years, at the end of which it will not have any scrap value. All washing-up is at present done manually and the annual costs for the next six years are estimated as follows:

Year	1	2	3	4	5	6
	£	£	£	£	£	£
Labour costs	110,000	110,000	115,000	115,000	120,000	120,000
Supplies	3,000	3,000	3,000	3,000	3,000	3,000
Total cost	113,000	113,000	118,000	118,000	123,000	123,000

The costs of the automatic dishwashing machine have been projected as follows:

Year	1	2	3	4	5	6
	£	£	£	£	£	£
Labour costs	60,000	60,000	60,000	65,000	65,000	65,000
Electric power	3,000	3,000	3,000	3,000	3,000	3,000
Supplies	4,000	4,000	4,000	4,000	4,000	4,000
Repairs	—	—	1,000	3,000	3,000	3,000
Total cost	67,000	67,000	68,000	75,000	75,000	75,000

You are required to calculate:

(a) the pay-back period
(b) the net present value of the project, assuming that the appropriate rate of interest is 10 per cent.

Uniform system of accounts for the lodging industry

20

INTRODUCTION

Uniform systems of accounting are by no means a recent development. Indeed one of the earliest uniform systems was the one introduced by the Federation of Master Printers in 1911. Subsequently a number of uniform systems were developed for various industries, and some of these have proved quite successful.

As far as the UK hospitality industry is concerned little was done in this area until the late 1960s. In 1969 HM Stationery Office published the 'Standard System of Hotel Accounting'. Two years later a companion publication appeared, and this was the 'Standard System of Catering Accounting'. Although both systems had considerable official backing, neither of them enjoyed sufficient acceptance in the hospitality industry and they have now fallen into disuse.

Corresponding developments in the USA have had a greater measure of success. In 1926 the Hotel Association of New York City adopted and recommended to its members the 'Uniform System of Accounts for Hotels'. This was revised from time to time; and in 1996 the ninth revision of the system appeared under the title 'Uniform System of Accounts for the Lodging Industry'. This replaced the previously published Uniform System of Accounts for Hotels; and now additionally contains information that used to be included in the 'Uniform System of Accounts and Expense Dictionary for Small Hotels'.

As far as the profit and loss account (variously described as the 'departmental statement of income', 'summary statement of income' or, simply, 'income statement) is concerned, the most important departure from the eighth revision is the division of the food and beverage schedule into two separate schedules—one for food and one for beverages.

From the illustrations given below students will appreciate that the Uniform System for the Lodging Industry is simple and easy to understand. Also it is a flexible system and one that may be adapted to all kinds of situations. Above all, it is a system that represents the best accounting practice in the international hospitality industry.

TERMINOLOGY

Students should be aware of the differences between British and American terminology.

(a) American hospitality accountants do not use the term 'profit', the term 'income' being used instead. Hence net profit is described as 'net income' and departmental profit as 'departmental income'. The term 'gross profit' is, however, in general use. Some British hospitality accountants still use the term 'gross operating profit'; this term was discontinued at the seventh revision of the uniform system and should no longer be used; the correct term to use is 'income before fixed charges'.

(b) What is described in the UK as 'sales or turnover' is in the uniform system described as 'revenue'. Hence net sales is referred to as 'net revenue'.

(c) Finally, the ninth revision of the system introduces some changes to the terminology used in the previous editions of the uniform system. Thus 'telephone' becomes 'telecommunications'; 'data processing' is now referred to as 'information systems' and 'energy costs' are now described as 'utility costs'.

SUMMARY STATEMENT OF INCOME
for year ended . . . (000)

	Net revenue	Cost of sales	Payroll related expenses	Other expenses	Income (Loss)
Operating departments	£	£	£	£	£
Rooms	3,280	—	575	255	2,450
Food	1,090	395	335	90	270
Beverage	420	85	110	40	185
Telecommunications	115	90	15	10	—
Rentals	95	—	—	—	95
	5,000	570	1,035	395	3,000
Undistributed operating expenses					
Administrative and General			120	180	
Marketing			65	230	
Property operation and maintenance			110	90	
Utility costs			–	295	
			295	795	1,090
Income after undistributed operating expenses					1,910
Rent, property taxes and insurance					345
Income before interest, depreciation, amortization and income taxes					1,565
Interest expense					250
Income before depreciation, amortization and income taxes					1,315
Depreciation and amortization					300
Income before income taxes					1,015
Income taxes					255
Net income					760

Figure 20.1 Summary statement of income

SUMMARY STATEMENT OF INCOME

The Summary Statement of Income is shown in Figure 20.1. It consists of three parts:

(a) The upper portion relates to departmental operations. From the net revenue of each department we deduct the cost of sales (if any), departmental payroll and related expenses as well as other departmental expenses, to arrive at the resulting figure of departmental income or departmental loss.

(b) The second (middle) part of the Summary Statement of Income lists the 'Undistributed Operating Expenses'. The total of these expenses is deducted from the total of departmental incomes to arrive at the income before fixed charges. The latter is, in the ninth edition of the system, referred to as 'Income after Undistributed Operating Expenses.'

(c) Finally, in the third part of the income statement we deduct fixed charges such as rent, taxes, insurance, interest, depreciation and amortization to arrive at 'Income before Income Taxes'. Net income is, of course, obtained after deducting the appropriate amount of income tax.

Students should note that all operating departments are treated in a uniform manner. Whether the department is the rooms department, food department or whatever, the method of arriving at the departmental income (or loss) is exactly the same.

	ROOMS
	£000
Revenue	3,310
Allowances	30
Net revenue	3,280
Expenses	
Salaries and wages	460
Employee benefits	115
Total payroll and related expenses	575
Other expenses	
Cable/satellite/television	11
Commissions	35
Contract services	18
Guest transportation	27
Laundry and dry cleaning	23
Linen	7
Operating supplies	63
Reservations	21
Telecommunications	7
Training	4
Uniforms	32
Other	7
	255
Departmental income	£2,450

Figure 20.2 Departmental statement for rooms

FOOD

	£000
Revenue	1,093
Allowances	3
Net revenue	1,090
Cost of sales	
Cost of food	402
Less cost of employee meals	5
Less Food transfers to beverage	3
Add Beverage transfers to food	1
Total cost of sales	395
Gross profit on food sales	695
Expenses	
Salaries and wages	260
Employee benefits	75
Total payroll and related expenses	335
Other expenses	
China, glassware, silver and linen	11
Contract services	12
Laundry and dry cleaning	5
Licences	1
Miscellaneous banquet expenses	8
Music and entertainment	2
Operating supplies	28
Telecommunications	4
Training	5
Uniforms	8
Other	6
Total other expenses	90
Total expenses	820
Departmental income	£270

Figure 20.3 Departmental statement for food

DEPARTMENTAL STATEMENTS

In addition to the Summary Statement of Income we prepare—for each operating department and all undistributed operating expenses—a detailed departmental statement. The purpose of such statements is to show more detailed results for each major division of the business. We show altogether four departmental statements for: rooms, food, beverage and administration and general expenses. Of course, all the other departmental statements would be written up in exactly the same manner.

Rooms department

In the departmental statement for rooms shown in Figure 20.2 we start with rooms revenue, and deduct departmental payroll and other departmental expenses, and, in this way, arrive at the figure of departmental income. As will be seen from subsequent examples, the procedure is the same for all operating departments.

Food department

As may be seen from Figure 20.3, the statement in respect of food operations shows a considerable amount of detail; students should, in particular, note the adjustments in respect of the cost of sales. In some hotels in addition to the ordinary revenue from food operations there are sundry items of revenue such as meeting-room charges and room rentals. Where such additional revenue exists, it should be added to the gross profit (in between 'Gross profit on food sales' and 'Expenses').

Beverage department

The beverage department statement, shown in Figure 20.4, is constructed in exactly the same manner as the food department statement. Here, too, we

BEVERAGE	£000
Revenue	427
Allowances	7
Net revenue	420
Cost of sales	
Cost of beverage	83
Less beverage transfers to food	1
Add Food transfers to beverage	3
Total cost of sales	85
Gross profit on beverage sales	335
Expenses	
Salaries and wages	88
Employee benefits	22
Total payroll and related expenses	110
Other expenses	
China, glassware, silver and linen	4
Contract services	5
Gratis food	1
Laundry and dry cleaning	2
Licences	3
Music and entertainment	9
Operating supplies	7
Training	2
Uniforms	4
Other	3
Total other expenses	40
Total expenses	235
Departmental income	£185

Figure 20.4 Departmental statement for beverages

show particulars of food and beverage transfers. Any addition to beverage cost will be shown in the food statement as a deduction from food cost, and vice versa.

Administration and general

This statement, shown in Figure 20.5, is different from the previous three statements in that it is wholly concerned with expenditure which we show under two headings: (a) 'Payroll and related expenses' and (b) 'Other expenses.'

In all the above department statements we have shown the relevant figures rounded off to the nearest £1,000. This we have done to ensure better clarity of the statements—though smaller hotels would probably prefer to show the actual detailed figures and refrain from rounding. Finally, we have had nothing to say about the balance sheet. The reason is two-fold. First, the structure and content of the balance sheet is not in any way affected by the uniform system. Secondly, whilst the income statement and the relevant statements are prepared quite frequently, the balance sheet is in many companies prepared just once a year and thus exists some distance from the actual operation of the uniform system.

	ADMINISTRATION AND GENERAL	
Payroll and related expenses		*£000*
Salaries and wages		100
Employee benefits		20
Total payroll and related expenses		120
Other expenses		
Bank charges		2
Communication systems		5
Credit collection		8
Credit card commissions		33
Donations		5
Dues and subscriptions		4
Head office		5
Human resources		16
Information systems		7
Internal audit		6
Meals and entertainment		3
Operating supplies and equipment		7
Postage		4
Printing and stationery		6
Prevision for doubtful accounts		15
Security		22
Telecommunications		7
Training		4
Travel		9
Other		12
Total other expenses		180
Total administrative and general expenses		£300

Figure 20.5 Departmental statement for administration and general expenses

ADVANTAGES OF THE UNIFORM SYSTEM

From what has already been said it will be readily appreciated that the Uniform System of Accounts for the Lodging Industry offers a number of advantages. It is essentially a simple, yet effective, system and one that non-accountants find easy to understand. As the system is periodically reviewed by senior hospitality accountants and hotel executives, it is clearly a system that represents the best accounting practice in the hospitality industry. The existence of the system means that there is no need for hotel operators to have tailor made systems prepared for them. The uniform system is there for every hotelier to use; and this benefit is now being increasingly appreciated in the international hospitality industry.

PROBLEMS

1. The following figures have been extracted from the records of the Green Valley Hotel at 31 December 1999. You are required to prepare the hotel's Summary Statement of Income for the year ended 31 December 1999.

		£000
Net revenue:	Rooms	1,700
	Food	540
	Beverage	255
	Telecommunications	60
Cost of sales	Food	215
	Beverage	55
	Telecommunications	60
Payroll and related expenses:	Rooms	305
	Food	175
	Beverage	60
	Telecommunications	10
Other (departmental) expenses	Rooms	135
	Food	50
	Beverage	20
	Telecommunications	5
Undistributed operating expenses		
Payroll and related expenses:	Admin and general	65
	Marketing	40
	Property operation and maintenance	60
Other expenses	Admin and general	95
	Marketing	150
	Property operation and maintenance	55
	Utility costs	165
Rent, property taxes and insurance		185
Interest expense		135
Depreciation and amortization		165
Income taxes		140

2. From the information given below prepare a departmental schedule for food and one for beverage for the year ended 31 December 1999.

	Food £000	Beverage £000
Revenue	550	245
Allowances	4	1
Cost of food/beverage	215	51
Cost of employee meals	4	—
Salaries and wages	140	49
Employee benefits	42	14
China, glassware and linen	6	3
Contract services	7	4
Laundry and dry cleaning	4	2
Licences	2	1
Music and entertainment	1	6
Training	4	2
Uniforms	5	3
Other	3	1

You are also informed that beverages transferred to the kitchen amounted to £12,000; food used in the beverage operation was valued at £3,000.

Appendix

Table I Present value of £1.00 received in the future

Periods hence	1%	2%	4%	6%	8%	10%	12%	14%	15%	16%	18%	20%	22%	24%	25%	26%	28%	30%	35%	40%
1	0.990	0.980	0.962	0.943	0.926	0.909	0.893	0.877	0.870	0.862	0.847	0.833	0.820	0.806	0.800	0.794	0.781	0.769	0.741	0.714
2	0.980	0.961	0.925	0.890	0.857	0.826	0.797	0.769	0.756	0.743	0.718	0.694	0.672	0.650	0.640	0.630	0.610	0.592	0.549	0.510
3	0.971	0.942	0.889	0.840	0.794	0.751	0.712	0.675	0.658	0.641	0.609	0.579	0.551	0.524	0.512	0.500	0.477	0.455	0.406	0.364
4	0.961	0.924	0.855	0.792	0.735	0.683	0.636	0.592	0.572	0.552	0.516	0.482	0.451	0.423	0.410	0.397	0.373	0.350	0.301	0.260
5	0.951	0.906	0.822	0.747	0.681	0.621	0.567	0.519	0.497	0.476	0.437	0.402	0.370	0.341	0.328	0.315	0.291	0.269	0.223	0.186
6	0.942	0.883	0.790	0.705	0.630	0.564	0.507	0.456	0.432	0.410	0.370	0.335	0.303	0.275	0.262	0.250	0.227	0.207	0.165	0.133
7	0.933	0.871	0.760	0.665	0.583	0.513	0.452	0.400	0.376	0.354	0.314	0.279	0.249	0.222	0.210	0.198	0.178	0.159	0.122	0.095
8	0.923	0.853	0.731	0.627	0.540	0.467	0.404	0.351	0.327	0.305	0.266	0.233	0.204	0.179	0.168	0.157	0.139	0.123	0.091	0.068
9	0.914	0.837	0.703	0.592	0.500	0.424	0.361	0.308	0.284	0.263	0.225	0.194	0.167	0.144	0.134	0.125	0.108	0.094	0.067	0.048
10	0.905	0.820	0.676	0.558	0.463	0.386	0.322	0.270	0.247	0.227	0.191	0.162	0.137	0.116	0.107	0.099	0.085	0.073	0.050	0.035
11	0.890	0.801	0.650	0.527	0.429	0.350	0.287	0.237	0.215	0.195	0.162	0.135	0.112	0.094	0.086	0.079	0.066	0.056	0.037	0.025
12	0.857	0.788	0.625	0.497	0.397	0.319	0.257	0.208	0.187	0.168	0.137	0.112	0.092	0.076	0.069	0.062	0.052	0.043	0.027	0.018
13	0.879	0.778	0.601	0.469	0.368	0.290	0.229	0.182	0.163	0.145	0.116	0.093	0.075	0.061	0.055	0.050	0.040	0.033	0.020	0.013
14	0.870	0.758	0.577	0.442	0.340	0.263	0.205	0.160	0.141	0.125	0.099	0.078	0.062	0.049	0.044	0.039	0.032	0.025	0.015	0.009
15	0.861	0.748	0.555	0.417	0.315	0.239	0.183	0.140	0.123	0.108	0.084	0.067	0.051	0.040	0.035	0.031	0.025	0.020	0.011	0.006

Table II Present value of £1.00 received at the end of each of N years

Periods hence	1%	2%	4%	6%	8%	10%	12%	14%	15%	16%	18%	20%	22%	24%	25%	26%	28%	30%	35%	40%
1	0.990	0.980	0.962	0.943	0.926	0.909	0.893	0.877	0.870	0.862	0.874	0.833	0.820	0.806	0.800	0.794	0.781	0.769	0.741	0.714
2	1.970	1.942	1.886	1.833	1.783	1.736	1.690	1.647	1.626	1.605	1.566	1.528	1.492	1.457	1.440	1.424	1.392	1.361	1.289	1.224
3	2.941	2.884	2.775	2.673	2.577	2.487	2.402	2.322	2.283	2.246	2.174	2.106	2.042	1.981	1.952	1.923	1.868	1.816	1.696	1.589
4	3.902	3.808	3.630	3.465	3.312	3.170	3.037	2.914	2.855	2.798	2.690	2.589	2.494	2.404	2.362	2.320	2.241	2.166	1.997	1.849
5	4.853	4.713	4.452	4.212	3.993	3.791	3.605	3.433	3.352	3.274	3.127	2.991	2.864	2.745	2.689	2.635	2.532	2.436	2.220	2.035
6	5.795	5.601	5.242	4.917	4.623	4.355	4.111	3.889	3.784	3.685	3.498	3.326	3.167	3.020	2.951	2.885	2.759	2.643	2.385	2.168
7	6.728	6.472	6.002	5.582	5.206	4.868	4.564	4.288	4.160	4.039	3.812	3.605	3.416	3.242	3.161	3.083	2.937	2.802	2.508	2.263
8	7.652	7.325	6.733	6.210	5.747	5.335	4.968	4.639	4.487	4.344	4.078	3.837	3.619	3.421	3.329	3.241	3.076	2.925	2.598	2.331
9	8.566	8.162	7.435	6.802	6.247	5.759	5.328	4.946	4.772	4.607	4.303	4.031	3.786	3.566	3.463	3.366	3.184	3.019	2.665	2.379
10	9.471	8.983	8.111	7.360	6.710	6.145	5.650	5.216	5.019	4.833	4.494	4.192	3.923	3.682	3.571	3.465	3.269	3.092	2.715	2.414
11	10.368	9.787	8.760	7.887	7.139	6.495	5.988	5.453	5.234	5.029	4.656	4.327	4.035	3.776	3.656	3.544	3.335	3.147	2.752	2.438
12	11.255	10.575	9.385	8.884	7.536	6.814	6.194	5.660	5.421	5.197	4.798	4.439	4.127	3.851	3.725	3.606	3.387	3.190	2.779	2.456
13	12.434	11.848	9.986	8.873	7.904	7.103	6.424	5.842	5.533	5.342	4.910	4.533	4.203	3.912	3.780	3.656	3.427	3.223	2.799	2.468
14	13.004	12.106	10.568	9.295	8.244	7.367	6.628	6.002	5.724	5.468	5.008	4.611	4.265	3.962	3.824	3.695	3.459	3.249	2.814	2.477
15	13.865	12.849	11.118	9.712	8.559	7.606	6.811	6.142	5.847	5.575	5.092	4.675	4.315	4.001	3.859	3.726	3.483	3.268	2.825	2.484

Index